AF361398

Neo-Firthian Approaches to Linguistic Typology

Key Concepts in Systemic Functional Linguistics

Series Editors
Gerard O'Grady, Cardiff University
Rebekah Wegener, University of Salzburg
Tom Bartlett, University of Glasgow

Books in this series provide monographic treatments of core theoretical concepts within Systemic Functional Linguistics, together with coverage of more recent concerns in Systemic Functional Linguistic theory and important areas of application and trans-disciplinary collaboration.

Each monograph is organized around a description of the historical factors that led to the emergence of the concept within Systemic Functional Linguistics and a detailed theoretical description of the concept within the overall architecture of the theory.

Published
Systemic Functional Translation Studies: Theoretical Insights and New Directions
Bo Wang and Yuanyi Ma

Forthcoming
Verbal Art and Systemic Functional Linguistics
Donna R. Miller

Neo-Firthian Approaches to Linguistic Typology

William B. McGregor

SHEFFIELD UK   BRISTOL CT

Published by Equinox Publishing Ltd.

UK: Office 415, The Workstation, 15 Paternoster Row, Sheffield, South Yorkshire S1 2BX
USA: ISD, 70 Enterprise Drive, Bristol, CT 06010

www.equinoxpub.com

First published 2021

© William B. McGregor 2021

All rights reserved. No part of this publication may be reproduced or transmitted in any form or by any means, electronic or mechanical, including photocopying, recording or any information storage or retrieval system, without prior permission in writing from the publishers.

ISBN-13   978 1 78179 666 5   (hardback)
            978 1 78179 667 2   (paperback)
            978 1 78179 668 9   (ePDF)
            978 1 80050 045 7   (ePub)

British Library Cataloguing-in-Publication Data

A catalogue record for this book is available from the British Library.

Library of Congress Cataloging-in-Publication Data

Names: McGregor, William, 1952- author.
Title: Neo-Firthian approaches to linguistic typology / William B. McGregor.
Description: Sheffield, UK ; Bristol, CT : Equinox Publishing Ltd, 2021. | Series: Key concepts in systemic functional linguistics | Includes bibliographical references and index. | Summary: 'This book identifies the inadequacies of the dominant "atheoretical" approaches to linguistic typology, and shows how these can be circumvented through a firm foundation in a Neo-Firthian theoretical framework. It also contends that Neo-Firthian approaches must take typology seriously as a criterion of theoretical adequacy, and be able to account for the full range of grammatical phenomena and their variation across languages, as well as those features that are universal. Case studies illustrate this argument through a selection of grammatical phenomena' – Provided by publisher.
Identifiers: LCCN 2020054039 (print) | LCCN 2020054040 (ebook) | ISBN 9781781796665 (hardback) | ISBN 9781781796672 (paperback) | ISBN 9781781796689 (pdf) | ISBN 9781800500457 (epub)
Subjects: LCSH: Typology (Linguistics)
Classification: LCC P204 .M325 2021 (print) | LCC P204 (ebook) | DDC 415.01—dc23
LC record available at https://lccn.loc.gov/2020054039
LC ebook record available at https://lccn.loc.gov/2020054040

Typeset by JS Typesetting Ltd, Porthcawl, Mid Glamorgan

Contents

List of Tables

List of Figures

Preface

This book aims on the one hand to give an idea of how linguistic typology might be conceptualized within the parameters of Neo-Firthian linguistics, and on the other hand what Neo-Firthian theories might learn from linguistic typology. It is addressed to two main audiences – Systemic Functional linguists and other linguists working within the parameters of Neo-Firthian linguistics and linguistic typologists. I hope it will convince both audiences of the need for meaningful interaction with one another, and the potential of cooperation – though I doubt either group will be very happy with many of the ideas expressed.

I am grateful to Tom Bartlett, Gerard O'Grady, and Rebekah Wegener for the invitation to write this contribution on typology for the series *Key Concepts in Systemic Functional Linguistics*. I saw the invitation as a welcome indication that Systemic Functional linguists were at last seriously appreciating the importance of linguistic typology – and the diversity of human languages – to theory building and renovation. In accepting the invitation, I was partly motivated by the desire to reveal to systemicists something of this diversity (and limitations on it), and to highlight some topics that have fallen through the cracks in a theory that has shown an inordinate focus on English. I also wanted to underline the immense importance of language description to linguistic theorizing. These two domains, linguistic typology and descriptive linguistics, have been my major research foci since 1980, when I began my PhD research in the University of Sydney on a language of the far north-west of Australia, with Michael Halliday as one of my supervisors. His influence led me to Systemic Functional Linguistics. This was a welcome replacement for the type of approach I had been exposed to in my undergraduate training under Bob Dixon at the Australian National University, which I had increasingly felt to be intellectually stagnant.

Although this book belongs to a Systemic Functional Linguistics series, it is not a Systemic Functional account of linguistic typology. Rather, it presents an approach to linguistic typology that fits within the parameters of Neo-Firthian linguistics – an approach, or rather a set of approaches, to language inspired by ideas of the British linguist J.R. Firth (see further §1.1). Firth's influence can be seen in the architectural foundations of the approach adopted in this book. With the benefit of hindsight, having now completed the text it seems to me that I might as well have referred to the guiding theoretical parameters as Neo-Hallidayan, highlighting the significance of some of Halliday's ideas to linguistic typology and description, while rejecting and/or modifying others. In primary place on the positive side, I would put his notion of 'metafunctions', which have been reconstrued in a somewhat different way (§1.1.3). On the negative side are according a primary place to paradigmatic oppositions over syntagmatic, and the notion of grammatical metaphor.

I have long believed that the typological and descriptive enterprises are dependent on linguistic theory – that contrary to common belief among practitioners they are no more data-driven than theory-driven. Thus, I saw the invitation to contribute to this series as an opportunity to also speak to linguistic typologists and descriptive linguists, and highlight some domains in which more attention to theory would be beneficial to their enterprise. These include domains that are central to linguistic typology and have attracted considerable attention, including grammatical relations (see Chapter 2), the noun phrase (Chapter 3) and complex sentence constructions (Chapter 4). This book has provided me with an opportunity to bring together some of my misgivings about the standard typological and descriptive treatments of these domains that I have voiced over the years in various places, without, however, bringing them together into comprehensive stand-alone critiques.

More generally, I believe it is important to comment on methodological issues. This takes us to some recent debates in linguistic typology, especially concerning the nature of the objects (linguistic categories) that are brought into the cross-language comparisons. In this context I reiterate remarks that I made over 20 years before this debate erupted on cross-language comparison of linguistic signs in a semiotically informed linguistic typology (see §1.2.4.2).

For comments on earlier versions of some of the chapters, I am most grateful to Jan Rijkhoff, Jean-Christophe Verstraete, and Kristin Davidse; thanks also go to the editors of the series for commentary on the penultimate draft. None of these are to be blamed for any of the shortcomings of the present book, nor do they necessarily agree with everything (indeed anything) I say. Others, too many to name here, have influenced my thought on the topics dealt with in the chapters (including grammatical relations, the NP, classification, ergativity, optional case marking); I am grateful to all these unnamed linguists for many challenging conversations.

Hobro, December 2019

Abbreviations and Conventions

A	transitive subject
ABL	ablative
ABS	absolutive
ACC	accusative
ALL	allative
AO	agent-oriented verb
APiCS	*Atlas of Pidgin and Creole Language Structures*
APP	applicative
ART	article
AUG	augmented (number)
BLT	Basic Linguistic Theory
C	consonant
CAUS	causative
CL	class (or gender); classifier
CL1, CL2, …	class 1, 2, …
CM	conjugation marker
CNT	continuous
COM	comitative
COMP	complementizer
COP	copula
CRD	cardinal (a case contrasting with the oblique)
DAT	dative
DEF	definite
DECL	declarative
DU	dual
EMP	emphatic
EN	epenthetic nasal
ERG	ergative
EXC	exclusive
F	feminine (gender)
FCT	factive (mood)
fERG	focal ergative
FOC	focus (marker)
FUT	future

GEN	genitive
II	gender-number series II
ILL	illative
IMP	imperfective
INS	instrumental
INT	interrogative
IRR	irrealis
J	juncture morpheme
LO	location-oriented verb
LOC	locative
LOG	logophoric
LP	lexical prefix
M	masculine (gender)
MED	medial
MIN	minimal (number)
N	noun/nominal; neuter gender
NEG	negative
NF	non-feminine
NFUT	non-future
NOM	nominative
NP	noun phrase
NPST	non-past
NPV	non-pivot form
NRL	nominalizer
NSG	non-singular
N_W	w-class neuter
O	object
OBJ	objective
OBL	oblique
PART	participle
PF	perfective
PL	plural
PO	patient-oriented verb
POS	possessive
POT	potential (mood)
PP	prepositional/postpositional phrase
PROG	progressive
PRS	present
PST	past (tense)
PURP	purposive
REDUP	reduplicated

REL	relative (clause marker)
REP	repetition ('again')
RLS	realis
RP	remote past
S	subject; intransitive subject
SAA	Standard Average Australian (language)
SAE	Standard Average European (language)
SDPST	same day past
SFL	Systemic Functional Linguistics
SG	Semiotic Grammar; singular
SIM	simultaneous converb
SoA	State of Affairs
SP	speaker
SUB	subjunctive (mood)
SUBORD	subordinate
TP	today past
V	verb; vowel
VP	verb phrase
WALS	*The World Atlas of Language Structures*
YEST	yesterday (past tense)
1	first person
2	second person
3	third person
-	morpheme boundary
+	a morpheme boundary type in Gooniyandi verbs
/	boundary of intonation contour

Example sentences are laid out according to the usual conventions (see https://www.eva.mpg.de/lingua/pdf/Glossing-Rules.pdf); a period (.) separates multiple metalanguage glosses for single items in the object-language, while a slash (/) separates glosses for composite unanalysed (but analysable) forms in the object-language. In the glossing verbs of Gooniyandi I follow the convention of citing the classifier in its basic form in capitals. Inflecting verbs in other northern Australian languages are cited in capitals in the text and tables, though not in example sentences.

On first mention of each language I provide information on its genealogical classification and approximate geographical location. Genealogical classifications of many if not most languages are highly contentious, so I have decided to restrict the genealogical information to just the family designation. In many cases this is also a matter of dispute. For languages of the regions that I have personal knowledge of I employ the classification I believe to be most viable. For example, I eschew the term Khoisan, since this is not a genealogical family but a convenience label for three distinct families spoken in southern Africa, plus two other languages of uncertain lineage spoken further north. For other languages I have by and large employed the classifications of *Ethnologue* (https://www.ethnologue.com/) and *Glottolog* (https://glottolog.org/). In many cases these are to be taken with a grain of salt. While families such as Indo-European, Tibeto-Burman, and Austronesian are well established (possibly with some uncertainties as to exact boundaries), others are more contentious and not necessarily agreed to by all experts – for instance, Nilo-Saharan, Niger-Congo, Australian.

Chapter 1

Introduction

1.1 Firthian and Neo-Firthian Traditions in Linguistics

The ideas of John Rupert Firth (1890–1960)[1] form the backdrop to the Firthian tradition of linguistics, generally referred to as the London School of Linguistics, which was prominent in the UK from the 1930s to the early 1960s, and after Firth's death, to various Neo-Firthian schools of thought. Firth himself never produced a coherent linguistic theory, though he did develop a theory of phonology. It was his students who developed his other ideas into theories. In this section I begin by highlighting Firth's most influential ideas (§1.1.1). Following this, I attempt to give a brief overview of the range of Neo-Firthian approaches (§1.1.2). What counts as a Neo-Firthian approach is not uncontentious: ideas of Firth have been adopted by many who would not call themselves Neo-Firthians, and many students of Firth, as well as their students, hardly count as Neo-Firthians given the limited apparent influence of Firth on their thought. In the final subsection of the section (§1.1.3), I outline one Neo-Firthian notion of particular significance to descriptive linguistics and linguistic typology, which is taken up in the discussion of typological topics in Chapters 2–6.

1.1.1 Key Ideas of Firth

Firth's major contribution to linguistics can be summarized in terms of three notions: (i) the centrality and ubiquity of meaning in human language; (ii) the polysystemicity of languages; and (iii) the fundamental place of prosodies in phonology, and the rejection of the notion of the phoneme. In addition to these three notions, Firth showed an abiding interest in linguistic historiography, and many of his publications begin by setting the topic in a historical context; indeed, some papers are primarily historical in nature. It seems likely that Firth's interest in the history of linguistics inspired his student R.H. Robins (1921–2000), who wrote an influential history of linguistics (Robins 1967). In what follows we provide a brief discussion of Firth's three key ideas; his historiographical contribution is not discussed further.

(i) Meaning occupies centre stage in Firth's linguistics, and Firth was committed to the idea that meaning infuses all levels of linguistic organization. It is not restricted to the lexicon and grammar, but extends into other components, including phonetics and phonology. Firth illustrated the extension of meaning into phonetics/phonology with two examples (as I understand him, Firth was not arguing that everything in phonetics and phonology is organized according to meaning). First, phonological processes represent a mode of meaning in that they 'are characteristic of persons, of social groups, even of nations' (Firth 1957: 192). He continues:

> Moreover, the general feature of voice quality is part of the phonetic mode of meaning of an English boy, a Frenchman, or a lady from New York. Surely it is part of the meaning of an American to sound like one.

Despite the somewhat confusing wording of the final sentence – surely he should have put it the other way around, though he repeats this ordering elsewhere in discussing other examples; for example, Firth (1957: 226) – Firth seems to be wanting to say that phonetic features can index social meanings such as group membership. Indeed, he extends the story from phonetics to broader patterns in grammar and lexicon – so that, ultimately, entire languages express meaning: '[s]urely the pattern of these relations is part of the meaning of Danish as used by Danes' (Firth 1957: 228). It is difficult not to see here the seeds of Labovian variationist sociolinguistics (especially the 'third wave' – Eckert 2018: 144–145) and the Hallidayan notion of language as social semiotic.

Second, Firth recognized that certain segments or sequences – for example, *sl* at the beginning of English words and *ump* in the rhymes – are meaningful, despite the fact that they are not morphemes (Firth 1964: 183–188, 190–194). By virtue of their recurrence in English words, speakers associate initial *sl* with a pejorative sense (*slut, slack, slouch, slovenly*). Firth dubbed this phenomenon *phonaesthesia*, and drew a sharp contrast with onomatopoeia and sound symbolism – which he spoke of as a 'fallacy' (Firth 1957: 194). Recently there has been an explosion of interest in phonaesthesia and iconicity not only in English but also other languages (e.g. Hinton, Nichols and Ohala 1994; McGregor 1996b; Nuckolls 1999; Bartens 2000; Urban 2011; Haynie, Bowern and LaPalombara 2014; Willett 2014; Kwon 2015; Blake 2017; Slonimska and Roberts 2017; Willemsen and Hjort Miltersen 2020),[2] as well as a more general questioning of the Saussurean doctrine of the arbitrariness of the linguistic sign.

In Firth's view semantics is the investigation of meanings of all types, regardless of the locus of expression. Central to his semantics was the notion of the context of situation (Firth 1957: 27), which phrase he borrowed from his one-time colleague the Polish anthropologist Bronisław Malinowski (1884–1942). Firth's semantics was a contextual theory of meaning, according to which the meanings of utterances derive from the situation in which they occur as much as from the uttered sounds. This was a serial contextualization, with an expanding set of contexts extending from the phonetic out to the widest context of culture. Firth attempted to make a classification of these contexts of situation (Firth 1968: 177–178), but this remained rather rudimentary. Meanings are found in each of the widening circle of contexts in terms of the function of linguistic elements in their context of situation. The total meaning of an utterance would be made up of the meanings in each level (Firth 1968: 200–201), though by what processes is not discussed in detail.

Not all linguistic meaning is contextual in this sense. One of Firth's most significant insights was that there are mutual expectancies between words in sentences, such that the English word *coffee*, for example, tends to co-occur with *white*, *black*, *weak* and *strong* and is less likely to co-occur with *grey*, *brown*, *soft* and *hard* (compare *soft* and *hard liquor*). Firth termed such biases in the mutual expectancies of words *collocations* (Firth 1957: 194–195). Collocations provide a component of the meaning of words according to Firth. However, he is explicit that this is a different type of meaning to contextual meaning (Firth 1957: 195). Though he does not develop this point, it seems that Firth saw contextual meaning as the vertical dimension: the function of a linguistic item in the larger context in which it occurs. Collocational meaning, by contrast, relates to the horizontal dimension of relations between things within the same context.

(ii) Firth strongly objected to the conceptualization of a language as a unitary phenomenon:

> Unity is the last concept that should be applied to language. Unity of language is the most fugitive of all unities, whether it be historical, geographical, national, or personal. There is no such thing as *une langue une* and there never has been.
>
> (Firth 1957: 29)

On the one hand, people serve in multiple social roles, and along with this use different 'situationally appropriate forms of language' (Firth 1968: 207). On the other hand, Firth spoke of language as *polysystemic*: a language consists of heterogenous coexisting systems. There is systematicity in many small domains of language, without there being an overarching uniformity – '[f]or any given language there is no coherent system ... which can handle and state all the facts' (Firth 1968: 24). Firth thus recognized variation as central to language. There may be no such thing as the phonological system of a language. For example, different phonologies might exist for words of different parts of speech. And, indeed, it is not uncommon to find that certain parts of speech in a language show phonotactic peculiarities that differentiate them from other parts of speech (for example, ideophones in many languages, and verbs in some languages). Firth also observed that different phonologies may be in operation in different syllabic positions: for instance, in languages such as German and Danish there would be different consonantal systems in syllable onsets and codas. Firth took the rather extreme line on this variation in regarding the systems as quite independent of one another and refusing to concede any commonality.

(iii) Firth objected strongly to the phonological theories of his contemporaries, especially those of the Prague School and American structuralism. In many places he refuses to countenance the phoneme as a unit, though occasionally this is tempered somewhat and he does admit the utility of the phoneme in transcription of speech. Firth's theory, prosodic analysis, divided the speech chain into phonematic units and prosodies.

Phonematic units are segments, comparable with phonemes though more abstract, and are sequenced in the speech chain. Prosodies are non-segmental, and can be spread over entire words, syllabic units, parts of syllables, and so on. Prosodies permit a non-process account of phenomena such as vowel harmony and assimilation: instead of processes, the description is in terms of the span of the prosody, for example to a word, the final syllable of a word plus a suffix, or adjacent units over which 'assimilation' applies.

Firth's ideas on phonology are the most completely developed component of his linguistics, and much work by Firth and his students in the 1950s was in this domain. This is also the widest known of his contributions to linguistics and, some would argue, represents his major contribution. For present purposes, however, Firth's phonological ideas are of less significance than his notions of meaning and polysystemicity, and I do not discuss them in more detail. For fuller accounts see, for example, Monaghan (1979: 41–44) and Ogden (2006).

One further component of Firth's thought is worth mentioning in winding up this section, even though it is by no means a Firthian peculiarity. This is the idea that both paradigmatic and syntagmatic relations are central, and neither can be derived from the other. They motivate Firth's distinction between system (the paradigmatic axis) and structure (the syntagmatic axis) (Firth 1968: 186). Neo-Firthians differ in terms of whether or not they assign equal prominence to both paradigmatic and syntagmatic relations (see below).

1.1.2 Neo-Firthian Approaches

The most prominent Neo-Firthian tradition is without a doubt Systemic Functional Linguistics (SFL), a tradition that was largely inspired by the work of Firth's student Michael A.K. Halliday (1925–2018),[3] beginning in the late 1950s. The term itself highlights two primary features of the theory. First, it takes the system as fundamental – and hence syntagmatic relations are derivable from paradigmatic relations. Second, it is a functional theory in that it is premised on the notion that language external explanations are to be sought for the organization of language – enshrined in the Hallidayan aphorism 'language is as it is because of the functions it serves in the life of man'. More specifically:

> Language has evolved to satisfy human needs; and the way it is organized is functional with respect to these needs — it is not arbitrary. A functional grammar is essentially a 'natural' grammar, in the sense that everything in it can be explained, ultimately, by reference to how language is used.
>
> (Halliday 1985: xiii)

SFL is by no means a completely homogeneous tradition, and three major approaches can be identified: the standard Hallidayan variety, the Sydney model associated with James Martin, and the Cardiff model, largely inspired by Robin Fawcett. This is not the place to go further into the theory. Two recent handbooks, Bartlett and O'Grady (2017) and Thompson et al. (2019), give a comprehensive picture of the present state of SFL; Butler (2003a, 2003b) provides an overview of the theory and situates it with respect to other functional approaches – see Butler and Gonzálvez-García (2014) and Butler (2019) for further comparison between SFL and other functional theories.

Various students of Halliday have, since the 1960s, developed their own theoretical approaches, initially inspired by Firthian and Hallidayan thought. Among them might be mentioned Robert M.W. Dixon, Rodney Huddleston and Richard Hudson, all of whom contributed to the early development of SFL. It is not clear to me that their current approaches are sufficiently inspired by Firth to warrant the label Neo-Firthian, and I doubt whether they would see themselves as Neo-Firthians.

Another student of Halliday, Kristin Davidse, has fostered a group of linguists centred in Leuven, and extending to other parts of Belgium. Davidse's own approach falls within the broad SFL tradition, though more than other systemicists she has cross-fertilized SFL with other functionally oriented traditions including Cognitive Grammar (e.g. Langacker 1987, 1991) and grammaticalization theory (e.g. Hopper and Traugott 2003; Traugott 2003). Also notable about this approach is the focus on detail and argumentation, which are seriously lacking in SFL generally. The Davidse-inspired Leuven School might be regarded as Neo-Firthian in that it shares some of the approaches of the Firthian and Hallidayan traditions, and places meaning in the centre of the picture. It cannot, however, be regarded as a school of SFL.

My own thought has been inspired by Halliday, though I diverge from him on a number of key issues, to the extent that my own approach, Semiotic Grammar (SG) (McGregor 1997b), cannot be seen as a sub-tradition of SFL.

SFL is not just a theory of grammar, but aims to be a comprehensive theory of language in all of its aspects. A particular focus has been on the social aspect of language – also inspired by Firth (see above), enshrined in Halliday's 'language as social semiotic' (Halliday 1978). The theory has also a manifest strong interest in first language learning by the child, the study of text and discourse, and has shown a strong orientation to applications: SFL is (allegedly) 'an appliable theory'. Other Neo-Firthians have developed Firth's ideas primarily in domains other than grammar, including John McH. Sinclair (1933–2007) in corpus linguistics, Malcolm Coulthard (1943–) in discourse analysis and forensic linguistics, and Norman Fairclough (1941–) in critical discourse analysis (Fairclough 1995; Chouliaraki and Fairclough 1999). These aspects of SFL and Neo-Firthian thought are of little relevance to the present book.

1.1.3 Metafunctions/Semiotic Components

In this section I introduce one Hallidayan notion that seems to me particularly significant, perhaps his most important insight: the notion of *metafunction* (Halliday 1985) or *semiotic component*, as I prefer to call it (McGregor 1997b). This is a cornerstone of Hallidayan SFL, though some systemicists consider it has no theoretical place – that it merely permits a notional categorization of grammatical phenomena (Fawcett 1980: 35–38).

Halliday proposes that the grammars of all languages are organized around three broad groupings of functions, hence metafunctions: ideational, interpersonal and textual (Halliday 1985).

The ideational metafunction concerns representation of the world of experience of a language user, whether it be the external world of 'reality' or an internal one of the user's construal or imagination. A clause such as *they followed his dripping blood until nightfall*, for instance, construes a world in which a certain group of people are doing something in a particular circumstance. Halliday distinguishes two subtypes of ideational meaning, experiential and logical. The experiential metafunction concerns the categorization of the construed world into persons, things, events and the like. The logical metafunction also concerns the world of experience, but attends instead to the interrelations between the experienced phenomena. For instance, the logical metafunction construes relations between situations specified by clauses: the sentence *they followed his dripping blood until nightfall, when they made camp* connects two situations (experiential phenomena) in a temporal relation (a logical phenomenon).

The interpersonal metafunction concerns the relationship constructed between speaker and hearer: the speaker's use of 'language as the means of his own intrusion into the speech event: the expression of his comments, his attitudes and evaluations, and also of the relationship that he sets up between himself and the listener' (Halliday 1973: 106). The interpersonal metafunction accounts for the illocutionary mood differences between *they followed his dripping blood until nightfall, did they follow his dripping blood until nightfall?, when did they follow his dripping blood until?,* and *follow his dripping blood until nightfall.*

Unlike the other metafunctions, the textual metafunction is language-internal, language turned back on itself, and concerns the organization of grammatical units as message-bearing items. According to Halliday's 1985 model, the clause is organized in terms of textual dimensions of information (Given and New – roughly, what is evaluated as predictable or recoverable vs what is evaluated as not predictable) and thematic structure (Theme and Rheme – the point of departure of the message vs what is added to that point of departure). In the English clause, Given typically precedes New. However, information is primarily marked prosodically, not by order, and utterance of a clause on different intonation contours correspond to different organizations of the expressed information. The unmarked utterance of *they followed his dripping blood until nightfall* will have tonic prominence on the final lexical item, *nightfall*. All other lexical words, as well as the pronoun *they*, can instead take the prominent syllable. These more marked choices give more marked choices of information focus, and invoke presuppositions. Information focus on *followed* invokes the presupposition that they did something to his dripping blood. In terms of thematic structure, the clause begins with the Theme *they*, which the clause is about; this is followed by the remainder, the Rheme, which represents what is said about the Theme. By contrast, *his dripping blood they followed until nightfall* is about *his dripping blood*, which represents the Theme; the remainder of the clause represents what is said about the blood.

In Halliday's conceptualization, the three-way grouping of linguistic functions into metafunctions is not a mere notional categorization, not merely a means of conceptualizing the immense range of functions to which languages may be put. Rather, it represents a principle according to which the grammars of human languages are organized. The metafunctional groupings are incorporated into the architecture of grammar, and belong to the very system of grammar. The metafunctions are, as it were, crystallizations of functions of language within the fabric of language. They serve to link the external functions of language (as a communicative system) with internal functions (functions of linguistic units within their linguistic contexts – grammatical relations or roles, broadly conceived). Metafunctions are emic categories within a language – indeed, it is hypothesized, within every language.[4]

The metafunctions are not hierarchically related, and simultaneously apply to and structure the clause; they may also structure other grammatical phenomena such as sentences (clause complexes) and groups or phrases. However, in Halliday's view the metafunctional organization of units other than the clause need not be so clear-cut, and the group, for example, combines the metafunctions into one 'line' of organization (Halliday 1985: 158).

Halliday motivates identification of the metafunctions in two ways. First, he proposes that they correlate with four different types of structure: constituency (experiential), recursive (logical), prosodic (interpersonal) and periodic (textual). These distinct structural types are inspired by Pike (1959)'s three-way view of language as particle (constituency and recursivity), wave (periodic) and field (prosodic). Second, Halliday observes that clausal networks of paradigmatic oppositions fall largely into separate subsystems that have few connections between them. These separate subnetworks correspond to the metafunctions and the metafunctional organization of the clause.

SG assumes a somewhat different conceptualization of Hallidayan metafunctions as semiotic components (McGregor 1997b). Four semiotic components are distinguished: experiential, logical, interpersonal and textural. In terms of notional 'content' the first three are understood in basically the same way as in Hallidayan SFL. The fourth, the textural semiotic, is construed rather differently to Halliday's textual metafunction: it is defined by syntagmatic relations of the linking type, whereby one item serves to link to something else via associative relations. Textural relations serve to hold grammatical constructions together and unify them; they also establish links between utterances and their contexts of use – and thus represent meaning-making resources available to the speaker for referring purposes. The grammatical relations comprising the textural semiotic are indexes in Peircean terms.

As in Hallidayan thought, the semiotic components are considered to be emic phenomena that structure grammatical units in each and every particular language, and in this sense can be said to be emic universals. However, in SG they are defined primarily syntagmatically, in terms of the type of syntagmatic relation by which they are expressed or realized. Specifically, the experiential semiotic is expounded through constituency (part-whole) relations; the logical semiotic through dependency (part-part) relations;[5] and textural through indexical relations (which are not bound to any structural elements in particular). The interpersonal semiotic is somewhat less easily described in syntagmatic terms. McGregor (1997b) characterizes them as whole-whole relations. More recently I have come to question this, and instead view it in terms of a model of action on a linguistic object (McGregor 2017a, 2019a). A linguistic entity is either used or 'shaped' in some fashion or other, and this contrasts with either its non-use or alternative shaping in terms of the interpersonal dimension. Effectively this is analogical in nature: action on another person is represented linguistically by means of action on a linguistic item.

Along with the different conceptualizations of the metafunctions/semiotic components come a number of different placements of particular grammatical categories and phenomena. I summarize some of the main similarities and differences in Table 1.1. There is no scope in the present book to enter into detailed discussion of the motivation for the differences in assignment of the phenomena; see, however, McGregor (2019a).

The notion of metafunction/semiotic component is what distinguishes SFL and SG most prominently from most other functional theories of grammar. These by and large focus on explaining grammatical phenomena in terms of specific functional motivations for structural phenomena (e.g. Givón 1995; Dik 1986), and do not make higher-level groupings among these motivations.

According to all versions of SFL, the lexicon and grammar go together to form a single 'level' of lexicogrammar. The lexicon is conceived of 'as most delicate grammar' (Halliday 1961). There is a serious problem with this suggestion, however. The notion of metafunction/semiotic component implies a very clear-cut division between the lexicon and the grammar. Only grammar is organized around the semiotic components; the lexicon cannot be strictly divided in terms of these components. At least in this regard lexicon and grammar emerge as semiotically separate resources.

1.2 An Overview of Linguistic Typology

The primary concern of the discipline of linguistic typology is with variation in human languages, and the extent of and the limits on that variation. It is concerned with both what is recurrent in linguistic systems and how they can differ. Thus, typology is concerned with universals of language as well as the variation and patterns in the variation of linguistic phenomena. Aside from documenting and describing the similarities and differences among languages, it is concerned with explaining them. Typologists want to know why certain structures or systems occur or do not occur, and why some are more frequent than others.

Table 1.1 Comparison of SFL and SG classification of some grammatical phenomena

Standard SFL	Grammatical phenomenon	SG
Ideational		[not recognized]
Experiential	Participant roles (arguments)	Experiential
	Process/Situation clause types	
	Relational clauses (A *is* B – range of types)	Logical
	Circumstantial relations (location, cause, reason, etc.)	
Logical	Clause/phrase/group complexes: expansion (extension, elaboration, enhancement)	
	Reported speech & thought (projection)	Interpersonal
Metaphorically interpersonal	Clausal complementation (belief, knowledge, etc. complements)	
Interpersonal	Illocutionary mood	
	Polarity	
	Epistemic mood ('modality')	
	Evidentiality	
	Finite element	
	Subject	[unplaced; the status of Subject is unclear to me]
Textual	Information structure	
	Thematic structure	Textural
[not recognized: markers emerge via realization statements, but there is no theoretical place for marking relations]	Marking relations	

1.2.1 Origins and Development of Typology

The nineteenth century saw the blossoming of comparative research on languages that focused on establishing genealogical relations among languages; this culminated in the Neogrammarian programme, which formed the background for the emergence of comparative and historical linguistics. A less conspicuous trend was initiated simultaneously which aimed to compare languages on a non-historical basis; this formed the backdrop for the emergence of linguistic typology.

In the early nineteenth century, Friedrich von Schlegel (1772–1829) and August von Schlegel (1767–1845) introduced a classification of languages according to morphological properties. This classification was developed further in the nineteenth and early twentieth centuries by Wilhelm von Humboldt (1767–1835), Edward Sapir (1884–1939) and others. A refined version of this enormously influential classification is still habitually employed today, if only to give an initial idea of the structural properties of a language. It distinguishes four language types: isolating (where words typically comprise a single morpheme), agglutinating (where words are typically made up of a number of morphemes in a string, with fairly clear divisions between them), fusional (in which words are typically polymorphemic, but the division between the morphemes is often blurry) and polysynthetic (highly morphologically complex languages in which what is a sentence in other types of language is often expressed by a single word).

Although this morphological classification is synchronic, a number of nineteenth- and early twentieth-century linguists imposed a diachronic evolutionary perspective on it, such that language begin as isolating, becoming agglutinating and ultimately fusional (the evolutionarily most developed status according to some). If the fusional contrasts are lost, a new cycle could begin.

The term *typology* was not employed until the turn of the twentieth century. It is generally attributed to Georg von der Gabelentz (1840–1893), who in the second edition of his book *Die Sprachwissenschaft* (Gabelentz 1901 [1891]: 481) says: 'If one had to baptize a not yet born child, I would choose the name typology' (cited in Ramat 2010: 21). Gabelentz stressed that typological classification is a very different thing from genealogical classification of languages.

Modern typology as such is generally considered to have begun with Joseph Greenberg (1915–2001) in the early 1960s, although others – including (to mention just a few) Edward Sapir, Pater Wilhelm Schmidt (1868–1954), Roman Jakobson (1896–1982) and Nikolai Trubetzkoy (1890–1938) – made some notable contributions in the first half of the twentieth century. Greenberg's seminal paper (1963) provided a cross-linguistic survey of word order in three different domains: (a) the order of adpositions with respect to the 'head'; (b) the position of the verb (V) with respect to subject (S) and object (O); and (c) the position of the adjective with respect to the noun it modifies. In regard to (b), according to Greenberg three orders are dominant cross-linguistically: SOV, SVO and VSO. Word order typology figures prominently in modern typology and descriptive linguistics, and recent studies support these as the dominant word orders, though the other three orders – OVS, OSV and VOS – are also attested. It is also increasingly realized that many languages (given the inadequacies of the sources it is difficult to estimate how many) should be regarded as showing no dominant word order. In these free word order languages the different orders may differ strongly in preference, and the language-internal frequencies sometimes replicate the cross-linguistic tendencies. Greenberg also observed significant correlations among the three ordering phenomena. For instance, SVO word order is more strongly correlated with prepositions and adjective following the noun than it is with postpositions and adjective-noun order. Furthermore, Greenberg attempted to set typology on a firmer empirical base by selecting a motivated sample of languages and establishing quantificational methods.

Today linguistic typology is a mature discipline of considerable scope. The core domains – phonetics and phonology, lexicon and grammar – are all grist for the mill and are the sites for a great deal of contemporary research. Semantics, pragmatics and sociolinguistics are also investigated typologically.

To wind up this overview of the historical background to the subject,[6] a note on terminology is in order. Following contemporary usage, I speak in this book of *linguistic typology* rather than *language typology*. The term *linguistic typology* registers the concern of modern typology with the classification of phenomena within languages rather than the classification of entire languages. The nineteenth-century morphological typology, by contrast, was a typology of languages – although linguists such as Sapir realized that no language could be classified as a single morphological type. The morphological typology of languages could easily become a linguistic typology by reorienting attention to the morphological properties of different parts of speech cross-linguistically.

1.2.2 Scope of Linguistic Typology

To give a feel for the discipline of typology, in this section I outline in a very broad sweep the nature of typological work in the three core domains, without going into great depth or breadth of treatment. Semantic and pragmatic typology, the typology of discourse and text, and sociolinguistic typology are left out of this overview, since these would take us too far from the concerns of this book; see, for example, Evans (2011) on semantic typology, Myhill (1992) on discourse typology, and Trudgill (2011) on sociolinguistic typology.

1.2.2.1 Phonological typology

Languages vary considerably phonetically and phonologically. Some languages have only around ten phonemes while others have over 100. Rotokas (West Bougainville, Papua New Guinea) has just six consonants and five vowels; !Xóõ (Tuu, Botswana) is generally considered to be the language with the largest inventory of phonemes, though there is considerable disagreement as to the exact number, which ranges from about 100 to almost 150. (The difference of opinion depends on how click accompaniments are analysed.) As this indicates, there are also limits on the variation: all languages have at least some phonemes, and none have more than 500 (perhaps 200 is a more accurate estimate of the least upper bound, but I am inclined to be cautious). This statement of course requires an important qualification so far left implicit: we are dealing with spoken languages. Sign languages don't have phones or phonemes as such, since they employ the visual-gestural rather than the auditory-vocal medium. True, sign language linguists speak of phonetics and phonology. However, there is nothing akin to the segment, phonetic or phonemic, in sign languages. Rather, what is fundamental to sign language phonetics and phonology are features such as handshape, location and movement. In sign languages Firth's mistrust of the phoneme is most clearly motivated.

Having mentioned sign languages, it is important to state a caveat: this book is concerned exclusively with spoken languages. To add sign languages would be problematic for various reasons, including the relative dearth of typological and descriptive research on these languages.

Phonological typologies can be based on a wide variety of factors, among which we might single out as most common: inventories of phonemes (e.g. the types of segment found, the features distinguishing them, and interrelations among these – for example, if a language has a voicing contrast in nasals it will have a voicing contrast in stops), phonotactics (e.g. permissible syllable shapes, and patterning in consonant clusters), phonological processes (such as sandhi processes applying within and across words), and prosodic or suprasegmental features. We now briefly outline some broad typological characteristics of prosodic systems.

In English and many languages of Europe the syllables of a word are pronounced with different degrees of stress (a complex factor that involves a combination of pitch, intensity and sometimes length), giving rise to patterns of prominence in the sequence of syllables. But in many languages of Asia and Africa (e.g. Mandarin Chinese (Tibeto-Burman, China) and Setswana (Niger-Congo, southern Africa)) stress is not employed in this way. We could distinguish between stress languages and non-stress languages depending on whether or not syllables of words inherently take different degrees of stress. In some languages, such as Japanese (Japonic, Japan), the syllables of a word are not more or less prominent by virtue of different degrees of stress, but by differences in pitch. These are called pitch-accent languages: the prominent (accented) syllable(s) of a word is typically produced with a relatively high pitch. There are some languages, for instance Swedish, that employ both stress and pitch-accent.

Among stress languages, some, including English, show phonemic stress. Stress in such languages is employed contrastively, and can distinguish words, as shown by minimal pairs such as the noun-verb pair ['ɪmpɔːt] vs [ɪmˈpɔːt]. In many stress languages, however, the placement of stress is entirely predictable; stress in these languages is delimitative in the sense that it indicates the phonological extent of words (not necessarily fully precisely). This is the case in languages as diverse as Polish (Indo-European, Poland), Hungarian (Uralic, Hungary), Dyirbal (Pama-Nyungan, Australia) and Gooniyandi (Bunuban, Australia). In Gooniyandi, simple monomorphemic lexical words take stress on the first syllable; if the word has more than three syllables it also typically gets stress on the penultimate syllable.[2] Stress in Hungarian also goes on the first syllable of a word; in Polish, however, it typically goes on the penultimate syllable. (The above remarks concern stress in simple lexical roots; stress placement in inflected and derived forms, as well as in word sequences, is sometimes more complex.)

In tone languages different patterns of pitch and/or their placement serve to distinguish between lexical words. Tone languages are found in almost all geographical regions, and make up somewhat over half of the world's languages; Africa, Asia and the Americas are well known for their high prevalence. Various typologies of tone languages or tone systems have been proposed. Best known is Pike's distinction between contour tone systems (where direction of tone movement is relevant) and register tone systems (where the relative height of the tone on a syllable is crucial) (Pike 1948). Thai (Tai-Kadai, Thailand), Lao (Tai-Kadai, Laos), Mandarin Chinese, Hakka (Tibeto-Burman, China), Cantonese (Tibeto-Burman, China) and many other languages of south-east Asia are contour tone languages. Many African languages have register tone systems, including Yoruba (Niger-Congo, Benin), Twi (Niger-Congo, Ghana), Bemba (Niger-Congo, Zambia), Sango (a creole, Central African Republic) and Shua (Khoe-Kwadi, Botswana). Donohue (1997) proposes (for languages of New Guinea) a typology based not on the shapes of the tones but rather on the domains of the tonal contrasts, whether they apply to entire words or to each syllable independently.

1.2.2.2 *Lexical typology*

Parts of speech categories play a central role in grammatical description and theory, lexicology and lexicography, as they have since Dionysios Thrax's (217–145 BC) grammar of Greek (*téxnē grammatikē* 'art of grammar'). Many, if not most, ancient and modern descriptive grammars employ terms such as noun, verb, adjective and adverb, as do the majority of linguistic theories. The ways in which the parts of speech are defined for different languages and in different theories differ considerably, however, raising serious difficulties for the typologist. A cross-linguistic comparison of systems can only be sustained if the systems in the various languages are defined in sufficiently similar ways so that one can be sure that what are compared are indeed comparables.

Typologists themselves, of course, also have their own theoretical proclivities which shape their approaches to parts of speech systems. Some take the view that parts of speech categories such as verb, noun and adjective are universals of human language. According to Croft (2000) these word classes are not categories of particular languages; rather, they are universals in the sense that they serve as typological prototypes for noun, verb and adjective, thus permitting cross-language comparison. Also in the universalist camp is Baker (2000), who by contrast defines noun, verb and adjective in terms of specific syntactic features.

Many typologists consider parts of speech systems and categories to be language particular, and thus that it is not necessarily the case that all languages distinguish categories of verb, noun and adjective (or adverb). This view is taken, for example, by Schachter (1985); Schachter and Shopen (2007); Hengeveld (1992); Rijkhoff (2007), among others. At the same time, some of these authors accept the universality of some of the parts of speech: Schachter and Shopen (2007) propose that all languages distinguish at least two primary lexical categories, verbs and nouns. However, in contrast to universalists such as Baker, this is posited as an empirical universal that could be falsified.

Criteria for distinguishing parts of speech categories tend to align with the formalist-functionalist divide. Formalists such as Baker (2000) employ formal syntactic features. Functionalists typically employ functional criteria. Various functionalists take as crucial the functions served by words of different categories. For instance, Hopper and Thompson (1984) employ discourse function, while Croft (2000) associates parts of speech with 'pragmatic' functions of predication, reference and modification. Dik's Functional Grammar has spawned a considerable amount of typological work on parts of speech systems; fundamental to this approach are definitions in terms of the grammatical relations served by the categories – for instance, verbs are words that can only be used as the head of 'predicate phrases' (roughly verb phrases) (e.g. Hengeveld 1992; Rijkhoff 2007; and various contributions in van Lier and Rijkhoff 2013).

The challenge for those who adopt a non-universalist stance lies in the cross-linguistic comparison of categories. There are two main ways in which this issue has been addressed. On the one hand, one may be satisfied with comparing items on the basis of a degree of similarity of meaning. This is the approach taken by Schachter (1985: 4): first parts of speech are set up for the separate languages; the members of the individual categories are then compared and named according to the majority notional meanings of the members – if most specify events, this category is appropriately named verb, and the categories with this label in different languages are comparable. On the other hand, one might attempt to specify defining characteristics of the parts of speech. This is the approach taken by Hengeveld (1992) and Rijkhoff (2007): only words that can be used exclusively as heads of verb phrases count as verbs in any language.

I highlight these two approaches to the cross-linguistic comparison of language-specific categories since both are employed in this book: the former in the typology of grammatical relations (Chapter 2), the latter in optional case marking (Chapter 5) and verb classification (Chapter 6). We return to this point in §1.2.4.2.

To return to the topic of word categories, there seems to me to be no reason to believe that parts of speech categories are universal or theoretical givens. They are categories that should be defined in terms of the different patterns of behaviour of words (and morphemes) in a given language rather than identified by fiat. They should be of descriptive use in the grammar of any language for which they are proposed. Parts of speech systems show considerable diversity reflecting marked differences among languages, as well as differences among those who describe the systems. There also appear to be some strong tendencies, and limits to the diversity. For instance, while it seems likely that there are some languages that do not distinguish nouns from verbs – indeed, perhaps do not make any category distinctions among lexical items (e.g. Samoan (Austronesian, Samoa) and Cayuga (Iroquoian, Canada and USA), see Rijkhoff 2007: 715–716) – there are relatively few languages for which this is the case. At the other extreme, it seems improbable that in any language each word will behave in such unique fashions that it is impossible to establish categories larger than singleton ones. Indeed, the available evidence suggests that for each language there will be a smallish number of categories (of the order of a score or so) to which words can be assigned on the basis of general patterns of behaviour. More specific behaviours might define subcategories of these categories, and there might conceivably be outlier words that don't fit any category but their own.

The categories adjective and adverb are less frequently distinguished. Indeed, it seems unlikely that any language would fail to draw a noun-verb distinction while showing a category of adjectives or adverbs. Many languages of Australia (e.g. Warrwa (Nyulnyulan), Gooniyandi, Dyirbal) lack adjectives as a separate part of speech; there is a single class of nominals that serve both to specify the referent type and to indicate a quality. In those Australian languages that do distinguish adjectives, they often comprise a small (perhaps closed) class. Galela (Papuan, Halmahera) also has no adjectives; to specify qualities it employs a construction with a verb participle (Rijkhoff 2007).

There are languages that lack adverbs (in the sense of words that prototypically modify verbs, like *quickly, happily*). This is the case for Dyirbal: a single part of speech is employed in both event and manner specification (Dixon 1972: 54). Ngiti (Nilo-Saharan, Zaire) distinguishes nouns, verbs and a single class of words that serve both as modifiers of nouns and verbs (Rijkhoff 2007: 717).

The four classes, noun, verb, adjective and adverb, are often considered to be the most central lexical classes, the lexemes most relevant to grammar, and are the focus of much typological work (Hengeveld 1992; Schachter 1985; Schachter and Shopen 2007; Rijkhoff 2007; Croft 2000; and others). They do not, however, exhaust the range of lexical parts of speech that may be distinguished in a language.[8] All languages, presumably, have a category of interjections (Ameka 1992). Many have a class of ideophones, words – often sound-symbolic – that evoke sensory images, like *boom, bang, thud* (see e.g. Voeltz and Kilian-Hatz 2001; Dingemanse 2012); in some languages – especially in Africa – ideophones form a large open class. Both interjections and ideophones are arguably lexical categories, though they are often considered to be syntactically inert, and thus of marginal concern to grammar – which assumption I would take issue with. Moreover, they typically play a prominent role in communication.[9]

1.2.2.3 *Grammatical typology*

An enormous volume of typological research concerns grammar in the narrow sense of morphology and syntax, and much of the contents of handbooks and textbooks is devoted to grammatical typology, as is a large fraction of the research published in journals such as *Linguistic Typology*. Some of the most popular topics in grammatical typology include: word order; nominal systems of case and case marking, gender and number; the noun phrase; possession; negation; grammatical relations; transitivity; voice systems; person marking; verbal systems of tense, mood, and aspect; and complex sentences. Some of these are treated in this book (grammatical relations, transitivity, the noun phrase, complex sentence constructions), others are touched on briefly in passing (e.g. gender systems, word order typology). Since it helps to illustrate issues and methods that will be relevant throughout the book, in what follows I discuss one of the above topics that is not treated elsewhere, the typology of case and case marking systems. For fuller treatment, see Blake (2001); Primus (2011); and various articles in Malchukov and Spencer (2009).

Case is a category that concerns the indication of the grammatical relationship or role that a nominal or noun phrase (NP) bears in another NP or clause (e.g. Blake 2001: 1). It concerns morphological marking of the nominal units themselves – NPs and the parts of speech that typically occur in them, including nouns, pronouns, determiners, etc. Indexation of grammatical relations of NPs is sometimes achieved by morphemes that occur elsewhere, such as verbal agreement markers and cross-referencing pronominals (which may occur on verbs or elsewhere in the sentence); these phenomena are not usually included under case.[10]

One dimension we can typologize case systems on is the locus of the marking. In some languages this is at the level of the word, while in others it is at phrase level. Many languages, including Latin (Indo-European, Vatican City), indicate case inflectionally on nouns (and many or all other units in NPs), as in example (1.1): each word of the NP 'a few months' occurs in the same inflectional case. Latin is a fusional language, and identification of segmental morphemes marking case is problematic: case and number are marked together in the same inflections. In some African languages cases are marked prosodically by tonal distinctions (König 2008a: 204–224). This has been proposed somewhat controversially for some Bantu languages; in Shua the accusative case has low tone as an allomorph, alternating with segmental realization as -(ʔ)à. By contrast, there are many other languages in which case marking morphemes can be readily identified, including Pitta-Pitta (Pama-Nyungan, Australia).

> (1.1)   *rēgnāvit*   *cōnsul*   *paucōs*   *mensīs*   Latin
>   rule.PF.3SG   consul.SG.NOM   few.PL.ACC   month.PL.ACC
>   'The consul ruled for a few months.'

Some languages mark case instead on NPs rather than separately on each word; in such languages case is a phrasal system rather than a word system. Most languages of the Kimberley region of Western Australia are of this type, as shown by the Ungarinyin (Worrorran, Australia) example (1.2). The case marking morpheme is a phrase-level clitic that typically occurs at the end of an NP, regardless of the part of speech membership of the final word. In contrast to Latin, other words in the NP are unmarked. In nearby Nyulnyulan languages, such as Bardi, Nyulnyul, Nyikina and Warrwa, the phrasal enclitic attaches to the first word of the NP regardless of its part of speech membership – in Wackernagel position (e.g. McGregor 2004: 138). In Gooniyandi the marker is encliticized to the most informationally salient word of the NP, regardless of its linear position (McGregor 1990a: 282–283).

> (1.2)   *ada budmara dambun nginin.ga-ra*   Ungarinyin
>   sit   they.did   camp   my-LOC
>   'They sat down at my camp.' (Rumsey 1982: 62)

Similarly, in English NPs are the locus of case marking, though here the markers are instead free words, prepositions, that occur in front of the NP. Japanese is similar, except that the free words are postpositions.

Languages are not necessarily completely uniform in terms of the locus of case marking. Thus, in many languages with NP marking, pronouns are inflected for case, as in English and Ungarinyin. A pronominal NP in these languages may be marked phrasally, while the pronoun is also case marked (as in *to me*), the case marking being 'governed' by the adposition, not the role of the NP in the clause. This brings us to a typological generalization, namely that pronominals are the most likely category to show inflectional case marking. If a language shows inflectional case marking on nouns, it will also show inflectional case marking on pronouns. Typologists often formulate such generalizations, which they refer to as implicational universals.

A second dimension we can typologize case systems on is the distinctions they make. Languages differ considerably in the number of cases they distinguish – more accurately, lest we compare apples and bicycles, we should say that systems of cases differ considerably in terms of the number of contrasts they make. Inflectional case in languages such as English and Ungarinyin is by and large limited to pronouns, and the case distinctions made are few. The system is more extensive in Latin and Pitta-Pitta, where nominals and pronominals distinguish cases (not necessarily with the same systems). More category distinctions are also made. Latin grammars typically distinguish six cases for nouns. For Pitta-Pitta, ten distinct inflectional case suffixes are distinguished for nominals (Blake 1979: 193), though these comprise two different systems according to whether tense is non-future or future. For pronominals in Pitta-Pitta, the same case systems are distinguished but they are marked differently (Blake 1979: 194–195).

Case system typologies focus attention on so-called 'core' or 'syntactic' cases, the cases associated with 'core' grammatical roles or argument roles – effectively those roles that are inherent to clauses of various transitivity values. In the following discussion I will use traditional terms subject and object, transitive and intransitive, loosely and in the traditional ways, ignoring the highly problematic status of all of them as conceptual, theoretical, and/or language-particular categories (see further Chapter 2 for some difficulties).

Many of the world's languages show nominative-accusative case marking systems, systems in which (words in) subject NPs appear in one case while (words in) object NPs appear in a different case form. (Below I will drop this convoluted wording and simply refer to the case of NPs, regardless of the locus of the marking.) This is the situation for case marking of pronouns of English, where different forms such as *I* and *me* exist for many of the person-number categories. Latin also had a nominative-accusative system. The word *cōnsul* in example (1.1) is in nominative case form. As the object of a transitive clause, the form *cōnsulem* would be employed instead. In nominative-accusative languages the nominative form is typically morphologically unmarked, or less morphologically marked than the accusative. In Hungarian, for instance, the nominative form of a noun is the bare form, while the accusative form takes the suffix -*(V)t*, as in *vonat-at* (train-ACC). The nominative case is also functionally unmarked in the typical nominative-accusative system: it is typically employed in the widest range of contexts (including in citation), and with the widest range of senses.

There are, however, a small number of languages in which it is the nominative case that is formally marked, while the accusative is formally unmarked. These so-called marked nominative systems are found in African languages of various genetic lineages, including Nilo-Saharan, Afro-Asiatic and possibly Niger-Congo (König 2006, 2008a: 138–139, 2008b, 2009); they are, however, rare elsewhere in the world. In marked nominative systems it is also normally the case that the accusative is the functionally unmarked case, with the widest range of uses and/or senses.

Perhaps a fifth of the world's languages show an ergative-absolutive case system, a system in which the case of transitive subjects (ergative) is different from the case of intransitive subjects and transitive objects, which are the same (absolutive). Chukchee (Chukotko-Kamchatkan, north-eastern Siberia) has such a case system, as shown by examples (1.3) and (1.4). In (1.3) the intransitive subject occurs in its citation form, the absolutive case, as does the transitive object in (1.4). By contrast the transitive subject in (1.4) is marked by the ergative morpheme -*nan*.

<table>
<tr><td>(1.3)</td><td>ŋinqeq-ø</td><td>gətg-etə</td><td>qət-gʔi</td><td>Chukchee</td></tr>
<tr><td></td><td>boy-ABS.SG</td><td>lake-DAT</td><td>went-3SG</td><td></td></tr>
<tr><td></td><td colspan="4">'The boy went to the lake.'</td></tr>
</table>

<table>
<tr><td>(1.4)</td><td>gəm-nan</td><td>walə-ø</td><td>tə-mne-gʔen</td><td>Chukchee</td></tr>
<tr><td></td><td>I-ERG</td><td>knife-ABS.SG</td><td>1SG-sharpen-3SG</td><td></td></tr>
<tr><td></td><td colspan="4">'I sharpened the knife.'</td></tr>
</table>

Ergative case marking systems show regional focus in distribution, and are particularly common in the languages of Australia and Papua New Guinea, the Himalayas, the Caucasus, and Amazonia.

In ergative-absolutive systems it seems to be always the case that the absolutive is formally unmarked, the ergative formally marked, as illustrated by the Chuckchee examples (1.3) and (1.4) above. There are languages – including perhaps Chuckchee – in which a zero absolutive morpheme can be motivated. But there are also languages in which postulation of a zero absolutive is not motivated, namely where there is no evidence that there is any morpheme there at all. In other words, the absolutive form is simply the unmarked citation form of nominal (and not that form together with a zero morpheme). Many grammatical descriptions, unfortunately, fail to draw this important distinction, and speak alternately of zero-marking and non-marking of the absolutive, as though they were the same phenomenon (e.g. Hercus 1982: 54 vs 112 on Paakantyi, Dixon 1994: 221 vs Dixon 1977: 124, 126 and Dixon 1994: 59–61). I have argued that in some languages of Australia (including Bunuban and Nyulnyulan languages) not only is there no marker of the absolutive case, but there is no absolutive case at all (McGregor 2012b). These are in other words systems with an ergative but no contrasting absolutive case. My guess is that there are accusative languages that likewise lack nominative cases. The implication to the typology of case marking systems is that we need to distinguish ergative-absolutive and nominative-accusative systems from plain ergative and plain accusative systems – and perhaps also plain nominative systems (lacking an accusative) in marked nominative systems.

Languages are not always monosystemic in terms of their case systems (see also §5.2). It is not uncommon to find both nominative-accusative and ergative-absolutive systems within a single language. For example, nouns in Anguthimri (Pama-Nyungan, Australia) inflect on an ergative-absolutive basis, while pronouns inflect according to a nominative-accusative system. The distribution of the two systems is not random. Four factors are relevant to the distribution of the different systems within languages: features of the nominal, the nature of the lexical verb, categories of tense, mood and aspect, and construction type (e.g. main vs subordinate clause).

In systems in which features of the nominal are relevant to the choice of case system, as was first observed by Silverstein (1976) (see also Moravcsik 1978), nominal types can be organized into a universal hierarchy – called the animacy hierarchy or Silverstein's hierarchy – that accounts for distribution of case systems within languages. Figure 1.1 shows a version of this hierarchy. As indicated, nominative-accusative marking is most strongly associated with the left end, with first and second person pronouns, and may extend rightwards: if a language shows nominative-accusative marking at any point on the hierarchy it will show nominative-accusative marking everywhere to the left.

Significantly, this hierarchy accounts for systems that distinguish three 'core' cases: ergative (for transitive subjects), nominative (for intransitive subjects) and accusative (for transitive objects). For instance, if nominative-accusative marking extends as far right as human nouns, and ergative-absolutive extends to third person pronouns, the case system for third person pronouns through to human nouns will be a three-way one.

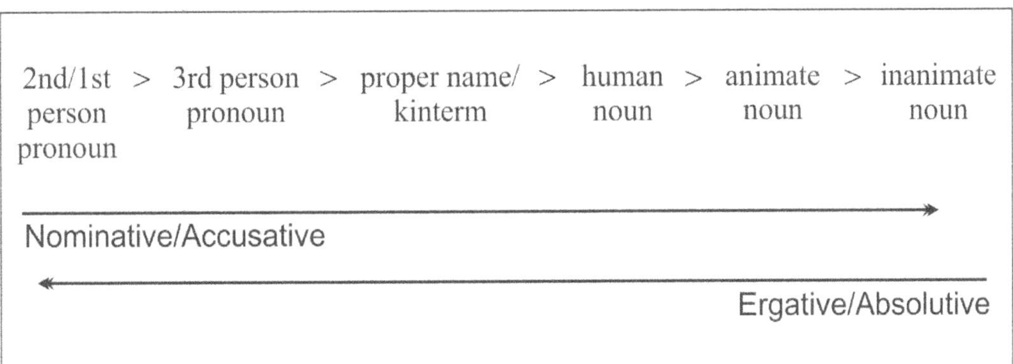

Figure 1.1 The animacy hierarchy (after Silverstein 1976)

It has emerged since Silverstein (1976) that there are problems with the universality of the hierarchy. There are languages in which the second person pronouns must be higher than the first person, and languages where things go the other way around. There are languages, for instance Kala Lagaw Ya (Pama-Nyungan, Torres Strait Islands), that seem to contradict the hierarchy (Comrie 1981a) – and attempts have been made to deal with these (apparent) exceptions (e.g. Round and Stirling 2015 on Kala Lagaw Ya). Nonetheless, the hierarchy is useful as a generalization and heuristic, albeit imperfect.

The above merely scratches the surface of typological variation in case and case marking systems; it is sufficient to show some of the major dimensions along which the systems may be typologized. These are active domains of research in linguistic typology and description. What has not been underlined sufficiently in the discussion is the theoretical dimension, and the dependence of any typology on grammatical theory.

1.2.3 Methodology and Data

Linguistic typology is an empirical discipline in that it is based on language data, which should surely come from more than a single language. (This does not mean that it is non-theoretical or atheoretical, as should be clear from the discussion of §1.2.2.2 and §1.2.2.3; see also §1.2.4.1 below.) This raises significant methodological issues concerning the language data we use and its selection, as well as of the languages we include in any investigation. We need to know what to look for so we can be confident that what we compare is comparable (recall §1.2.2.2 above; see also §1.2.4.2 below); we also need to know where to find the information and ascertain its reliability. For most research projects we need to make a selection from the approximately 7,000 languages spoken in the world. Given the breadth of linguistic typology and the wide range of different types of question that can be asked, it should not be surprising that there is no one-size-fits-all methodology. In this section we remark on each of the two major issues just raised, taking them in order in the following subsections.

1.2.3.1 Data

For most typological investigations, at least in the core linguistic domains, data comes from descriptive grammars. To address many typological questions in phonology, parts of speech systems and grammar, this is the obvious place to begin. However, there are some important caveats.

First, modern comprehensive grammars of languages are in the order of about 300 to 1,000 pages in length, and this sized grammar cannot include mention and discussion of all grammatical features of a language. Indeed, so-called comprehensive grammars are far from comprehensive, as most writers of descriptive grammars (such as myself) would readily admit. This limits the typological questions we can address. I personally would like to do a typological study of nominal tautologies (constructions like *boys will be boys*). Few comprehensive grammars mention such expressions – most likely not because they don't exist in the language, but because they tend to be rare, and not the sort of thing that descriptive grammarians tend to look for. Indeed, treatment of such phenomena in a 1,000-page grammar is arguably not normally warranted: space should be allocated to more central and frequent phenomena. Thus, I have never undertaken the project.

There are, of course, other avenues I could pursue that might yield relevant data: I could contact experts and ask them about the expressions in the languages of their expertise. This is unlikely to be very successful. Few non-native speaker experts would know the relevant mode of expression for 'their' languages, and anyway it is improbable that many of them would have the time or inclination to answer my questions. I could look at corpora for languages, though there are relatively few languages for which sufficiently large corpora are available. I could search for articles that deal with the topic. While this approach might yield pay-dirt for some questions (and would be an essential component of a typological study of possession), it is unlikely to do so for nominal tautologies. The only really satisfactory approach would be to go and gather the data from languages myself – a hardly feasible option.

Many more mundane topics are poorly treated in the average comprehensive grammar. For example, relational clauses – clauses that attribute properties of things (as in e.g. *Einstein was a genius*) or identify referents (e.g. *the one on the left is Einstein*) – are generally accorded a page or two, with little discussion of the range of meanings expressed. The range of typological questions one can successfully address about these clauses is quite limited.

A second caveat concerns the sort of information that is almost certainly contained in the grammar: information on phonetics and phonology, parts of speech, morphology and basic noun phrase and clause structures. Aside from the issues of comparability that have been raised already, the typologist must be aware that grammarians use the same terminology for very different things, and different terminology for what is at some level of granularity the same. If one were to undertake a typological investigation of ergativity it is not simply a matter of searching grammars for mention of ergative or ergativity: not everything under that rubric will be what you are looking for, and what you are looking for may go under a different label in the grammar. One needs to muck around in grammars, as Joseph Greenberg once said.

A third point concerns the reliability of claims that the grammarian makes. Grammars of the majority of languages of the world are written by linguists who are not native speakers. They investigate the language in the field – ideally, in the geographical region within which the language is spoken – for a relatively short time (often about a year). They gather a corpus on the language, which they analyse with the tools of modern linguistics, and within some theoretical framework(s). Relatively few grammars are based on significantly larger corpora, or are written by native speakers – and these are mainly of major European and Asian languages such as English, Spanish (Indo-European), French (Indo-European), German (Indo-European), Mandarin Chinese and Japanese. Whatever the grammar, it cannot be regarded as presenting god's truth about the language.

Here the typologist must bring to the descriptive grammar expertise of their own, and intuitions as to what is more or less likely to be true. At some level, the claims that the grammarian makes about the phonemic inventory of a language might be taken at face value, perhaps with some qualifications concerning the treatment of complex segments (should a nasalized click be treated as a single segment?) – and assuming that the typologist is not J.R. Firth!

But many claims immediately raise the suspicions of the reader – and rightly so. For my part, among other things, I am always highly suspicious of claims that in a given language the verb or copula in attributing or identifying clauses is completely optional, and its presence or absence makes no difference to the meaning. (Such claims have been made for a number of languages of Australia and elsewhere.) I am suspicious in part for an overarching theoretical reason: absolute synonymy in a language is implausible from a functional perspective (Bolinger 1977; Haiman 1983: 782). I am also suspicious of the claim because of my own work on languages that apparently fit the bill for optional verbs. Thus, in Gooniyandi there is a clear meaning difference between attributing clauses with and those without the verb (McGregor 1990a: 308–312, 1996a). Again, one needs to muck around in the grammar, not just read the section on the clausal expression of attribution – or worse just the relevant claim in the typological overview in the introductory chapter.

The bulk of data the typologist uses in most typological investigations will be secondary, and thus must be treated with the usual cautions. Even a corpus of naturalistic data in a language such as one might find in an online documentation of a language must be secondary to be usable by non-speakers: it requires the prior analysis and interpretation of the compiler. A corpus of Warrwa texts that did not include analysis into words (and morphemes) and sentence-sized units along with glosses and free translations would hardly be usable by anyone except perhaps – with difficulty – a speaker of another Nyulnyulan language or a Nyulnyulanist. Even primary linguistic data is processed in the mind of the speaker and analyst, both of whom can make mistakes.

Another data source that has become prominent in recent years is online databases such as *The World Atlas of Language Structures* (WALS) and the *Atlas of Pidgin and Creole Language Structures* (APiCS). These can be useful resources for certain typological investigations. They are, however, rather more limited than the average comprehensive grammar in terms of the features covered and the depth of treatment they provide of them. Serious gaps include exceptions, quirks, irregularities and, more importantly, sufficient tokens to test the veracity of the analytical decisions of the compiler. If comprehensive grammars provide a view of the terrain of a language from a low-flying helicopter, typological databases provide a view from a jumbo in the troposphere. These databases must be addressed with at least the degree of caution one would address to a grammar – and for myself, I am *much* more cautious. (Back to Greenberg's mucking around in grammars yet again!)

1.2.3.2 *Language sampling*

Whatever typological question one addresses, a selection of languages must be made, a corpus of languages chosen. Depending on the question, different criteria will be invoked. There is no single set of criteria that works for all questions. The choice may be fairly obvious if I want to address the expression of possession in the Khoe languages of southern Africa. It would be feasible to include all the languages believed to belong to this family, since there are fewer than fifty named varieties known. The number would be whittled down further when one looked for relevant data in the form of descriptive grammars and other readily retrievable sources. In a project of this type, comprehensiveness of treatment is desirable, and I would not like to overlook a mode of expression employed in any one of the languages. I have used such a sampling procedure in an ongoing typological investigation of the words 'one', 'some' and 'other' in Australian languages. All indigenous languages of the continent were potentially included in the language corpus. The corpus was reduced to a little over 200 named varieties I could find a grammar, grammatical outline and/or lexicon of. I considered this to be the most appropriate choice since I wanted maximum coverage of the range of morphological, syntactic and semantic features of these words (given available information), not just the most frequent characteristics.

For some typological projects a rather different approach is necessary. For instance, to do an investigation of parts of speech systems across the world's languages it will hardly be feasible to aim to include all languages, even all languages with accessible grammatical descriptions. As will be clear from §1.2.2.2, the typologist will necessarily engage in analysis of the systems described in the grammars – they will be interested in knowing what criteria the grammarian employed, and will need to reinterpret the 'facts' of the grammar in the theoretical framework they adopt themselves. This will only be feasible for a smallish number of languages, for a single investigator, presumably the order of a hundred (if they want to complete the project within a few years, the usual lifetime for such projects).

Which languages should be included? If one is doing a general typology of parts of speech systems in the world's languages one wants a representative sample of languages: a sample of languages that does not overrepresent any geographical region or genetic lineage. Various sampling methods have been devised that take these considerations into account: see Rijkhoff et al. (1993); Rijkhoff and Bakker (1998) for one approach. However, there are many very different ideas about the genetic constitution of the world's languages (only a small number of families have been established reliably through application of the comparative method). Samples would be very different for different genetic assumptions. For instance, the assumption of a single Australian family would yield a different number of languages than the assumption of a score or so of families plus a handful of isolates (which represents the current state of knowledge, Harvey and Mailhammer 2018 notwithstanding).

But balanced diversity samples are not ideal for all world-scale typological projects: for example, in an investigation of the typology of tense marking it would be pointless to include in the sample languages that don't have the grammatical category of tense. (Initial inclusion of languages claimed not to have the category might be motivated, and the claim tested.) On the other hand, one would surely want to include a sufficient diversity of languages that do have tense to be sure that the categories and modes of marking are adequately represented. Much more could be said about the selection of languages (see e.g. Bakker 2011); the above is sufficient to show that the criteria depend on the question asked.

1.2.4 Two Topical Issues in Linguistic Typology

To wind up this overview of linguistic typology, brief discussion of two topical issues is in order. These are the role of theory in typology (§1.2.4.1) and the nature of categories employed in linguistic typology (§1.2.4.2).

1.2.4.1 Typology and theory

The need for theory is underlined in a well-known passage penned by Charles Darwin (1809–1882) over 150 years ago in a letter dated 18 September 1861 to one of his early supporters, Henry Fawcett (1833–1884):

> About thirty years ago there was much talk that geologists ought only to observe and not theorise; and I well remember some one saying that at this rate a man might as well go into a gravel-pit and count the pebbles and describe the colours. How odd it is that anyone should not see that all observations must be for or against some view if it is to be of any service![11]

Without a theory, you wouldn't know where to look, or what counts as data – it would be impossible to decide what was relevant to your enterprise. (In fact, in the absence of a theory it is doubtful whether you could have an enterprise.) Data is only data in relation to theory. Even the mucking around in grammars recommended by Greenberg is motivated looking: he encouraged one to seek phenomena that are in some sense interesting or striking, which is clearly possible only if one has expectations – and thus some theoretical standpoint, no matter how rudimentary. Different things will be striking to observers employing different theories.

Immaculate perception (in the words of Francis Bacon and Friedrich Nietzsche) is an impossibility, certainly for us humans. As Kuhn (1970) observed, all data is 'theory-laden'. The data in grammars is dependent on the theoretical stance of the grammar-writer, as should be clear from the discussion of §1.2.2. This does not mean that data from grammars operating within different theories is incommensurable, as Kuhn put it. If it were, linguistic typology would be impossible. It is possible to translate between theories, and to be aware of qualifications on the translations. The onus is on the typologist to make the translations, to understand how the descriptive grammarian uses a particular term. The translations will be into the theory adopted by the typologist, who cannot even begin without adopting some stance.

If these remarks seem to belabour the point, it is for a reason. It is not uncommon for both descriptive linguists and typologists to claim to work within a theory-neutral approach. One such approach is Basic Linguistic Theory (BLT) (e.g. Dixon 2010a, 2010b). This approach is quite popular and has been explicitly adopted by many descriptive grammarians and typologists. However, as the name indicates, this is in fact a theory, albeit one that allegedly bases itself on the set of propositions about language held by all linguists. (This, however, is almost certainly the empty set.) A rather different approach is advocated by Haspelmath (2010b), who proposes that grammatical descriptions are best situated in framework-free theory. His discussion centres on grammatical relations in Schachter and Otanes (1972)'s grammar of Tagalog and Drach (1963 [1937])'s field theory of German syntax. It seems that they are framework free in that the authors eschew universal categories and attempt to identify language-particular categories. How this makes them framework free is completely opaque to me.

Of course, adoption of a theory comes with a price. It limits the questions you may think of asking – though you would have no questions at all without a theory. It potentially limits the readership of the grammar, especially if it employs a theory that is not well known – this is especially a problem for theories that were well known at some time, but since have been consigned to the graveyard of theories. (The theoretical tenets are unlikely to be made explicit in such descriptions.)

I leave the summing up of this section to J.R. Firth:

> For me, a *fact* must be technically stated and find a place in a system of related statements, all of them arising from a theory and found applicable in renewal of connection in experience.
>
> (Firth 1968: 43)

1.2.4.2 *Categories in linguistic typology*

Categorization – the assignment of things to categories – is fundamental to grammar. Grammatical phenomena of a language are assigned to a range of categories, including units (phonemes, morphemes, words, phrases and so on), relations (syntagmatic, paradigmatic, grammatical roles, etc.). Categorization is likewise fundamental to linguistic typology, which is centrally concerned with categories of linguistic phenomena in a cross-linguistic context. As we have already seen, serious difficulties arise in the comparison of the categories, including how we can be confident that what we compare are comparable. Put in another way, what sorts of categories can we operate with in linguistic typology?

There has long been difference of opinion among typologists in terms of the categories they operate with. Recently, an intense debate erupted on the Lingtyp list, followed by a collection of discussion papers in the journal *Linguistic Typology* (volume 20, issue 2) presenting the two main sides of the debate. On one side, LaPolla (2016) and Rijkhoff (2016) argue for employment of language-particular categories in typology. On the other side, Haspelmath (2016) argues there is a place for comparative categories or concepts, notional categories invented by the linguist to facilitate cross-language comparison (see also Haspelmath 2010a).

For those who argue for use of emic categories, the question of comparison of these categories immediately arises. Being emic, these categories are inherently language-specific, and thus different from categories in any other language. This does not mean, however, that it is impossible to compare them cross-linguistically – that they are incommensurable. They can be compared in terms of formal marking and their coded meanings, for example, and those that show sufficient similarities in either or both might be taken as the comparanda. This approach is advocated by McGregor (1997b: 15–16); Rijkhoff (2016: 333). This is a variant on what many linguists do when making lexical comparisons between languages, and claim, for example, that all languages have a core lexicon comprising words for concepts such as 'sun', 'moon', 'water' and so on. Clearly, the lexical signs of a language are inherently language particular; nonetheless they can be compared in terms of their meanings, so that, for example, *mirri* in Gooniyandi is identified as the lexeme for 'sun'. This does not mean that *mirri* means precisely the same thing as the English word *sun*.

A second approach is to provide explicit criteria that must be met for a certain emic category to be regarded as an instance of a particular phenomenon. Only those emic categories that satisfy these requirements would be compared in the typology. Examples of this approach include Hengeveld (1992) on parts of speech system (see §1.2.2.2 above); McGregor (2002b) on systems of grammatical classification such as genders and noun classification; McGregor (2013c) on optional grammatical markers; and Spronck and Nikitina (2019) on reported speech and thought constructions.

Cross-linguistic comparison may seem simpler if one employs comparative categories. The simplicity, however, comes at a considerable price. Rijkhoff (2016) discusses problems with doing word order typology with comparative categories such as adjectives defined notionally in terms of their modifying function, and what these problems mean in terms of the viability of resulting typologies. Chapter 2 of this book reveals serious problems with this approach to the typology of grammatical roles.

1.3 Contribution of Neo-Firthian Theories to Linguistic Typology and Description: Accomplishments and Prospects

1.3.1 The Contribution of Neo-Firthian Theories

It is fair to say that Neo-Firthian theories have contributed far less to language description and linguistic typology than most other functional theories, claims by Mwinlaaru and Xuan (2016) and Kashyap (2019) notwithstanding. And unlike, for example,

Functional (Discourse) Grammar and Role and Reference Grammar, typological adequacy is not taken seriously as a criterion of theoretical adequacy within the dominant Neo-Firthian tradition – instead, it tends to be seen as an 'application' of the theory (Caffarel, Martin and Matthiessen 2004: 4–5; Kashyap 2019 appears in the third part of *The Cambridge Handbook of Systemic Functional Linguistics* labelled 'SFL in Application'). This may seem surprising given that Firth revelled in variety and diversity at all levels of language; however, as noted above, this was not tempered by any serious concern with unity – an essential ingredient in any approach to typology.

Relatively few comprehensive descriptive grammars have been written in any Neo-Firthian framework.[12] The majority of these employ SFL. The following is a fairly comprehensive listing: Mbembe (Niger-Congo, Nigeria) (Barnwell 1970), Gooniyandi (McGregor 1984, 1990a), Wangurri (Pama-Nyungan, Australia) (McLellan 1992), Finnish (Uralic, Finland) (Shore 1992), Pitjantjatjara (Pama-Nyungan, Australia) (Rose 2001), Ọ̀kọ́ (Niger-Congo, Nigeria) (Akerejola 2005), French (Caffarel 2006), Mandarin Chinese (Li 2007), and Japanese (Teruya 2007).[13] As to other Neo-Firthian theories, there is a grammar of Nyulnyul (Nyulnyulan, Australia) (McGregor 2012a) and one of Warrwa (Nyulnyulan, Australia) in progress, both written within the parameters of SG.

Descriptively oriented accounts of the phonology – or aspects of the phonology – of a smallish number of languages other than English have been written from a Neo-Firthian perspective, again mostly SFL. These include (ignoring descriptive grammars): Arabic (Afro-Asiatic, Middle East and Northern Africa) (Eddaikra and Tench 1992), Mandarin Chinese (Halliday 1992; Lock 1992; Yali and Chengyu 2014), Gooniyandi (McGregor 1992b), Isthmus Zapotec (Otomanguean, Mesoamerica) (Mock 1992), Telugu (Dravidian, India) (Prakasam 1972, 1992), Swahili (Niger-Congo, Tanzania) (Maw 1992) and Welsh (Indo-European, Wales) (Kelly 1992). I am not aware, however, of any SFL typological studies in phonology (or typological studies in any other Neo-Firthian framework).

Typological investigations of morphosyntactic phenomena within Neo-Firthian paradigms are also few and far between. Within the systemic tradition there is, of course, the edited collection *Language Typology: A Functional Perspective* (Caffarel, Martin and Matthiessen 2004). The bulk of this book comprises 'metafunctional profiles' for eight languages belonging to seven different genetic families. These are primarily theoretically informed descriptive accounts of the fundamental features of the clausal grammar of the eight languages; a number of these descriptions do, however, include typological remarks. Each description attempts to provide a 'holistic' perspective on the clause in the targeted language, and is organized according to the perspectives of each of the metafunctions. It seems that it is because of this attention to entire systems of languages rather than to isolated constructions that the editors speak of 'language typology', and apparently want to distance themselves from mainstream linguistic typology (Caffarel, Martin and Matthiessen 2004: 1); see also §1.2.1.

The final chapter of the book, Matthiessen (2004), attempts to draw out typological generalizations – 'descriptive motifs and generalizations' – from the individual language profiles. The focus is on a comparison of the ways in which the metafunctions organize the clause paradigmatically in the targeted languages, and to a somewhat lesser extent syntagmatically. A number of additional languages are brought into this comparative enterprise. Also included in this final chapter is discussion of a range of categories of interest to typologists, including negation, grammatical relations such as subject, mood, modality, voice, thematization, tense and aspect, and so on. Existing typological work in these domains is largely overlooked – and is certainly not critically engaged with.

Given its neglect in SFL, Caffarel, Martin and Matthiessen (2004) is a positive indication that typology has begun to appear on the SFL radar. Unfortunately, however, it reads more as an application of SFL to the typological domain than as a work on typology inspired by or informed by SFL.

Systemicists frequently point to Halliday (1966) as evidence of an interest in typology from the earliest days of the theory. Halliday does in fact identify some key problems for typology of the time (this paper was written at around the time Greenberg began his typological programme). These include: word order as a marker of grammatical relations (effectively whether clausal order is ever entirely consistent – Halliday 1966: 167); the lack of evidence for cyclic change in morphological type of languages, and that the morphological type of a language may remain stable over very long periods (Halliday 1966: 171); the problem of what is to be compared; and the role of the exotic. However, the paper is a flash in the pan, and nothing was seriously followed up in subsequent SFL research. It is notable that Halliday spoke of *linguistic typology* already in this piece (1966), whereas the recent SFL accounts revert to *language typology*, and evidently invoke the very un-Firthian assumption of *une langue une* (see also Bartlett 2017: 379).

Less impressive is Halliday's suggestion that '[t]ypology is, so to speak, generalized comparative descriptive linguistics; or generalized "contrastive" linguistics' (1966: 173). The issues that confront a typologist are rather different to those that confront a descriptive or contrastive linguist. The central concerns of the enterprises are quite distinct, and what works methodologically for one need not for the others.

The only Neo-Firthian approaches I am aware of that have tackled linguistic typology seriously are SG and the Leuven School (see §1.1.2 above). Both of these approaches take typology seriously, and assign it a central place. Over the past thirty or so years I have addressed a range of typological questions mostly from the perspective of SG (a selection of these are discussed in Chapters 2–6 of the present book; others include possession, ergative case marking, mood, lexical typology, typology and grammaticalization and areal typology). Members of the Leuven School have addressed the typology of, among other things, the NP (e.g. Louagie 2017, 2020; Louagie and Verstraete 2015, 2016), mood (e.g. Verstraete 2005a), case marking asymmetries (Verstraete 2010; Chappell and Verstraete 2019), complementation (the topic of a recent workshop *The syntagmatic properties of complementation patterns*, 9–10 May 2019, University of Liège), clause combining (e.g. Verstraete 2002) and insubordination (e.g. Verstraete, D'Hertefelt and Van linden 2012).

1.3.2 What Can Neo-Firthian Theories Offer to Linguistic Typology and Description?

It will be clear from the previous subsection that I consider the contribution of Neo-Firthian theories to both typology and grammatical description to be underwhelming. Can these approaches make a significant contribution to these domains? On this question my answer is a positive one, as I hope the bulk of the book will demonstrate. (Were it otherwise I would not have agreed to write the book in the first place.) In my opinion Neo-Firthian linguistics has the as yet largely unrealized potential to make a mark on linguistic typology and description. In this section I identify some of the features of Neo-Firthian thinking that, in my view, could inform and reshape the fields. (In §7.2.2 I address the same issue from the opposite direction, and identify topics in linguistic typology that challenge Neo-Firthian theorizing.) But in order to make this contribution, major theoretical rethinking and renovation is in order, as are major changes in approach to description and typology. The interaction between theory, typology and description must become more of a two-way street than it currently is in the major Neo-Firthian player, SFL.

To begin with, there are in my opinion a few key ideas shared by many (though not all) Neo-Firthian approaches that are of significance to both typology and description. Most significant of these is the notion that the phenomena of primary concern in grammar in the narrow sense – that is, excluding phonetics and phonology – are signs, form-meaning pairings. Thus, both form and meaning are central to the description of the morphology and syntax of any language. This view continues and expands on Firth's notion that meaning is central to language, and is present at all levels of analysis. Halliday does not actually talk about grammatical signs, and has indeed on occasions implied that he does not see the sign as central to linguistic semiosis: language is a semiotic system 'not in the sense of a system of signs, but a systemic resource for meaning' (Halliday 2003 [1985]: 190). However, it is clear that the grammatical phenomena he identifies in Halliday (1985) – in particular, the grammatical roles of the various semiotic/metafunctional types, such as, for example, Actor, Agent, Theme, Subject, etc. – are grammatical signs, comparable in conceptualization with the constructions of Construction Grammar (e.g. Goldberg 1995). They are, that is, not merely either purely formal or functional categories, but defined by an inherent connection between form and function (or meaning). Indeed, Halliday leans to the view that all formal patterning is the realization side of some sign.[14] There is no place for formal patterns that are essentially meaningless, instances of form for no other purpose than form. To other Neo-Firthians, such as myself, this is too strong an assumption, and it is a proper subset of formal patterns that comprise the form aspect of signs (McGregor 1997b: 2).

The implication to language description is that central to the description of the grammar of any language is the identification of its grammatical signs. The descriptive linguist's primary job is to attempt to establish what is emic in the language. Roles such as Agent, Actor, Subject, Object and the like must be motivated by language-internal evidence, and are not mere objects of either form or meaning. This does not mean that universals are necessarily eschewed. Rather, any universal is taken to be empirical, subject to test in each and every particular language, not posited for theoretical reasons alone. In line with remarks in §1.2.4.2 the emic roles of a particular language may be compared with those of another language by virtue of either similarity or the fact that they share certain essentials. (This also means that the objects of comparison might be disputed.)

This has profound implications for doing typology. To begin with, many categories identified in modern descriptive grammars are not emic, but rather are etic, notional categories – Haspelmath's comparative categories. This holds for grammatical roles or relations, which are often construed within notional paradigms (see Chapter 2). A Neo-Firthian typologist cannot use the categories of such descriptions. The terms Agent and Subject in Neo-Firthian approaches are labels for grammatical signs, and confusing these with notionally characterized agents and subjects would be misguided. The Neo-Firthian typologist is hampered by the dearth of grammatical description that can be deployed. It also means that online databases such as WALS are not usable for most questions that a Neo-Firthian typologist would ask.[15]

There are ways in which existing descriptive grammars can be employed, with provisos, in addressing questions that a Neo-Firthian typologist might find interesting. For instance, as outlined in Chapter 2, a typology of grammatical relations could begin by taking the formal features of argument marking as a beginning; this would need to be accompanied by some attention to meaning to determine the type of the grammatical relation indexed. Louagie and Verstraete (2016) show how the emic structure of NPs can be addressed using comparative-category based descriptions. The approach of Rijkhoff (2002, 2016), which combines formal, meaning and functional considerations, also lends itself to Neo-Firthian theories. These methodologies, of course, require further analysis and interpretation of the facts as laid out in the sources. Whereas this is to a greater or lesser degree possible for grammars, information in online databases is almost always too sparse to permit reanalysis.

Neo-Firthian approaches are not, of course, unique in their adoption of the sign as fundamental to grammar, and Dik-inspired Functional (Discourse) Grammar, Cognitive Grammar, Construction Grammar and others instate the sign in a central place. More peculiar to (some) Neo-Firthian theories is the Hallidayan conceptualization of 'metafunctions' – my semiotic components (see §1.1.3). Caffarel, Martin and Matthiessen (2004) can be seen as an attempt to apply this notion to language description and typology. My own descriptive and typological work is also based on this assumption. What can it offer to description or typology?

I would argue that it can enrich our understanding of the range of structure types found in languages, and that it attests to the inadequacies of the constituency relation – and equally dependency – as the sole syntagmatic relation (as argued in McGregor

1997b, 2003a). The enriched range of structural types recognized permits more adequate descriptions, which can account for more in terms of both expression and meaning. It can also reveal deep and unexpected links between phenomena that appear on the face of it to be unrelated – for instance, negation, mood and modality, clause complementation, and information structure.

Attempts to employ the theoretical notion of semiotic type in the description of particular languages and in linguistic typology can input to the theory itself, and potentially reshape it. This, however, is something that practitioners of SFL have strongly resisted in their practice: as observed above, the direction of enrichment is exclusively one-way, from theory to description and typology. Halliday's conception of the 'metafunctions' and how they parcel up the emic domain of a language is regarded as inviolable – see again Caffarel, Martin and Matthiessen (2004). There is no Firthian 'renewal of connection'.

The paradigmatic orientation of SFL is almost unique among modern grammatical theories. Accordingly, SFL might be expected to be potentially beneficial to description and typology in directing more attention to this relatively overlooked domain. The conceptualization of paradigmatic oppositions in terms of system networks could also offer something to the understanding of the structure of paradigms. The most obvious places where one might think of employing a paradigmatic perspective is in the description and typology of relatively closed grammatical paradigms such as, for example, tense, mood, aspect, gender classes, pronominal systems and the like. But this potential is largely unrealized in the typological domain, where at best there are some hints at the types of paradigmatic choices that might be available in some systems.

To take just one example, a paradigmatic approach to illocutionary mood (clausal mood that relates to the illocutionary or speech function value of the utterance) could raise and address typological questions concerning the range of moods identified, how they are organized paradigmatically (e.g. is there hierarchy in the system?), and what features define them as separate emic categories. Such a typological investigation would be feasible given available resources of grammatical description (along with a good dose of interpretation). What I have in mind is clearly a very different approach to the typology of illocutionary mood than that sketched in Matthiessen (2004: 610–625), which begins with the assumption that the English features of 'orientation' (giving vs demanding) and 'commodity type' (information vs goods-&-services) provides a general organizing principle for mood systems. Languages demonstrably carve up the illocutionary roast in very different ways. Modal types such as interrogative and imperative do not exist in all languages, including Gooniyandi. There is, however, in Gooniyandi an exclamative mood (as a distinct emic modal type) that contrasts with an assertive (perhaps declarative) mood and two other non-assertive moods, subjunctive and factive, which effectively mark the proposition as something entertained or assumed as fact – and thus beyond questions of truth or falsity.

Many of the system networks of Caffarel, Martin and Matthiessen (2004) concern much more complex grammatical territory, where an immense range of choices is available – and an even more immense range of ways they might be put together (even granted the 'metafunctional hypothesis'). One wonders about the advisability of beginning with the complex. Moreover, syntagmatic relations come to the fore in clausal and super-clausal syntax, and these are obscured in any approach that treats them as derivative, and merely realizations of underlying systems of oppositions. In a similar way linguistic forms are understood purely as realizations of features; marking relations – the typological importance of which will be revealed in this book – are hidden in realization statements.

Paradigmatic oppositions play an important role in this book, though this role is regrettably obscured by the focus on syntagmatic relations. However, these oppositions are neither conceived nor represented in terms of networks of oppositions of the type employed in SFL, which I do not believe provide a good conceptualization of the nature of choice in all contexts. Consider, for example, the choice between use and non-use of a case marker (Chapter 5). The choice is at the level of use: use or don't use the morpheme. This is a completely different matter to the paradigmatic choices one might make among the cases or case markers themselves. The only obvious way of representing such a choice in an SFL network is with a system that opposes use of the case marker to its non-use. However, I fail to see what might be gained by drawing such a system: where would it be located, and what would the realizations of the oppositions be? (Use clearly cannot be the morpheme itself, but must rather be the act of putting it there, which has only one place in SFL networks, the realization statements.) Ultimately, it is not helpful to construe all paradigmatic relations as though they were fundamentally the same, and well represented by SFL style networks of choices – even if they can be so represented.

Finally, it seems likely that Neo-Firthian linguistics has the potential to contribute to the description and typology of phonetics and phonology. These traditions inherit Firth's focus on prosodies, which is shared by other modern theories of phonology. The paradigmatic-based approach might also rejuvenate feature theory, especially (in my view) if it takes aboard some of the key ideas of Nikolai Trubetzkoy (1890–1938) concerning the paradigmatic nature of feature systems (Trubetzkoy 1969), and refocus attention on what is emic in particular languages.

1.4 Contents and Organization of the Book

The following five chapters comprise the main body of the book and deal with the typology of a small selection of grammatical phenomena, which they address from a Neo-Firthian standpoint. These are: grammatical relations and transitivity (Chapter 2); the noun phrase (Chapter 3); complex sentence constructions (Chapter 4); optional case marking (Chapter 5); and systems of verb classification – grammatical systems that overtly categorize verbs in a way comparable with systems of noun classes (or genders) and classification (Chapter 6).

The selected phenomena do not constitute a representative selection of grammatical phenomena (whatever that might be) and nor do they comprise a representative selection of phenomena dealt with in the linguistic typology literature (see §1.2 for an overview). Rather, they reflect my own personal interests, and include some topics that have barely begun to be investigated from a cross-linguistic perspective – in particular, optional case marking and verb classification. All are topics I have published on from typological, descriptive and/or theoretical perspectives. My purpose is not so much to propose new typologies as to show that typology can be done better from a Neo-Firthian perspective. On the other hand, I also want to show that for a Neo-Firthian theory to be adequate it must address typology more seriously than has been the case hitherto.

In the concluding chapter, Chapter 7, I discuss linguistic typology in relation to other domains of linguistics, including theory, description, documentation, and diachronic linguistics. I also highlight an important lacuna in the book, namely the omission of sign languages. A few remarks are made on sign language typology and the relevance of sign languages to linguistic typology and Neo-Firthian linguistics.

Chapter 2

Grammatical Relations and Transitivity

2.1 The Clause as a Fundamental Unit of Grammar

The simple clause plays a central role in modern linguistics, in theoretical linguistics, language description and linguistic typology. Indeed, in some respects the clause may be regarded as the fundamental unit of grammar; it competes with the word for primary status. The rich and varied structure of the clause and its classification into types are among the chief concerns of grammar.

This view finds stout adherents among followers of Firth, and is manifested in SFL. For instance, Halliday (1985) is organized around the clause, and it is this grammatical unit that Halliday chooses to showcase the metafunctions/semiotic components (see §1.1.3). All major clauses (basically, all clauses other than minor clauses that by and large express interjections, e.g. *Hi!*) are structured, according to Halliday (1985), in terms of three of the four semiotics: experiential, interpersonal and textural. The logical semiotic does not figure in the grammar of the clause in the Hallidayan scheme. I have taken issue with this, and argued that some phenomena that Halliday treats as experiential – including his circumstantial roles, as represented by the prepositional phrase in *the farmer kissed the duckling in the woodshed* – are in fact logical (McGregor 1997b: 140–175).

Clauses are typically structured in terms of grammatical relations of the various semiotic types, the number, types, and perhaps orders of which may permit a semiotic classification of the clause. There are two 'completeness' assumptions of Hallidayan SFL that seem to me to be too strong. First is the assumption that each and every major clause is structured in terms of each semiotic. This assumption forces one to analyse copula relational clauses in English as showing experiential structure, and thus that clauses like *the president is Donald Duck* specify 'processes' occurring in some world of experience or imagination. Like most linguists, I would argue that such clauses do not construe a process, and the *be* verb serves a purely copula function, a language-internal connecting function. Second is the assumption that every unit in the clause fulfils some role in each semiotic, or is a component of a larger unit that does. This assumption forces standard SFL to identify along with the clausal role of New information a corresponding role of Given information, motivation for which is weak (Dik 1989: 277ff; McGregor 1997b: 272–273).

From a Neo-Firthian perspective, this chapter is concerned with grammatical relations of the experiential type, and the clause as an experiential unit. We begin by outlining and critiquing an approach that has been dominant for some decades in linguistic typology and in descriptive linguistics – especially as applied to small, under-described and often endangered languages. I then go on to argue that a Neo-Firthian approach affords an alternative approach to the typology of grammatical relations that does not suffer from the fundamental problems that we identify for the received approach in typology and description. This approach, moreover, reveals the advantages of an approach to linguistic typology that begins with emic units in languages, with descriptive categories, and eschews comparative categories (see §1.2.4.2).

2.2 The S, A, O Theory of Grammatical Relations and What Is Wrong With It

2.2.1 Grammatical Relations in Linguistic Typology

In both modern linguistic typology and 'atheoretical' descriptive linguistics grammatical relations play a significant role. These, however, are not construed as language-particular relations defined by the grammars of those language, but as comparative categories that are identifiable in abstract conceptual space, platonic ideals in the minds of linguists (see above §1.2.4.2).

Following Fillmore (1968), semantic roles are often identified, which are effectively a set of roles that are defined purely in notional terms, in accordance with the broad meaning they express. Thus, a semantic role of agent is commonly distinguished as the entity that is responsible for the performance of an event, and that has control over it (e.g. Velupillai 2012: 231). These are notional roles, distinguishable by inspection of the meaning of a clause, though in practice features of particular languages are sometimes brought into account. These somewhat resemble the experiential roles identified in Neo-Firthian grammars, but are fundamentally different in that the latter are language-particular emic categories (Davidse 2017: 79). Another set of roles frequently presumed in typology are pragmatic roles, which concern information status of components of clauses, for example topic and comment. These are again comparative categories, identifiable by inspection of the apparent expressed meaning of a clause. Although in terms of labels and expressed meaning they are like the textual relations of SFL, the latter are once again emic categories.

Our concern here is not with these so-called semantic and pragmatic relations, but rather with one of two distinct but partly related more abstract sets of relations that are closer in conception to argument roles – the binary system distinguishing subject and object, and the ternary one distinguishing S, A and O (see below for explanation). These are again comparative categories, and are sometimes contrasted with semantic and pragmatic roles as grammatical or syntactic relations. In accordance with this conceptualization, they are – unlike semantic and pragmatic roles – purely abstract and meaningless categories. As such, they are anathema to Neo-Firthian linguistics, which abhors the meaning-vacuum.

The first system is effectively the traditional one that distinguishes subject and object. These are comparative categories, presumed to be distinguishable by inspection. They form the centrepiece of so-called word order typology, which classifies languages in terms of the relative orders of subject, object, and verb, and the rigidity of this ordering. Word order typology has been influential in linguistic typology and descriptive linguistics (see §1.2.1), and its influence has extended into historical and theoretical linguistics – and into general linguistic parlance and a widely used typological classification of languages. To enter into a discussion of the inadequacies of word order typology would take us too far from the main concerns of this chapter.[1]

My concern in this chapter is with a different set of grammatical relations (I use the term advisedly, since they are not really grammatical relations at all, but primitive units of some undisclosed type) that has been widely invoked in linguistic typology to get a grip on phenomena such as agreement, cross-reference, case marking, conditions on ellipsis and/or argument sharing in clause combinations, and word order. Three primitive grammatical relations are identified in this theory, S, A and O. It is presumed that in all languages there are two (primary) clause types, intransitive and transitive. Intransitive clauses have a single argument, S, while transitive clauses have two arguments, an A and an O (sometimes labelled P or U). S, A and O are considered universal primitives, identifiable in all languages. This begot alignment theory, a theory that is concerned with how the different grammatical relations align themselves in different grammatical circumstances.

The theory of alignment is based on the three primitives, and addresses the question of how S, A and O are 'treated' in some specified component of the grammar of the language. Which – if any – are treated alike in specified circumstances and which are treated differently? For instance, the circumstances might concern word order, morphological marking of the NP, or agreement or cross-reference in the verb. This gives the scheme for the possible 'treatments' of the relations as same or different in a given context for a given language as shown in Figure 2.1.

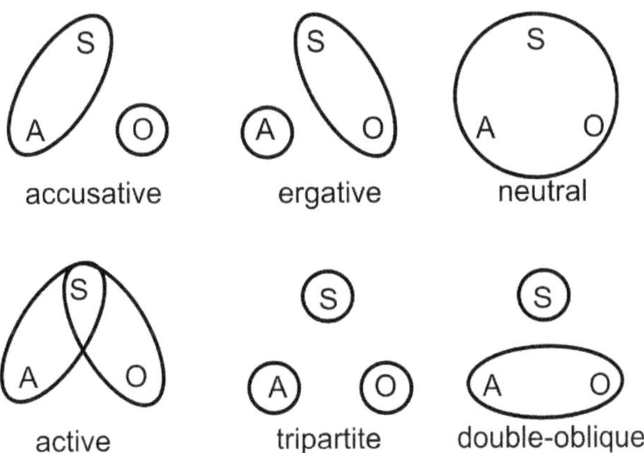

Figure 2.1 Possible alignments of S, A and O in specified grammatical environments

It is not assumed that a language will be consistent across all grammatical environments in its treatment of the primitives. For instance, case marking and verbal agreement or cross-referencing might show different treatments. The scheme of Figure 2.1 is thus not seen as providing a typology of entire languages.

As already mentioned, most typological work on case marking and grammatical relations employs alignment theory. Textbooks such as Comrie (1981b), Velupillai (2012) and Moravcsik (2013) repeat it with approval, albeit in places with emendations. Handbooks of typology such as Song (2011) feature it prominently in chapters on case and grammatical relations typology, again sometimes with emendations; it is assumed throughout Malchukov and Spencer (2009). WALS employs this system, for example in Comrie's chapters on alignment of case marking of NPs and pronouns (Comrie 2013a, 2013b), and Siewierska's chapter on alignment in verbal person marking (Siewierska 2013). The vast bulk of typological treatments of phenomena such as accusativity, ergativity, etc. assume it, for example Blake (2001) on case; Dixon (1979, 1987, 1994) on ergativity; Tsunoda (1981) on splits in case marking; and many more. Numerous recent grammars written within the 'theory neutral' BLT paradigm employ alignment theory (e.g. Guirardello 1999; Liljegren 2008; Fehn 2014; Clendon 2014; and Epps 2008 to mention just a small and arbitrary selection).

One potential advantage of the S, A, O theory is its extreme conceptual simplicity. But there is a big but. The theory has been called to question by many investigators, including Mark Durie (1987), Marianne Mithun and Wallace Chafe (1999), Scott DeLancey (2006), Geoffrey Haig (2010), myself (McGregor 2002a, 2006a), and numerous others. Many investigators question the viability of the theory, but go on to say that it is the only available one, so we might as well presume it and get on with things. Thus, after presenting a number of damning critiques of the theory, Queixalós and Gildea in their introduction to Gildea and Queixalós (2010) go on to say:

> [I]t is beyond the scope of this work to further explore the theoretical implication of A, S and P – for now, we merely welcome their expository convenience while joining the skeptics in doubting the theoretical validity (or cognitive reality) of such a level of structure.
>
> (Queixalós and Gildea 2010: 7)

2.2.2 Problems with the S, A, O Theory

I now outline some of the problems with the S, A, O theory, many of which have been known for a very long time. The major criticisms are founded on the application of the conceptual primitives S, A, and O to particular languages. Thus, criticisms mostly hinge on whether the comparative categories actually correspond to any reality in particular languages.

To begin with we have the question of how we can identify the A and O in transitive clauses, and distinguish them from one another. This is left largely to the intuitions of the linguist – it is presumed to be obvious by inspection which NP is which. There are no fully workable and determinate criteria by which we can make the decision abstracted from the facts of specific languages.

One suggestion that has been made is that A and O can be identified by their relative degree of agentivity or activity, how much control they have over the event. For example, according to Dixon (1994: 52) the A is usually the thing that is 'most relevant to the success of an action'. So the A of a clause denoting hitting will be the hitter, the O the hittee. But what of events of receiving, where it is difficult to say – and it may depend on the context imagined – which is the more relevant to the success of the action: the recipient (*he received the guests in the living room*), the thing exchanged (*I received the letter from the taxation office*) or the initial possessor (*he received the degree from the dean*)? It is ultimately difficult to construe the question of what is A and what is O abstracted from a language and its lexicon. Another suggestion might be to recognize the relation of 'subject of' to distinguish the A. But to do this would invoke the problematic presumption of subject as a universal category, which the theory was designed to circumvent.

Perhaps the major and most persistent criticism that has been levelled at the S, A, O theory concerns the presumed unity of S. Particularly in active systems, the motivation for identifying a unified S category is dubious. Mark Durie's criticism of the theory in relation to Acehnese (Austronesian, Sumatra) is that there is no viable category S in the language (Durie 1987). Intransitive clauses come in two distinct types, with the single inherent role serving in different grammatical relations, as revealed by grammatical facts of the language. In one type of intransitive the putative S is cross-referenced by a pronominal prefix to the verb, as in example (2.1). In the other type of intransitive the 'S' is optionally cross-referenced by a pronominal enclitic to the verb, as in (2.2).

(2.1) *geu-jak gopnyan*   Acehnese
       3SG-go   3SG
       '(S)he goes.'

(2.2) *lôn   rhët-(lön)*   Acehnese
       1SG   fall-(1SG)
       'I fall.'

Durie argues at length that there is no language-internal reason to group together the 'S' roles of these two types of intransitive clause. They are different grammatical roles; the only commonality lies in the fact that they are the single inherent role of the corresponding clause types.

A similar problem arises in Gooniyandi, were we have three distinct 'intransitive' clause types, as illustrated by (2.3)–(2.5). In (2.3) and (2.5) the inherent NP is cross-referenced by a NOM prefix in the verb; in (2.4) it is cross-referenced by an ACC prefix (the third person plural nominative prefix in this example is a dummy element that does not cross-reference anything). In (2.3) and (2.4) the inherent NP is almost always unmarked by a case marking postposition; in (2.5) it is optionally marked by the ergative postposition. Again 'S' cannot be a unified category.

(2.3) *nganyi*   *ward-ng+i*   Gooniyandi
      1SG.CRD   go-1SG.NOM+I
      'I went.'

(2.4) *gooroongal-ya*   *gard-birr+ø+ini*   *yoowooloo* *yoowarni*
      Christmas.Creek-LOC   hit-3PL.NOM+3SG.ACC+BINI   man   one
      'At Christmas Creek a man was killed.'   Gooniyandi

(2.5) *nganyi-ngga*   *mila-ng+arni*   Gooniyandi
      1SG.CRD-ERG   see-1SG.NOM+ARNI
      'I saw myself.'

Further to the problem of the non-unified S are problems of the non-unified A and O. Consider Nyulnyul examples (2.6)–(2.8). Each of these is a bivalent clause, which thus has an A and an O argument. The obvious candidate for A argument in each case is the NP marked by the ergative postposition. However, whereas in (2.6) and (2.8) this NP is cross-referenced by the nominative pronominal prefix in the inflecting verb, in (2.7) it is not cross-referenced at all in the verb. Moreover, the ergative postposition is optional in (2.6) and (2.8), but obligatory in (2.7). The conclusion is inescapable: there cannot be a single A role shared across these three examples.

(2.6) *wamb-in*   *i-n-dam-ø*   *yiil*   *jan*   Nyulnyul
      man-ERG   3NOM-CM-hit-3MIN.ACC   dog   1MIN.OBL
      'The man hit my dog.'

(2.7) *bulji* *nga-n-ji*   *marriny-in* *ngay*   Nyulnyul
      tired 1MIN.NOM-CM-say   walk-ERG   1MIN.CRD
      'I'm tired from walking.'

(2.8) *kudirrawany-in* *i-n-di-jin /*   *winin /*   Nyulnyul
      bustard-ERG   3NOM-CM-say-3MIN.OBL   emu
      'The bustard spoke to the emu.'

Nor can the other role in these three examples be identified across the three clause types. Although in all instances it is realized by an unmarked NP, in (2.6) it is cross-referenced by an accusative enclitic to the inflecting verb (in this instance -ø); in (2.7) it is cross-referenced by a nominative prefix to the inflecting verb; and in (2.8) it is cross-referenced by an oblique enclitic to the inflecting verb. The grammatical facts of Nyulnyul reveal that – for exactly the same reasons as identified for the above Acehnese examples – there are at least two different roles corresponding to the putative A, and at least three different roles corresponding to the putative O. S, A, and O are unified only in the platonic space of comparative categories.

Many languages have trivalent clauses in addition to monovalent and bivalent clauses. This is the case, for instance, in Nyulnyul, as shown by (2.9). If we operate within the parameters of S, A, O theory the only option is to invoke three new roles, say G (Giver), T (Transferred thing), and R (Recipient).[2]

> (2.9) *ngay-in*   *nga-na-w-ø*   *mirlimirl*   Nyulnyul
> 1MIN.CRD-ERG   1MIN.NOM-CM-give-3MIN.ACC   paper
> *kinyingk   wamb   biird*
> DEF   man   yesterday
> 'I gave the book to the man yesterday.'

The above represent just a small selection of problematic examples that demonstrate the inadequacy of the presumption that clauses fall into two simple types, intransitive and transitive. Numerous other problem cases can be identified cross-linguistically. For instance, many languages show a distinct clause type of speech, different from transitive clauses, in which the addressee serves in a role that cannot be identified with the O of ordinary transitive clauses because of different formal marking or behaviour (see §2.3 for examples). Many languages show another distinct bivalent clause type that expresses referential identity of two NPs, but whose roles show properties distinguishing them from the two roles of the ordinary transitive clause – that cannot reasonably be identified with A and O roles – as in the English clause *Sean Connery is James Bond*.

2.3 A Neo-Firthian Approach to the Typology of Grammatical Relations

2.3.1 Preliminary Remarks

The criticisms levelled against the S, A, O theory in the previous section hinge on its failure to take language-particular categories seriously, and the implicit notion that comparative categories are fundamental. Language-particular grammatical phenomena emerge as mere reflexes of how the comparative categories are 'treated' in the language – it is as though S, A, and O are the central grammatical phenomena and the language-particular facts instantiations of their 'treatment' in the morphosyntax of the language. By contrast, in a Neo-Firthian approach to typology things are reversed.[3] The language-particular facts occupy the fundamental place, and represent the phenomena to be compared cross-linguistically. These are the emic grammatical relations of particular languages. These emic phenomena are compared on the basis of their likenesses to one another across languages. No set of comparative categories is required to draw the comparisons; they can be made without postulating notional categories. To put things in a slightly different way, in S, A, O theory morphosyntactic facts of languages provide windows into or overlays on S, A, and O, which are the fundamental or primitive relations (as depicted in Figure 2.1). In a Neo-Firthian approach morphosyntactic facts of a language are the fundamental ones, and all primitive categories are defined in terms of morphosyntactic facts.

A second feature of a Neo-Firthian approach to the typology of grammatical relations is that the targeted phenomena are presumed to be linguistic signs, defined as per Saussure, as two-faced entities displaying inherent forms (signifiers) and inherent meanings (signifieds). As indicated in §2.2.1 above there is no place for semantic, pragmatic and grammatical roles as understood in received linguistic typology. On the one hand, the roles express, indeed code meanings; on the other are identifiable only by virtue of their formal exponence.

In what follows I present one Neo-Firthian approach to the typology of grammatical relations, that of SG (McGregor 1997b), this being one of the few Neo-Firthian theories that has attempted to typologize the domain, or to describe grammatical relations in languages other than English – although there is a certain amount of SFL descriptive work on grammatical relations in other languages (see e.g. Shore 1992 on Finnish; Martin 1996 on Tagalog; and contributions in Caffarel, Martin and Matthiessen 2004 on French, German, Telegu, Vietnamese, Mandarin Chinese and Pitjantjatjara).

To begin with, we restrict attention to grammatical relations of the experiential type, which concern the domain of transitivity (§1.1.3). This qualification must be borne in mind throughout the discussion, where I will usually omit the qualifier *experiential*.

As stressed above, any typology of grammatical relations must be founded on grammatical relations in specific languages. What we need to do for each language in our typological sample is to identify the transitivity types, and how they can be defined in terms of emic grammatical roles. This implies that we need language-specific criteria for the identification of the roles. The experiential roles of very few languages have been described in SG, so a motivated typology is beyond the scope of the present work. It will only be possible when the phenomena in a representative sampling of the world's languages have been described. Of necessity, then, the approach to the problem in this chapter is largely top-down rather than bottom-up. I present the typology on the basis of the theory. Nevertheless, I begin outlining and constructing the SG theory in a bottom-up fashion, from the situation in a small selection of languages that I am most familiar with myself: three languages of the north-west of Australia, Gooniyandi (McGregor 1990a), Nyulnyul (McGregor 2012a, 2014a) and Warrwa (McGregor 2002a, 2006a, in preparation). We begin with Nyulnyul.

2.3.2 Grammatical Relations in Nyulnyul

McGregor (2014a) proposes that two tiers of experiential roles are identifiable in Nyulnyul in accordance with two formal parameters. One concerns how the NP fulfilling the role is cross-referenced by bound pronouns in the inflecting verb; the other concerns the morphological marking of the NP, how it is, or may be, marked by postpositions. The former is a set of so-called 'participant' (argument) roles: Actor (cross-referenced by a nominative pronominal prefix), Undergoer (cross-referenced by an accusative enclitic), and Implicated (cross-referenced by an oblique enclitic). The second system gives a set of 'connate' (or affiliated) roles: Agent (optionally marked by the ergative postposition), and Medium (realized by an unmarked NP, an NP without a case marking postposition).[4] The system of participant roles is an accusative one; the system of connate roles is an ergative one.

As discussed above, these grammatical roles are understood to be linguistic signs of the experiential type, and thus express meanings. These meanings are abstract and diffi-cult to specify with precision (see also Halliday 1988a). Table 2.1 provides an approximate explanation of the meanings of each of the roles. The crucial feature in each specifi-cation concerns an abstract action vector rather than notions such as intentionality, deliberation, and control. Transitivity as a semantic phenomenon is thus fundamentally concerned with direction of activity vectors in Nyulnyul.

Table 2.1 Characterizations of the meanings of participant and connate roles in Nyulnyul, after McGregor (2012a: 573)

Role	Meaning
Actor	The thing that is construed as enacting or performing the event, as engaged or involved most actively in the situation, regardless of whether they are acting deliberately or unintentionally.
Undergoer	An entity construed as the target of the activity engaged in by the Actor, towards which an action vector is directed and impinges on: it is something directly impacted on by, or that suffers in some way from, the event performed by the Actor.
Implicated	An entity, typically human, that is involved in the event, though less directly than Actor or Undergoer. They may be: • tangentially impacted on by the event, involved in passing; or • the action may be directed towards them without reaching them.
Agent	An entity that engages in directed activity, one that directs an activity vector to a conceptually distinct entity.
Medium	An entity involved in the event, from which further action does not emanate: the locus, or potential locus, of coming-to-being of the event.

The two tiers of roles differ in terms of their centrality. The participant roles repre-sent, I have suggested (McGregor 2014a), the more central tier, the nucleus, while the connate roles form a less central tier, though they still belong to the core of the experi-ential grammar of the clause. The motivation for this assignment to tiers derives from facts of Nyulnyul grammar. To begin with, participant roles observe a role-uniqueness condition – there may be just one instance of any such role in a clause – while connate roles do not, and more than one instance of a given connate role may be present in a clause. Participant roles always conflate with connate roles. Moreover, they construe the central 'directionality' of the situation specified by a clause, and each participant role is inherent to the clause type in which it occurs. Connate roles by contrast may be inherent or non-inherent, and may or may not conflate with participant roles. Those connate roles that are not conflated with participant roles stand somewhat outside of the nucleus of the clause in that they do not partake in the inherent 'directionality' of the situation. Connate roles are more marginal to the experiential construal of the situation than participant roles – and hence the label.

The above discussion applies just to verbal clauses that represent situations or ongoing happenings in a possible world of experience. Not all Nyulnyul clauses represent situations. There are clauses that are inherently verbless, and construe instead logical relations of attribution, identification and the like (McGregor 2012a: 552–562), or textural relations like indexing presence of something in a certain context (McGregor 2012a: 550–551). In verbal situation clauses the verb also serves in an experiential role: it specifies the event itself. This role is dubbed the State of Affairs (SoA), which is right at the centre of the clause. Figure 2.2 encapsulates these observations.

These grammatical relations permit an experiential classification of Nyulnyul clauses in terms of the combination and conflations of roles from the two tiers, as shown in Table 2.2. This language-particular account is descriptively adequate, and does not suffer from the problems of the S, A, O theory identified in §2.2.2. Only some of the possible conflations of roles from the two tiers actually occur. The attested conflations in Nyulnyul are represented diagrammatically in Figure 2.3. Inspection of the specifications in Table 2.1 will reveal that some of the conflations are ruled out semantically; others simply do not exist in Nyulnyul.

The six transitivity types of Nyulnyul range from 1-valent (intransitive) to 3-valent (ditransitive), with four intermediate 2-valent types. In some sense they differ in degree of transitivity, ranging from least to most transitive in order from top to bottom in Table 2.2. The intransitive type is the least transitive, and involves just an Actor/Medium, as in (2.10).

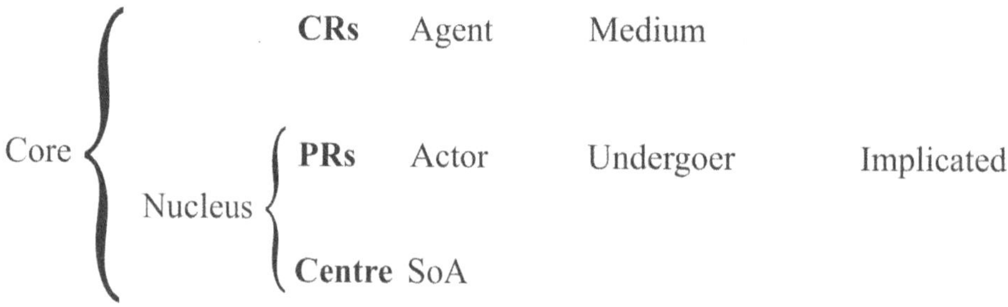

Figure 2.2   Tiers of experiential grammatical relations in Nyulnyul

Table 2.2 Transitivity types in Nyulnyul

Clause type	Nuclear and core conflations		Core role only
intransitive	Actor/Medium		
quasi-transitive	Actor/Medium		Medium
medio-active	Actor/Medium		Agent
middle	Actor/Agent	Implicated/Medium	
transitive	Actor/Agent	Undergoer/Medium	
ditransitive	Actor/Agent	Undergoer/Medium	Medium

(2.10)   *ngay*   *nga-ny-jurub*   Nyulnyul
                 1MIN.CRD   1MIN.NOM-PST-fart
                 Actor/Medium   SoA
                 'I farted.'

The 2-valent types differ also in apparent degree of transitivity according to the mappings of grammatical roles onto the inherent NPs of the clause. Quasi-transitive and medio-active clauses conflate Actor with Medium, and thus construe the Actor as not engaged in activity that extends beyond itself. These two clause types show just one participant role, the Actor. The other inherent role is a connate role. Quasi-transitive clauses have a second Medium role representing another locus of coming into being of the situation. One of the Mediums (the one conflated with the Actor) is more engaged or involved than the other, which represents what is effectively a means for realization of the event. Thus, in (2.11) the persons are the most engaged, the food represents the means by which they bring the exchange into being. This is a highly restricted transitivity type in Nyulnyul, and only one known VP type realizes the SoA role in quasi-transitive clauses. This involves the inflecting verb -BARNJ 'exchange'.

(2.11)   *wilamay*   *i-ngi-rr-barnj*   Nyulnyul
                 food   3NOM-PST-AUG-exchange
                 Medium   SoA
                 'They gave each other food.'

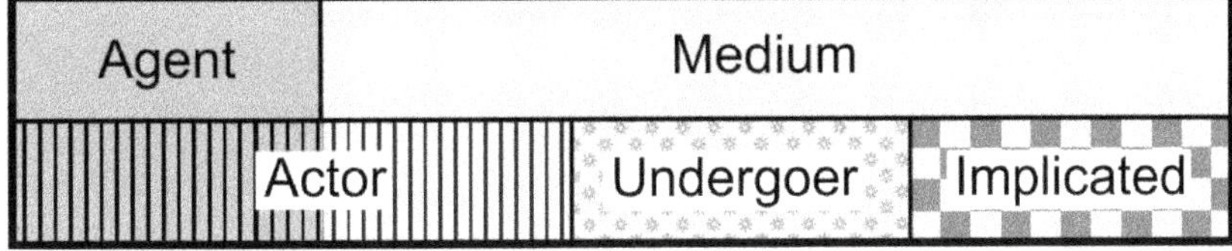

Figure 2.3 Conflations of participant and connate roles in Nyulnyul

By contrast, medio-active clauses – illustrated by (2.7), repeated below for convenience as (2.12) – have a second role that directs activity to some other entity, but is not construed as performing the event. Medio-actives construe happenings that befall animates, typically humans, as the result of some external cause, typically inanimate (McGregor 1999b, 2012a: 579–582).

<pre>
(2.12) bulji   nga-n-ji   marriny-in ngay   Nyulnyul
        tired   1MIN.NOM-CM-say   walk-ERG   1MIN.CRD
        SoA   Agent   Actor/Medium
        'I'm tired from walking.'
</pre>

The two other 2-valent types involve inherent NPs both of which involve conflations of participant and connate roles: both inherent NPs participate in the nuclear activity of the event as well as in its associated activity. Both have an Actor that is simultaneously an Agent. They differ in the involvement of the other entity. In transitive clauses such as (2.13) (= (2.6)) it is construed as a target of activity, and thus undergoes the situation, suffers from action on it. In middle clauses – for example (2.14) (= (2.8)) – the activity is less potent: the Medium is either impinged on tangentially or the activity does not quite reach it.

<pre>
(2.13) wamb-in   i-n-dam-ø   yiil   jan   Nyulnyul
        man-ERG   3NOM-CM-hit-3MIN.ACC   dog   1MIN.OBL
        Actor/Agent   SoA   Undergoer/Medium
        'The man hit my dog.'
</pre>

<pre>
(2.14) kudirrawany-in i-n-di-jin /   winin /   Nyulnyul
        bustard-ERG   3NOM-CM-say-3MIN.OBL   emu
        Actor/Agent   SoA   Implicated/Medium
        'The bustard spoke to the emu.'
</pre>

Ditransitive clauses – as illustrated by (2.15) (= (2.9)) – show an Actor/Agent and two Medium NPs, just one of which also fulfils a participant role, the Undergoer; this is invariably the recipient of an event of giving. In other situation types the Undergoer is normally an animate being, while the unconflated Medium NP is typically an inanimate.

<pre>
(2.15) ngay-in   nga-na-w-ø   mirlimirl   Nyulnyul
        1MIN.CRD-ERG   1MIN.NOM-CM-give-3MIN.ACC   paper
        Actor/Agent   SoA   Medium
        kinyingk   wamb   biird
        DEF   man   yesterday
        Undergoer/Medium
        'I gave the book to the man yesterday.'
</pre>

The six transitivity types differ strikingly in terms of their degree of semantic specificity. Quasi-transitive, medio-active and middle clauses are quite specific semantically, while intransitive, transitive and ditransitive are much more schematic. This is as might be predicted given that the former are more language particular, the latter transitivity types being expected in most languages. Moreover, the meanings of intransitive, transitive and ditransitive clauses appear to be largely compositional, a sum of the meanings of the inherent roles comprising them. For the quasi-transitive, medio-active and middle, the meanings are more specific and less compositional: they cannot be fully predicted from the meanings of their grammatical roles.

This brief overview of experiential grammatical roles in Nyulnyul serves to illustrate the main parameters of a Neo-Firthian approach to the description of transitivity in a given language. The formal and semantic phenomena overviewed serve as the basis for a typology of experiential relations, as outlined in the following section.

2.3.3 A Neo-Firthian Typology of Grammatical Relations

As already acknowledged, there is a paucity of descriptive SG accounts of transitivity in the world's languages, thus precluding a bottom-up typology. Of necessity we are forced to assume the universality of experiential roles, that all languages will show an emic set of grammatical roles of this type. As linguistic signs these will be language-particular, with both form (signifiers) and meaning (signifieds). The particular grammatical roles will be different in any pair of languages, as stressed by Dryer (1997). However, the roles in different languages can be expected to show similarities in form and/or meaning, sufficient to permit us to employ the same label for those roles that are most alike in the different languages (see §1.2.4.2). In some sense the different roles can be regarded as the same – not because they are manifestations of the same platonic ideal but because they share significant attributes of form and meaning.

Experiential roles share a significant formal attribute, namely they are realized by meaningful constituency relations, part-whole relations in which the part serves a function in the whole (see §1.1.3 and McGregor 1997b: 21–31, 74; 2003a). The hypothesis is that roles of this type – expressed by constituency relations – will be identifiable in all languages. At the same time the theory suggests that the relations showing this formal attribute will share something in their meaning, namely that they relate to the construal of a world of experience. More specifically, we might hypothesize that in any language there will be an experiential role like the SoA of Nyulnyul that specifies a type of 'event'. It also seems reasonable to presume that in any language it will be possible to identify a role that is sufficiently close in meaning to the Actor role of Nyulnyul to permit use of this term, and the identification of the roles for typological purposes. For present purposes, I will assume that all languages select grammatical relations from a set including those identified for Nyulnyul. There is no claim to exhaustiveness. This does not open the floodgates to any role at the analyst's whim: these are emic roles, demanded by the facts of the particular language.

A final aspect of the theory is the notion that there are tiers of grammatical roles, and that these tiers differ in orientation, accusative or ergative. This hypothesis also has potential to show cross-language variation. Let us now turn to specifics, and outline some typological hypotheses afforded by the theory.

2.3.3.1 *Identification and marking of the roles*

How the experiential roles are formally manifested in different languages is expected to show some degree of variation, though this variation is expected to be within limits. In Nyulnyul we saw that they are marked by verbal and nominal morphology. The same holds true for Gooniyandi (McGregor 1990a: 317) and Warrwa (McGregor 2002a, in preparation). In Acehnese the situation is not dissimilar, with verbal morphology (cross-referencing pronominals and derivational morphemes) and nominal markers (here free prepositions) marking the relations. Wangkajunga (Pama-Nyungan, Australia) employs a system of enclitic pronouns that attach to the first unit of a clause together with NP marking (my own fieldwork and Jones 2011).

A plausible typological hypothesis that bears investigation is that if a language marks experiential roles by both cross-referencing bound pronominals (whether verbal or not) and NP marking, the former will mark participant roles, the latter connate roles. The system of participant roles is more likely to be accusative than ergative. In terms of alignment theory this corresponds to the observation that systems of bound pronouns are more likely to be accusatively than ergatively oriented.

Experiential roles are not always formally marked: they are not always overt categories. In English, for instance, there are no morphological indexes of experiential roles. Even pronominal case marking does not identify experiential roles – nominative pronouns can serve in Agent roles in transitive clauses (*she kissed him*) and in Undergoer role in the corresponding passive (*he was kissed*). This lack of overt marking does not mean that experiential roles are not present in English. Rather, as per, for example, Halliday (1967, 1968, 1985) and Davidse (2017), experiential roles in this language are covert categories and 'strongly cryptotypical' (Davidse 2017: 87), identifiable by patterns of agnation, i.e. diathesis alternations. Active-passive pairs argue for distinguishing between Actor and Undergoer, as do pairs like *the farmer ate the duckling* and *the farmer ate*. On the other hand, there is evidence of another tier of experiential roles in alternations such as *the farmer broke the glass* and *the glass broke*. Alternants such as these motivate identification of a Medium role served by *the glass*, and an Agent role served by *the farmer*.

There is scope for investigation of the cross-linguistic range of modes of marking participant and connate roles in languages, their relative frequencies, and whether these correlate with any other grammatical features. In the S, A, O theory modes of marking are not distinguished as such, but are simply one of the means of 'treating' these primitives in a language. The facts of the language are effectively window-dressing on linguists' ideals.

2.3.3.2 *Meanings of the roles*

Experiential roles differ cross-linguistically also in meaning, in their signifieds. We assign the same role labels to roles that differ in both their formal indexation and their meanings. But there must be sufficient commonality on both dimensions to warrant the same label. Thus, for both Nyulnyul and Gooniyandi I recognize an Agent role. The formal indexation in both languages is by means of (optional) deployment of the ergative postposition. In terms of meaning, there is a difference in that in Gooniyandi the action vector need not necessarily be directed to a conceptually distinct entity. It may be self- or internally directed, as in reflexive-reciprocal clauses, which represent a separate transitivity type in Gooniyandi, but are simple intransitives in Nyulnyul. The Medium roles of Gooniyandi and Nyulnyul are very similar, but Nyulnyul's is slightly more general, and is systematically vague between potential and actual coming into being through some entity. Gooniyandi Mediums by contrast serve as actual loci, and potential loci are realized through another role (see below).

Less similar are the Actor and Undergoer roles of Nyulnyul and Acehnese. As we have seen deliberation, control and intentionality are not part of the meaning of the Actor role in Nyulnyul. However, they are in Acehnese (Durie 1985, 1987). The single inherent role of an intransitive clause of motion is an Actor only when the moving object is one that is prototypically in control of the motion. Otherwise, for uncontrolled motion like falling, there is no Actor role. Instead, the moving entity is represented as an Undergoer. In Acehnese, in contrast with Nyulnyul, the Undergoer role does not code the meaning that an action vector is directed towards it.

The ranges of meanings coded by experiential roles is surely a topic of great interest to linguistic typology,[5] permitting a window on the semantic features deployed in the construal of events. In turn this raises the Whorfian question of whether there is any connection between the linguistic construal of roles and habitual ways of thinking about the world of experience – for speaking (*a la* Slobin) and more generally (*a la* Whorf).

2.3.3.3 *A transitivity typology of clauses*

Another domain for typological investigation afforded by the Neo-Firthian approach concerns a transitivity typology of situation types. This is a non-issue in the S, A, O theory, which begins from the premise that the clauses of any language fall exhaustively into two types, intransitive and transitive. Ditransitives sneak in by the back door, but attract scant attention. Voice options such as passives, antipassives, reflexives and the like emerge as deformations of, or derivations from, the two fundamental types. They are not seen as genuine construction types worthy of places alongside intransitive and transitive clauses, in paradigmatic opposition with them. In the Neo-Firthian approach voice options represent distinct constructions, on a par with ordinary transitive and intransitive clauses – and in no sense derivative from them.

According to the Neo-Firthian approach situation types are defined in terms of conflations of participant and connate roles, and the combinations of these conflations, as illustrated for Nyulnyul in Table 2.2 above. In Gooniyandi, as we have seen, the formal marking of the roles is similar to that in Nyulnyul, and the set of roles and their meanings is also remarkable similar. However, a rather different set of transitivity types are distinguished in Gooniyandi, as shown in Table 2.3, a revision and expansion of McGregor (1998: 500).

Table 2.3 Transitivity typology of situation clauses in Gooniyandi

Clause type	Participant and connate conflations		Connate role only
intransitive	Actor/Medium		
impersonal	Undergoer/Medium		
reflexive/reciprocal	Actor/Agent		
middle	Actor/Agent	Implicated/Target	
transitive	Actor/Agent	Undergoer/Medium	
ditransitive	Actor/Agent	Undergoer/Medium	Medium

Despite the employment of a similar set of participant and connate roles, with very similar meanings, they are put together in rather different ways in the two languages. Both languages distinguish the same number of transitivity types, but Gooniyandi divides the domain more evenly with respect to number of inherent roles: three monovalent, three polyvalent. It makes a ternary division in monovalent clauses between intransitive, impersonal and reflexive/reciprocal clauses. Nyulnyul by contrast divides up the polyvalent domain into five different types, leaving the monovalent domain undifferentiated.

Both languages also distinguish a category of middle clause, like many languages of the region. In both languages this category includes situations of seeking or looking for, as well as speaking to someone. In Nyulnyul the thing sought and the addressee are treated as though the situation comes into being through them; they are the locus of the situation's occurrence, even if it does not actually ensue. However, in Gooniyandi the corresponding things are treated as Target of the activity vector. This role is served by an NP marked by the dative postposition; it specifies something as the intended target of an action, but (in contrast with the Undergoer) connection is not necessarily achieved with it. Thus, in (2.16) an activity vector is directed towards the child, but need not necessarily reach it for the situation to have come into being. By contrast, in (2.17) the activity vector must reach the child, a connection must be made with the child, for the situation to have occurred.

(2.16) *nganyi-ngga*   *jiginya-yoo*   *moow-l+a-nhi*   Gooniyandi
   1SG.CRD-ERG   child-DAT   search-1SG.NOM+A-3SG.OBL
   Actor/Agent   Implicated/Target SoA
   'I looked for the child.'

(2.17) *nganyi-ngga   jiginya   gilba-l+ø+i*   Gooniyandi
      1SG.CRD-ERG   child   find-1SG.NOM+3SG.ACC+DI
      Actor/Agent   Undergoer/Medium   SoA
      'I found the child.'

The classifications suggested for Nyulnyul and Gooniyandi clauses are rather abstract ones, distinguishing types according to very general action-vector features of situations. It is possible that other classifications of clauses are possible that distinguish according to more concrete features of the referent situations. For instance, it might be possible to classify situations cross-linguistically into categories resembling Halliday's classification of English clauses into material, mental, behavioural, etc. (Halliday 1985: 131), or according to other systems found in the literature invoking Aktionsart (e.g. Dik 1989; Dowty 1979; Van Valin 1993: 35).[6]

I have suggested that patterns of alternation among the transitivity types of Table 2.3 permit a comparable classification of situation clause types in Gooniyandi (McGregor 1997b: 106–112). Here I refer to the sets of transitivity types that enter into paradigmatic alternations in the representation of situations of particular types, i.e. what has been called 'agnation patterns' in some SFL work. This is shown in Figure 2.4, which distinguishes four primary types: being (roughly, situations specifying the general mode or stance of being of some entity), receptive (roughly, situations of undergoing, in which some entity undergoes a change of state), active (roughly, situations of doing-embracing situations of stasis, motion, impact and violence, vocalization, bodily functions, etc.), and behavioural (roughly, situations of bodily behaviour).

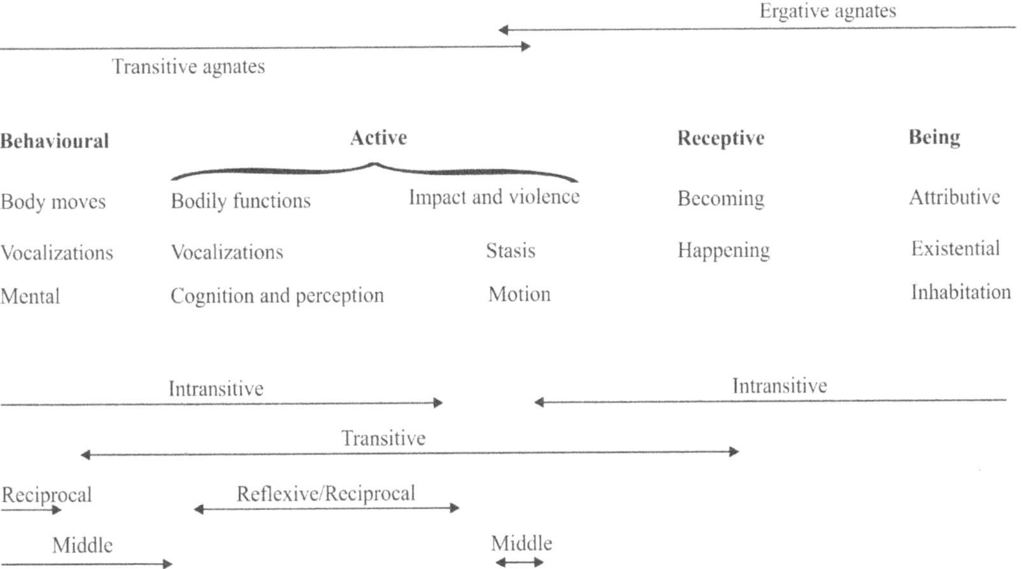

Figure 2.4 Another classification of Gooniyandi clause types, after McGregor (1997b: 111)

These types are identified by virtue of the alternative modes of representation in transitivity types. Being clauses are represented by just intransitive clauses; there are no minimal pairs of other transitivity values for these clauses. Behavioural clauses by contrast may show alternation between intransitive, middle, reflexive/reciprocal and rarely transitive clauses; the reflexive/reciprocal agnates are, however, restricted to reciprocals: singular Actors are precluded, and the reflexive interpretation is ruled out for plural Actors. Receptive clauses are typically intransitive, though occasionally transitive agnates are found; these are normally causatives. Active clauses are overall transitive, though intransitive and reflexive/reciprocal agnates usually exist, and middle agnates rarely exist. For clauses of violence impersonal agnates may also exist (not shown in the figure). These alternations pattern ergatively towards the right of the figure, accusatively towards the left (see again §2.3.3.1). That is to say, the corresponding roles in the intransitive-transitive agnates are the Medium/Actors and Medium/Undergoers for receptive clauses, but Medium/Actors and Agent/Actors for behavioural clauses. Both patterns are found in active clauses.

My previous critical remarks on some universal claims should not be taken as implying that there are no universals in grammatical roles – I have tried to characterize ways that grammatical roles might be considered universal – or that there are no universals of situation types. Like other typologists, I consider the formulation of potential universals to be an important goal. These of course must be theoretically motivated and empirically tested. Thus, I have suggested (McGregor 1997b: 110), building on the language-particular observations of the prevous paragraphs, a possible universal hierarchy of situation types as shown in Figure 2.5. These range from the least to most restrictive in terms of selection restrictions on the Actor role. Clauses at the far left (bodily moves and functions, vocalizations, and cognition and perception) require an animate, prototypically human Actor, whereas those at the far right (becoming, inhabitation, attribution and existential) impose no animacy restrictions. The intermediate types

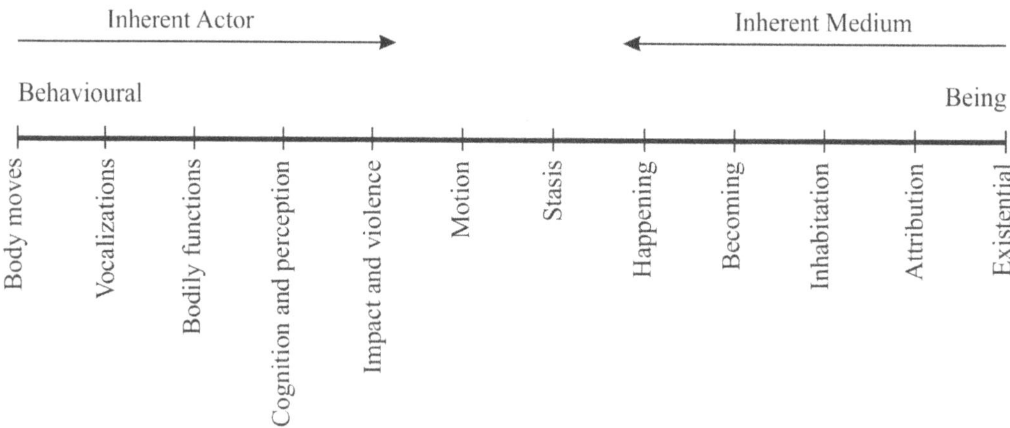

Figure 2.5 Hypothetical universal hierarchy of situation types

show weaker statistical associations between the Actor role and animacy. This hierarchy represents a clausal analogue for Silverstein's animacy hierarchy for the NP (Silverstein 1976; Figure 1.1) and permits predictions concerning the agnation patterns found in different clause types. (See §3.1.1 and Rijkhoff 2002, 2008b on correlations between the grammar of the clause and the NP.)

2.3.3.4 *A further issue in the typology of experiential roles*

The above just scratches the surface of possible typological implications of a Neo-Firthian approach. The loci and relative weights of ergative and accusative patterning in experiential roles would be interesting to study from a typological perspective. Do all languages organize their experiential roles into two tiers, and if so, to what extent are they identifiable with the two tiers proposed for Nyulnyul? Are there formal indexes of the contrast, as in Gooniyandi and Nyulnyul? Halliday has suggested that all languages show both ergative and accusative patterning in their experiential roles (Halliday 1985: 149), but show variation in the locus and extent of these patternings. Indeed, Halliday (1985: 144–147) proposes that the ergative system of English (as per §2.3.3.1) applies to all clause types in the language, while the accusative system of Actor and Goal are restricted to material processes; other transitivity types – for example, mental and behavioural clauses – show different participant role types. In Halliday's scheme, the ergative system would presumably be the nuclear tier of roles in English, the accusative one the core tier.

2.4 Concluding Remarks

To do the typology of experiential roles in a Neo-Firthian framework is clearly a challenging task that requires much more from grammatical descriptions than currently on offer from 'comprehensive' grammars set in an S, A, O based 'atheoretical' framework. Richer and more theoretically informed grammars are essential. We have a long way to go before we can effectively do a bottom-up Neo-Firthian typology of grammatical relations.

An important consequence of the approach to grammatical relations advocated in this chapter is that there is no such thing as alignment – except in the minds of linguists. We do not need a theory of alignment; indeed, such a theory is nonsensical. It can only be founded on a mapping between language-particular facts of marking ('treated the same' vs. 'treated differently') and a notional level of platonic ideals. This implies that recent forays into alignment in discourse – for example, Du Bois (1987, 2003) – are also fundamentally misguided. The issue of interest to a Neo-Firthian account is whether there are 'discourse' related correlates of grammatical roles, and if there are, what might motivate them.

One does not need to buy the full Neo-Firthian package of §2.3 to have something better than S, A, O theory. Most typologists would presumably be happier with the assumption that grammatical relations should be language particular ones, defined by the morphosyntactic features of the language in question than with the assumption that grammatical relations code meanings. Much of the typology outlined in the previous section is possible under the assumption that the grammatical relations are purely formal ones.

I end this chapter on a somewhat jaundiced note. The survival of the S, A, O theory over the past few decades is in many ways surprising, and one can almost hear Karl Popper turning over in his grave. In the discipline of modern linguistics, theories tend to have quite short half-lives, and are readily rejected for either theoretical inadequacies or failure to account for the facts of languages. Yet the S, A, O theory has survived in the face of a large weight of counterevidence that has constantly accumulated since the 1980s. Perhaps it is the apparent and/or alleged atheoretical status of the theory that appeals to many typologists, who tend to be highly suspicious of theory. The theory is simple enough to appear to be a non-theory and to belong to the set of propositions all linguists attest to – and hence is beyond question. I am thus sceptical that the critiques and alternative proposals outlined in this chapter will have the slightest effect on typologists, or result in abandonment of a cherished non-theory.

This story is reminiscent of the history of SFL. Like S, A, O and alignment SFL seems to have survived fundamentally unchanged over the decades, immune to problems. Fundamental difficulties known since the 1960s (for instance, with Halliday's version of the rank scale hypothesis – Halliday 1961; see, for example, Matthews 1966; Huddleston 1988; and McGregor 1991 for critiques) are massively ignored. The reason is not to do with suspicion of theory, but rather seems to be a consequence of the ever-widening spheres of interest, and widespread lack of concern with the architecture of the theory – concerns that many theorists put in primary place. As Halliday puts it, '[a] feature of systemic work is that it has tended to expand by moving into new spheres of activity, rather than revising earlier positions' (Halliday 1996: 324). Perhaps in part the same explanation applies to the S, A, O theory – where the ever-expanding spheres of activity are the descriptions of new languages.

Chapter 3

The Noun Phrase

3.1 Introduction

3.1.1 The Notion of NP (and PP)

Like the clause, the category of noun phrase (NP) – under whatever name – has wide currency in linguistic theory, and is identified as a syntactic category in a wide range of formal and functional theories. As with the clause, a precise definition is somewhat elusive. I will assume as a working characterization that NPs are grammatical units that specify and refer to entities (see also Rijkhoff 2002: 19, 27, who further restricts them to units involving nominals). These entities may be things in the external physical world, or mental representations of entities that are somehow construed in the minds of speakers. Sometimes, of course, only the latter obtains, and there may be no actual referent in the physical world – for instance, *the unicorn* may have just a mental representation. There are uncertain cases such as *the abominable snowman*; often an NP has both a physical and a mental referent, as in, for example, *the Great Wall* and *the computer in front of me*. The issue of the reality of referents takes us away from linguistics; one approach is to think of utterances as construing worlds of discourse referents. But we habitually act on the world and the world on us; referents are often real. Real things can be construed in many different ways, as discourse referents satisfying quite different characteristics. One needs to know when and how to make the connection between discourse referents and real ones.

NPs include both expressions involving pronominals (e.g. *you*, *the two of us*), lexical nouns (*the abominable snowman*), and/or both (*we linguists*). They may be simple, comprising just a single word, as in *you*, *cattle* (*there's cattle in the field*) or *Murdoch*. In some languages – for example, various Australian languages – single word lexical NPs are the norm, and these may construe both specific/definite and non-specific/indefinite referents, as in (3.1). NPs may be larger and more complex than this, as in *the cat that chased the mouse that ate the mouldy cheese*.

> (3.1) *kinya-n*   *ngi-rr-a-ma-na/*   *wanangarri/*   Warrwa
>   DEF-LOC   3NOM-AUG-CM-put-PST   rock
>   'They put stones/a stone there.' or 'They put the stone(s) there.'

As observed in §1.2.2.2 not all languages distinguish separate nominal and verbal lexical parts of speech. This does not mean that such languages lack NPs. There is nothing in the characterization of NP that refers to a part of speech. Tongan (Austronesian) shows no part of speech contrast between nominals and verbs. The lexeme *si'i* 'small' serves to specify an Event (being small) in (3.2), while in (3.3) and (3.4) it belongs to NP-like expressions referring to entities, the abstract entity 'childhood' and the concrete one 'little child', respectively.

(3.2) *na'e si'i   'ae   akó*   Tongan
      PST   small   ABS   school.DEF
      'The school was small.' (Tchekhoff 1981: 4)

(3.3) *'i   'ene   si'i*   Tongan
      in   3SG.POS   childhood.DEF
      'in his/her childhood' (Tchekhoff 1981: 4)

(3.4) *na'e ako   'ae   tamasi'i si'i   iate   au*   Tongan
      PST   study   ABS   child   little   LOC   1SG
      'The little child studied at my house.' (Tchekhoff 1981: 4)

Likewise, in languages with nominals an NP need not necessarily include a nominal (or related category such as pronominal). This seems to be the situation in Tuscarora (Iroquoian), which has just a small class of nominals. Verbs can be used to specify Events, or alternatively to refer to entities, in which case they may co-occur with determiners and be coordinated with genuine nominals (Mithun Williams 1976: 31).

Another component of the definition of NPs is that they represent grammatical units, syntagms that cohere in such a way that they form single unified grammatical entities.[1] It is in relation to this component of the definition that it has been claimed that a number of languages – including the Standard Average Australian (SAA) language – lack NPs. We address this issue in the next section (§3.1.2) and suggest that in fact there is little evidence for languages without the category of NP.

SFL, as mentioned in §2.4, assumes a rank scale, which distinguishes ranks of clause, phrase/group, word and morpheme (for English at least). Phrases and groups are at roughly the same position on the rank scale, according to Halliday (1985: 159), though he considers one (the group) to be an expansion of the word, while the other (the phrase) is the contraction of a clause. What I refer to as NPs Halliday construes as nominal groups; this analysis and terminology has gained wide currency in SFL. The term phrase is employed in SFL in reference to constructions such as the prepositional phrase (PP) of English. The PP shows, as Halliday (1985: 189) observes, a different structure to the nominal group (NP). It is not clear to me, however, that this structural difference warrants identification of a distinct rank, rather than merely a different category at the same rank.[2] Halliday makes a case for the reduced clause structure of the phrase by proposing that the preposition is in fact a minor verb, and that the structure of the phrase replicates the structure of the clause, such that this minor verb serves in comparable experiential and interpersonal functions within the PP as the typical verb in a clause.

There are two serious problems with these proposals. First, as has been observed by theoreticians of various persuasions (including functional – e.g. Rijkhoff 2002), there are striking parallels between the structure of the NP and the clause. It is not clear why such parallels do not motivate the NP as a reduced clause. Second, the suggestion that the preposition is a minor verb, and serves in functions in the phrase comparable with those of the verb in a clause lacks an evidential basis. It is not obvious that adpositions generally do anything more than relate NPs to other things, and hence serve purely textural functions. It is difficult to accept Halliday's suggestion that the adposition serves in an experiential role comparable with the role of Event served by a verb in a VP. And while there is evidence in some languages that adpositions have grammaticalized from verbs, there is no reason to believe that verbs are the sole (or even primary) source of adpositions cross-linguistically. Furthermore, with the grammaticalization of the verb surely comes reduction in its functional potential such that it no longer serves in an experiential role construing an event.

3.1.2 The NP as a Linguistic Universal

The universality of the phrasal category of NP has been challenged by some descriptive linguists and typologists. The primary grounds for this rejection are that in certain languages, including Australian languages such as Kalkatungu (Pama-Nyungan), Mangarayi (Arnhem) and Warlpiri (Pama-Nyungan): (i) nominal expressions that apparently specify a single referent are not necessarily continuous, indeed are frequently discontinuous; and (ii) the words of such nominal expressions often do not occur in a fixed order. To illustrate, consider the oft-repeated Kalkatungu examples from Blake (1983: 145), which show that the three words *cipa* 'this', *ṯuku* 'dog' and *yaun* 'big' which might be expected to form an NP can be separated from one another, and occur in various orders.

(3.5)   *cipa-yi*   *ṯuku-yu*   *yaun-tu*   *yaɲi*   *icayi*   Kalkatungu
          this-ERG   dog-ERG   big-ERG   white.man   bite
          'This big dog bit/bites the white man.'

(3.6)   *cipa-yi*   *ṯuku-yu*   *yaɲi*   *icayi*   *yaun-tu*   Kalkatungu
          this-ERG   dog-ERG   white.man   bite   big-ERG
          'This big dog bit/bites the white man.'

(3.7)   *ṯuku-yu*   *cipa-yi*   *icayi*   *yaɲi*   *yaun-tu*   Kalkatungu
          dog-ERG   this-ERG   bite   white.man   big-ERG
          'This big dog bit/bites the white man.'

(3.8)   *yaun-tu*   *cipa-yi*   *ṯuku-yu*   *icayi*   *yaɲi*   Kalkatungu
          big-ERG   this-ERG   dog-ERG   bite   white.man
          'This big dog bit/bites the white man.'

(3.9) *cipa-yi   icayi yaṇi   ṭuku-yu   yaun-tu*   Kalkatungu
       this-ERG bite   white.man   dog-ERG   big-ERG
       'This big dog bit/bites the white man.'

(3.10) *yaṇi   icayi cipa-yi   yaun-tu   ṭuku-yu*   Kalkatungu
       white.man   bite   this-ERG big-ERG   dog-ERG
       'This big dog bit/bites the white man.'

It has been proposed that in these languages nominals do not form larger units with one another, but occur in apposition, each word separately entering into a grammatical relation in the clause (Blake 1983: 145). These arguments have been widely accepted by typologists (e.g. Rijkhoff 2002: 19). I have always been sceptical of them.

First, it is not clear what is meant by apposition. Its nature as a syntagmatic relation is never made clear. Nor is it obvious why nominals in apposition to one another do not form a unit together. Lacking a clear specification of the apposition relation, it cannot be concluded that if two nominals are in apposition they do not at the same time form a single larger unit with one another.

Second, according to Blake's proposed analysis, each of the three words marked by the ergative case marker in (3.5)–(3.10) separately enters into a grammatical relation in the clause. This must presumably be one and the same participant role. But this implies that a given clause may have more than one instance of any participant role. In such an analysis we could not maintain a role-uniqueness hypothesis (as per §2.3.2), thus losing a significant grammatical generalization. There is another alternative, namely that just one of the nominals serves in the grammatical role (with the other nominals in an appositional relation to it). This, however, fares no better: which of the three nominals in (3.5)–(3.10) is the one that serves in the grammatical role? Why?

Third, even if discontinuity of nominal expressions is permissible in a language, it is – in languages that I have investigated myself, as well as many included in the typological sample of Louagie and Verstraete (2016) – far from the norm, and is subject to strong constraints (see further §3.3.2.1 below).

Fourth, the alleged freedom of order of the nominals in examples such as (3.5)–(3.10) above seems to be overstated, certainly in the languages that I am familiar with. In Gooniyandi, as in Kalkatungu the order of nominals in expressions denoting a single entity is typically fairly free. Demonstratives and numerals may occur in either order with respect to a lexical nominal without affecting the reference of the expression. However, as will be seen in §3.2 these differences in order are associated with different functions of the demonstratives and numerals, and there are definite, albeit often subtle, meaning differences associated with the different orders.

In some languages there is other evidence supporting the identification of a NP-sized units. For instance, in Bunuban, Worrorran and Nyulnyulan languages it is typically the case that a single case or number marking clitic occurs with a continuous nominal expression. In Bunuban and Nyulnyulan languages, in contrast with Kalkatungu, just a single instance of the ergative case marker would normally occur in clauses corresponding to (3.5). This attests to the unithood of continuous nominal expressions such as these.

Placement of Wackernagel enclitics in some languages provides evidence for the NP as a unit. For instance, in languages such as Ngaanyatjara (Pama-Nyungan, Australia) – along with a number of other Western Desert varieties – bound pronouns occur in Wackernagel's position in the clause. They are normally cliticized to the end of an NP unit if that occurs in clause initial position, though they occasionally occur on another word or words of the NP (Glass and Hackett 1970: 37–38). Of course, as Louagie and Verstraete (2016: 45) observe, this only provides evidence for unithood of the nominal expression when it occurs in clause initial position, and when the bound pronouns occur at the end of the expression. Although it is somewhat limited as a tool for determining phrasal status of an expression, it does provide evidence for the existence of this type of unit: if NPs are viable units in initial position, it would be very implausible to suggest that they are not also viable elsewhere.

Prosody may also provide evidence for phrasal units (Louagie and Verstraete 2016: 45–46; Schultze-Berndt and Simard 2012). However, the Australianist literature provides only limited information on prosody, and the best we can say is that it may be that in some languages there are prosodic differences between NPs and nominals in apposition. For instance, Hill (2015) proposes that NPs are typically produced on a single intonation contour, as distinct from nominals in apposition, which are not.

The upshot is that grammarians have too quickly rejected the NP as a unit in a number of small languages where ordering of words is considerably less constrained than in Standard Average European (SAE) languages (Whorf 1956: 138). Subtle meaning differences may not be apparent in the absence of depth studies, and the permissibility or grammaticality of certain modes of expression does not necessarily imply their normality or unmarkedness.

3.2 Grammatical Structure of NPs

In this section I argue that the NP is structured as a four-dimensional object in accordance with the four semiotic components, experiential, logical, interpersonal and textural. In some respects, the NP is perhaps not as richly structured as the clause in terms of these semiotics. Before getting down to details, it is worth briefly highlighting two significant differences between the approach taken here and the standard SFL approach to the description of the structure of the NP, aka 'nominal group'.

First, according to SFL the clause is structured simultaneously in three different ways according to the experiential, interpersonal and textu(r)al components (see §2.1). By contrast, for the NP, Halliday (1985: 158) avers that there is a single structural line involving experiential, interpersonal and textu(r)al components; the semiotic components do not, that is, contribute different structures to the NP. I have argued to the contrary (McGregor 1997b) that both clause and NP are typically (though not invariably) structured in accordance with each of the semiotics, though not every unit in them necessarily serves roles in each semiotic.

Second, according to SFL the ideational metafunction comprises two sub-metafunctions, the experiential and the logical (§1.1.3). The phrase ('group') shows a distinct logical structure separate from the fused experiential, interpersonal and textual structure (Halliday 1985: 170–175). This structure is assumed complete: every component of the phrasal unit fulfils a role in the logical structure. Again, this assumption seems to me to be too strong.

3.2.1 Experiential Structure

As seen in §3.1.1 the NP is a unit that is used to refer to things in the real world or in some discourse world. I have argued (McGregor 1997b: 120–122) that the experiential structure of the NP is trivial in that it comprises a single role, the Entity. This is the role served by the noun *blood* in the NP *his dripping blood*, by the nominal *wanangarri* 'rock' in Warrwa example (3.1), by the contentives *si'i* 'small' and *tamasi'i* 'child' in Tongan examples (3.3) and (3.4) respectively, and by the nominal *ṯuku* 'dog' in Kalkatungu examples (3.5)–(3.10). These lexical items specify the referent of the NP in terms of a conceptualization of the type of thing it is. Other types of item that frequently serve in the Entity role are pronominals (e.g. *you* in *you two*) and proper nouns (e.g. *John* in *Farmer John*).

The Entity role may be realized by something more complex than a single lexeme. For instance, conjoined or disjoined nominals may realize this role, as in *ladies and gentlemen* and *boys or girls*. Various languages, including English, Gooniyandi and Mandarin Chinese (Li 2017: 348–349), show systems of subclassification whereby one lexical nominal partitions the domain of another into subtypes, as in *electric train, steam train, passenger train, express train* and so on. In such systems two lexical items, often nominals, appear in a close syntagmatic relation with one another, and the syntagm formed by them arguably serves in the Entity role.

All NPs presumably have an Entity role, though of course not all NPs actually have a linguistic unit substantiating it. For instance, the two NPs *the large* and *the small* in a barista's question *Which do you want, the large or the small?* have no nominal serving in the Entity role. In such instances, however, it is clear that the nominal filling this role has been ellipsed, being retrievable from context. This seems to hold in various other languages, including Gooniyandi (McGregor 1990a: 254–255), Kayardild (Tangkic, Australia) (Evans 1995: 234), Gaagudju (Arnhem, Australia) (Harvey 2002: 317) and Finnish (Uralic, Finland) (Shore 1992: 121). (Notice that in languages like Gooniyandi that lack a category of adjectives, an NP such as *ngoorroo nyamani* (that big) is ambiguous between two interpretations: 'that boss', where *nyamani* 'big' serves in the Entity role, and 'that big (one)' where the Entity nominal has been ellipsed.)

3.2.2 Logical Structure

NPs frequently comprise more than just Entity nominals. They often include a range of other linguistic items that serve to modify the Entity nominal by attributing properties of it beyond the conceptual categorization by that nominal. These modifying units serve in various types of dependency relation to the Entity nominal. This is a hypotactic relation in which the Entity nominal serves as head. In terms of the grammatical model outlined in §1.1.3 these part-part relations assign logical structure to the NP. I have argued (McGregor 1997b: 60–64, building on Halliday's 1985: 196 notion of 'logico-semantic' relations of expansion) for a three-way typology of dependency relations, distinguishing: elaboration (restatement, provision of an alternative conceptualization), extension (adding something new) and enhancement (embellishment, provision of circumstantial information).

Elaboration in the simple NP comes in two main varieties: specification of a quality or property of the Entity, and specification of its numerosity. These two features are attributed of the Entity nominal in examples such as *the two old cats* and *the three hairy gits*. As Rijkhoff has shown, these two types of attribute strongly tend cross-linguistically to occur in certain orders: other things being equal, the quality attribute will be closer to the Entity head nominal than the quantity attribute if both occur on the same side of that head (Rijkhoff 2002, 2014). This ordering is found in various Australian languages, claims concerning radical freedom of word order notwithstanding, including Kuuk Thaayorre (Pama-Nyungan) (Gaby 2017: 195), Nyulnyul (McGregor 2012a: 402), Umpithamu (Pama-Nyungan) (Louagie and Verstraete 2016: 34), Tiwi (Tiwi) (Lee 1987: 224) and Kayardild (Evans 1995: 235).

NPs in many indigenous languages of Australia, Africa and the Americas rarely include many elaborating dependents, and it is unusual to find more than one in an NP. By contrast, in SAE languages stacking of attributing dependents is not uncommon. For instance, in both English and Finnish more than one quality attribute is possible in an NP, as shown by example (3.11). These attributes appear to be ordered in a fairly principled way, with those that indicate the most inherent properties closest to the Entity nominal (here either *taloon* 'house' or *puu taloon* 'wooden house').[3]

> (3.11) *tuohon*   *upeaan*   *isoon*   *valkoiseen* *puu*   *taloon*   Finnish
> that:GEN   magnificent:ILL   big:ILL   white:ILL   wood   house.ILL
> 'to that magnificent old white wooden house'

The positioning of quantity attributes in a less central position than quality attributes might also be understood as governed by this principle (see also Rijkhoff 2002). However, there are reasons to believe that quantity and quality attribution are (usually) grammatically and emically distinct. In many languages they are questioned by different interrogatives, and in a number they are typically (other things being equal) located on opposite sides of the Entity nominal. Moreover, in some languages presence of both quantity and quality dependents is permissible, whereas only one quality dependent is permitted.

Extending dependents add something new to the Entity nominal, rather than indicate a property or quality of it. Two main types are distinguishable: comitative and privative, as illustrated respectively by (3.12) and (3.13). These examples involve NPs (*jinali-ngarri* 'with a spear' and *ngoombarna marlami* 'without a husband') embedded within the larger NPs; it is these embedded NPs that enter into dependency relations with the Entity nominals. The prototypes of extension, 'and' and 'or', are paratactic relations, and as such, are typically found between units that serve together as a single unit in some role in an NP. Comitative extension can be regarded as a hypotactic version of the 'and' relation.

(3.12) NP[*yoowooloo jinali-ngarri*]NP-*ngga maa ngab-ga*   Gooniyandi
       man   spear-COM-ERG   meat eat-3SG.NOM/3SG.ACC/PRS/A
      'The man with the spear is eating meat.'

(3.13) NP[*goornboo ngoombarna marlami*]NP-*ngga mila-ngina*   Gooniyandi
       woman   husband   nothing-ERG   see-1SG.ACC/3sgNOM/A
      'The woman without a husband saw me.'

Enhancing dependents provide circumstantial information concerning the Entity nominal, modifying it in terms of its spatial, conditional or temporal circumstances. As for extending dependents, the dependent unit is frequently another phrase, as in *the man on the balcony*, *the meeting in the afternoon*, and (3.14), where *wirla-ya* 'on his back' provides a spatial location for *boolba* 'things'.

(3.14) NP[*boolba-ngarri wirla-ya*]NP *girragirra-ari*   Gooniyandi
       things-COM   back-LOC   run-run-3SG.NOM/PRS/I
      'He is running with a pack on his back.'

Adverbials sometimes also serve as enhancing dependents, as in *the shelf above*, *the wharf downstream*, *the meeting tomorrow*, and the like.

The analysis presented above bears some similarities to the scheme of Rijkhoff (2002, 2008a, 2014), which identifies three related layers, Quality, Quantity, and Locality. (There is another layer in his model, which is mentioned below, §3.2.4.) The first two, Quality and Quantity, correspond to the two types of attributing dependency in my model. The third, Locality, corresponds to both extending and enhancing dependency in my model (though it includes other things as well – see §3.2.4). My separation of extension from enhancement at the emic level is motivated by the meaning difference: extending elements do not locate or provide circumstantial modification of the Entity nominal, and only enhancing units can be (sometimes) realized by adverbials. Additionally, there is often a pattern of agnation between hypotactic extension (within the NP) and paratactic extension (between NPs and between nominals) – compare *the man with the dog* with the paratactic *the man and the dog* and *(the) man and dog*. In enhancement the enhancing unit is typically a dependent on the Entity nominal, and paratactic agnates do not represent single syntagmatic units. Thus, for *the dog in the car* there is a paratactic agnate *the dog, in the car* but this does not form a single unit, as evidenced by prosody. (Compare the unified prosody of *the man and the dog*.)

3.2.3 Interpersonal Structure

The interpersonal structure and potential of NPs is restricted compared to that of the clause, which typically serves as the locus of expression of propositions, which are more amenable to interpersonal modification than are entities. Nevertheless, NPs can and do show distinct interpersonal structure, as observed in McGregor (1997b: 120); see also Van de Velde (2007).

NPs may contain modifiers that express evidential or epistemic slants on the Entity nominal. There are a number of such modifiers in English, including *putative, alleged, possible, potential*, and so forth, as in, for example, *the putative ancestor, the alleged father, a possible answer*. These modifiers clearly do not indicate qualities or properties of the Entity nominals, and usually they do not admit rephrasing in attributing clauses – for example, *the alleged father* cannot be rephrased as *the father is alleged*. Rather the modifier expresses some concerns about the viability of the nominal serving the Entity role as an appropriate descriptor of the referent of the NP: it is a label that has been used, though the speaker does not necessarily subscribe to it.

It is not necessarily the viability of the nominal serving in the Entity role that may be called to question by an interpersonal modifier. Thus, *putative* in *Italy's putative new Prime Minister* indicates that the speaker has some reservations about the applicability of the expression *new Prime Minister* as a label for the referent of the phrase, and raises the issue of whether the referent will actually be the next Prime Minister.

I would also argue that intensifiers such as *very* and *real* serve as interpersonal modifiers in NPs, as in *a very old car* and *a real city slicker*. Intensifiers have scope over some component of the NP and indicate that a quality or designation obtains to an extent greater than expected. They are expectation-invoking, and as such express interpersonal modulations. I have also argued (McGregor 1997b: 224–227) that clausal negation provides modification of the interpersonal type in that it expresses a line on the proposition expressed by the clause, and invokes expectations of the truth of the proposition. The same holds for negation at the NP level. Thus, I would argue that *without* in *without a handkerchief* serves as an interpersonal modifier of the NP, holding *a handkerchief* in its scope. It is denied that there is an instance of the type expressed by the noun *handkerchief* in the context; at the same time an expectation is invoked that such an entity should be present.[4]

Other items that serve as interpersonal modifiers in NPs include focus markers, which may single out one component of the phrase as particularly noteworthy, assigning the remainder of the NP to the domain of presupposed. Also commonly found are expectation modifiers such as *only*, which invoke expectations that are evaluated as greater than what is asserted. The 'only' form holds the NP in its scope, with perhaps one of the units in the NP in the focus of the relation. In Gooniyandi, for instance, there is an enclitic *-moowa* 'only' that attaches to the focus of the assertion, as shown by example (3.15).

> (3.15) *yoowooloo   mirra-moowa   damboong-giri*   Gooniyandi
> man   head-only   exposed-3SG.NOM/PRS/I
> 'Only the man's head is showing.'

Gooniyandi has another enclitic *-nyali* REP that means 'again' when it has propositional scope. It also has uses in NPs, as shown in (3.16). In this instance an expectation is invoked that the name of the bird is not the same as its call (which is in fact the normal circumstance in the language). This is juxtaposed to the assertion that it is in fact the same – 'his name again'. Here the expectation of difference is counterposed to an asserted identity.

> (3.16) *nhoowoo-nyali   yingi   goowaj-goo-lagini*   *diyadiya   miga-nyali*
> 3SG.OBL-REP   name   call-PRS-3SG.NOM/ARNI$_2$ peewee   thus-REP
> '(The peewee) is called by the name of his song, *diyadiya*.'   Gooniyandi

These Gooniyandi examples show that interpersonal structure is not restricted to NPs in SAE languages.

It should be noted that the interpersonal structure of the NP concerns items that modulate the NP structurally, providing some line on the Entity nominal, such as its existence or otherwise. What is involved are units that hold some or all of the NP within their scope. Interpersonal structure cannot be identified from mere knowledge of the semantics of some lexical or grammatical item. Thus, words like *beautiful* and *ugly* invoke as part of their semantics the subjective attitude of the speaker. This does not mean that they function interpersonally in the NP: lexical meaning is independent of syntagmatic function. On the other hand, some putative modifiers such as *poor* may function interpersonally rather than logically, as in *poor John is always hurting himself*. It will be observed that *poor John* does not find an agnate in *John is poor*, whereas such agnates exist for *beautiful* and *ugly*. Presumably titles as per the first units of *Mr. Bloggs, Mrs. Thatcher, President Trump* also serve in interpersonal roles, as would honorifics in a number of Asian and other languages.

In English an abstract nominal serving as Entity can sometimes hold a proposition in its scope, as in *the possibility that he is lying is very strong* and *the fact that you have been there doesn't impress me in the slightest*. In examples of these types the *that* clause does not specify a quality of the Entity nominal in the manner of a relative clause (e.g. *the dog that got run over*). Rather, the Entity nominal indicates how the proposition is to be taken: in the examples just given, as a possibility or as a fact, respectively.

3.2.4 Textural Structure

The textural semiotic comprises syntagmatic relations of the linking type (§1.1.3), relations that associate one linguistic entity with another, or with a non-linguistic entity. Textural relations hold phenomena in a language together, unifying them and giving them perceivable shape. They are like the nuts, bolts and welding that hold a car together and distinguish it from a pile of spare parts. They give shape to linguistic units, including the NP, rather than provide a level of structure as such, as do the other semiotic components.

One of the most obvious ways in which NPs are textured is indexically, by pointing; a linguistic unit zeroes in on the referent 'locating' it deictically with respect to some deictic centre. This is typically achieved by use of items such as demonstratives. These are indexical items that situate the NP referent with respect to a deictic centre, and function in the 'determination' of the NP: *this computer* indicates that the referent is proximal to the deictic centre defined by the speech situation. Aside from items that index exophorically are linguistic items that do so endophorically. Demonstratives in languages like English are used both exophorically and endophorically. However, some languages have demonstratives that index exclusively endophorically. Gooniyandi, for instance, has in addition to the demonstratives *ngirndaji* 'this' and *ngoorroo* 'that' a pair of endophoric items *niyaji* 'this' and *niyi* 'that' used exclusively in establishing reference to entities previously or subsequently introduced into the discourse.

Other items that are habitually employed in NP determination include possessives and comparative determiners. These index the referent of an NP indirectly via some other entity as an intermediary. Possessives facilitate the reference of the NP by associating the referent with another referent via a possessive relation (a very general relation that embraces ownership, belonging to, right of usage, and other relations – see e.g. McGregor 2009). Comparative determiners include lexemes such as *other* and *same* that identify a referent in terms of its difference from or identity with some item serving as a standard of reference. (See Halliday and Hasan 1976 for more extensive discussion of reference items and relations.)

Determination is a very different phenomenon to modification by logical means (as per §3.2.2), where a linguistic unit indicates some attribute or quality of the referent. In determination the linguistic unit indexes the referent in some way, rather than picks out a property of it. This does not mean that units such as demonstratives, comparative determiners and possessives can only be used in NP determination. I have argued that in Gooniyandi and Nyulnyul the positioning of such units in the NP is not arbitrary but conveys a subtle meaning difference (McGregor 1990a: 268–270; 2012a: 411). In initial position, as in (3.17), a demonstrative serves to determine the referent of the NP: it serves to restrict the reference of the NP by directing attention to those candidates located distally with respect to the here-now of the speech situation. By contrast, in final position, as in (3.18), a demonstrative instead attributes a property of the referent;

this example is more accurately translated as the non-idiomatic '[the] boy who is this one'. It adds, as it were, to our knowledge about the referent in question rather than narrows down to the referent of the phrase.

(3.17) *ngoorroo yoowooloo nyamani*   Gooniyandi
   that   man   big
   'that big man'

(3.18) *gambayi ngirndaji*   Gooniyandi
   boy   this
   'this boy'

The pattern found in Gooniyandi and Nyulnyul is not unique. Determining elements in NPs in Australian languages tend to be constrained to the edges of NPs (Louagie and Verstraete 2015, 2016). In a number of languages, the determining elements tend to occur initially or finally; there are some languages where they are attested in both initial and final position. Whether in such languages (including e.g. Worrorra (Worrorran)) there is a functional difference along the lines of Gooniyandi and Nyulnyul is not known, though it warrants careful investigation.

In Rijkhoff's model (2002, 2014) demonstratives serve a localizing function in the NP since in some sense they situate the referent with respect to a deictic centre. In my view, this obscures a genuine functional difference in the way indexical items narrow down the reference of an NP and the way genuine locative modifiers (such as *on the hill* in *the house on the hill*, which serve in enhancing dependency relations) do. Rijkhoff's 'localizing modifiers' thus include both items that serve a determining function (a textural function) and items that serve an enhancing relation of location (or some other dependency relation). (This is not to suggest that demonstratives can only serve in textural functions: as indicated above, they may also serve in modifying functions.)

Rijkhoff (2002: 237; 2014) identifies a fifth layer of discourse-referential modifiers and operators, which indicate the status of the referent in the world of discourse construed by the speech interaction. This is the layer to which the English morphemes *the* and *a ~ an* belong. My analysis draws the boundaries between the localizing and discourse-referential layers in a different place. Items that are deployed as determining elements function texturally (Rijkhoff's discourse-referential layer), regardless of whether they index within the speech situation or discourse; many such items can also serve in logical relations (Rijkhoff's localizing layer).

Other items that texture the NP are markers of grammatical categories and relational markers. The former include markers of inflectional categories such as number in languages in which this is an inflectional category of nouns (see further Rijkhoff 2002: 34–46, 146–156 on number marking), and gender or noun class markers in a wide genetic and geographical spread of languages (see §6.1.1). In the majority of Bantu languages of

Africa as well as various languages of Australia and Papua New Guinea nouns or nominals are assigned to classes that are marked by agreement affixes that occur on other units of the NP, as in example (3.19), where the prefix *ki-* indicating noun class 7 occurs on all three lexemes making up the NP. (It also occurs on the verb.) The repetition of the prefix can also be seen as contributing to the unity of the NP.

(3.19) *ki-kapu*   *ki-kubwa*   *ki-moja*   *ki-li-anguka*   Swahili
        CL7-basket CL7-large   CL7-one   CL7-PST-fall
        'One large basket fell.'

Relational markers typically found in the NP include free or bound adpositions as well as inflectional markers of case. Adpositions are often (including in SFL) understood to construct a distinct type of phrase from the NP, whereas inflectional markers of case do not – what one has instead is simply an NP with its lexical items in a particular case form. If we take the view that adpositions are no more than markers of grammatical relations there is no reason to see the adpositional phrase as significantly distinct structurally from the ordinary NP, as discussed in §3.1.1: it just has a marker in it that is not present in the plain NP. This marker belongs to the NP unit, but does not serve in a constituency relation in it. Although it serves a marking function within the NP, it does not serve a function in its capacity as a component of the whole NP (see again §1.1.3) – compare screws which may function to hold a bookcase together, though the screws are not functional parts of a bookcase in the way that the shelves are. There is no compelling reason to distinguish two distinct ranks of phrase and group as per SFL.

The position of relational markers in NPs is not random, and in many languages tends to be sensitive to NP boundaries (Dik 1997a: 407; Rijkhoff 2002: 295). Three positions are common: NP-initial, NP-final, and Wackernagel's position, i.e. following the first unit of the NP. There are exceptions, including languages such as Gooniyandi in which the position of the relational marker is in accordance with the relative information values of the component words. There are also well-known correlations between the type of adposition (preposition vs postposition) and the widely accepted 'word order' typology (e.g. Dryer 1992).

3.2.5 Ordinals

One puzzle for the model of the structure of NPs presented here is where ordinals fit. These do not express quantity but rather invoke the sequencing of a set of entities of a given type, and use this order to select a particular referent. Reference is (as in possession) indirect. In English ordinals can co-occur with quantifying dependents, as in *the first two crabs (to cross the line)*. In some languages (e.g. many Australian languages) there are no ordinal numerals as such, but something akin to sequential position is indicated by spatial relations such as 'in front' (first), 'middle' (following) and 'behind' (last). My guess is that it is necessary to identify two additional types of attributing relation in addition to quality and quantity, namely sequence and arrangement. As non-inherent features of a referent set, these are typically found towards the periphery of NPs.

3.3 Word Order

As already remarked at the beginning of this chapter the order of words in NPs cross-linguistically is not always rigid in the sense that particular words or word types (parts of speech) must always occur in a certain order. Indeed, for a number of languages – including SAA languages – the order of words in putative NPs seems so unconstrained that the existence of this unit has been questioned (see again §3.1.2). In this section we argue that the alleged chaos in word order in NPs in some languages is more apparent than real. This in turn suggests that for other such languages deeper investigation may reveal the same thing, that ordering of words in NPs is in general not 'free' in the sense of being completely unconstrained.

We begin in the next subsection (§3.3.1) by discussing factors that motivate the ordering of words within NPs. Then in §3.3.2 we turn to discontinuity, suggesting that this is highly constrained in many languages, and rather than arguing for the absence of NP units, in fact presents further evidence for the viability of this rank of unit. This section also includes discussion of the related phenomenon, attested in some languages, whereby a continuous putative NP is split into two pieces, which remain contiguous.

3.3.1 Motivations for the Ordering of Words within NPs

My own fieldwork languages from the Kimberley region of north-west Australia are SAA languages in that (as in the Kalkatungu examples (3.5)–(3.10) above) words of a putative NP can be permuted in a wide range of ways without affecting grammaticality, or having a marked effect on the meaning of the syntagm. For instance, in Nyulnyul NPs, expressions of quality and quantity are found both before and after the entity-denoting lexeme, though there is a fairly strong preference for the former position. We find both *miid baab* (male child) and *baab miid* (child male) with the meaning 'boy, male child'; compare also *kujarr baab* (two child) and *baab kujarr* (child two) 'two children'. Comitative and ablative PPs also occur on either side of the entity-denoting lexeme, as in *uriny baab-inyirr* (woman child-COM) and *baab-inyirr uriny* (child-COM woman) both of which mean 'a woman with a child'. However, there is a preference for such PPs to occur after the nominal. The same goes for oblique pronouns specifying possessors: *jan wurrul* (my fingernail) and *wurrul jan* (fingernail my) 'my fingernail'.

McGregor (2012a: 402–420) argues that these contrasting word orders express different meanings, albeit sometimes quite subtle. More specifically, these meaning differences are a consequence of the different grammatical functions that the words discharge when they occur in different orders. When they precede the entity-denoting nominal of an NP, quantifier and qualifying words serve as attributing dependents on that nominal. They occur in a fixed order: quantifying dependent followed by qualifying dependent. When they follow the entity-denoting nominal they instead predicate a property of the referent of the NP. Similarly, items such as demonstratives and oblique pronominals, when they precede the Entity nominal, serve to make more precise the reference of that nominal, whereas when they follow it they predicate a deictic location or owner of the referent. In effect, what precedes the Entity nominal modifies its reference, whereas what follows this nominal modifies its referent. Pre-Entity items in the NP, that is, contribute to the specification of the referent, while post-Entity items add to what is known of the referent, presumed already identifiable. This explains the meaning differences conveyed by the different orders in the previous paragraph. Quantifiers such as *kujarr* 'two' typically serve to restrict the reference of lexical nominals, though they occasionally predicate a quantity of an entity. When the Entity is realized by a pronominal, however, the reverse order is typical – a pronominal typically designates an identifiable entity. And while *uriny baab-inyirr* (woman child-COM) and *baab-inyirr uriny* (child-COM woman) both mean 'a woman with a child', the latter is likely to refer to a pregnant woman, the comitative phrase narrowing down on the referent of the phrase. The former is more likely to refer to a woman who is temporarily with a child.

Similar arguments can be made for Warrwa (McGregor in preparation: chapter 10) and Gooniyandi (McGregor 1990a: 249–276), though in the latter language the order of words in the NP is considerably less constrained than in Nyulnyul, doubtless a consequence of the stronger status of Gooniyandi when I worked on it.

Other factors than the grammatical function served by a unit within an NP may be relevant to its ordering. For instance, in English prepositional phrases and relative clauses tend to occur following the Entity nominal, as in *two people with a dog*, *pigs at a trough*, and *the line that used to run from Silkeborg to Horsens*. The position of these phrasal and clausal units within the NP is evidently conditioned by the widely recognized heaviness principle, according to which units that convey large amounts of information are placed in NP-final position (see note 14, in Chapter 1). Similarly, in Tutrugbu (Kwa, Ghana) relative clauses occur in final position in NPs, following all other dependents, textural and interpersonal items (Essegbey 2019: 106). In Nyulnyul weight seems also to be relevant to the position of dependent units within NPs: qualifying and quantifying dependents precede the Entity nominal, where they serve as reference modifiers, as we have seen. When the quality is described in a heavier expression it may be positioned after the Entity nominal, as in *karrambal bindany aa murrul* (bird big and little) 'big and little birds', or 'birds large and small'.

3.3.2 Complications

3.3.2.1 Discontinuity

As remarked at various points above discontinuity is widely believed to be rife in Australian languages, and this has raised the question of the viability of the NP category in SAA languages such as Warlpiri (Hale 1983), Nunggubuyu (Heath 1984: 505–506), Kalkatungu (Blake 1983: 145), Ngalakan (Merlan 1983: 83), and others. However, I remain suspicious about these claims, which appear to be based principally on elicited data: speakers of the various languages find discontinuous expressions acceptable, as in the case of the Kalkatungu examples (3.5)–(3.10) above.

I have elicited similar reactions from speakers of Gooniyandi: they accept as grammatical utterances in which apparent NPs are split up by various types of intervening material. However, when actual usage is examined things are rather more constrained, and discontinuity emerges as a highly marked option. Thus, in a corpus of narrative texts comprising just over a thousand verbal clauses it was found that only 3% of NPs were discontinuous. However, 80% of the NPs consisted of just one word, and when this is corrected for, some 17% of NPs that could have been discontinuous actually were. This is still a relatively small proportion, indicative of the markedness of discontinuity. These facts are consistent with Behaghel's first law (Behaghel 1932: 4), according to which what belongs together mentally is placed together in language form: that is, grammatical units will – other things being equal – be contiguous.

Discontinuous nominal expressions that could potentially represent NPs (in that they satisfy the structural description of the NP) can be divided into two types according to whether or not the discontinuous pieces fall into a single intonation unit. There are reasons to believe that it is only when the discontinuous pieces belong to the same unit that they do comprise an NP (see below). Discontinuous NPs in Gooniyandi are subject to a number of quite strong restrictions, as per a.–f. below (a revision of McGregor 1997a: 93). Even in Warlpiri discontinuity is a highly marked option (Swartz 1988), and similar restrictions apply; see also Siewierska (1984: 62–64) on Polish, and Schultze-Berndt and Simard (2012) on Jaminjung (Mirndi, Australia).

a. Discontinuous NPs are always separated into just two parts.

b. Only one discontinuous NP may occur in any clause; there are no exceptions in the corpus.

c. Discontinuous NPs usually have just two words: only a fifth have more. If discontinuous phrase has more than two words, only one of the two separated pieces has more than a single word in it; this generalization is almost exceptionless.

d. Each piece of a discontinuous PP has a case marking postposition; normally only one such postposition is attached to each discontinuous piece. There are just a few exceptions in the corpus where the discontinuous parts are not identically marked.

e. Usually one part of a discontinuous phrase occurs clause initially, the other finally. Three quarters of discontinuous NPs show this maximal separation.

In the remaining quarter, the first piece always occurs preverbally, the second post-verbally.

f. Usually (for over 90% of tokens), nothing intervenes between the verb and the final piece of the discontinuous phrase.

Constraints a., b., d. – and perhaps to some extent c. – may facilitate processing. The other two constraints do not appear to be motivated by processing considerations, and indeed e. would seem to add to processing difficulties. Accordingly, I have argued that discontinuity in Gooniyandi is semiotically significant, that it expresses a specific and definable meaning (McGregor 1997a).

As per e., the first piece of a discontinuous NP is normally initial in the clause, and the second piece final, as in (3.20).

(3.20) *wanyjirri*   *ngarragi-ngga* *yoowooloo* *gard-bini*   Gooniyandi
         river:kangaroo 1SG.OBL-ERG man   hit-3SG.NOM/3SG.ACC/BINI
         jamarra /
         male:kangaroo
         'A male river kangaroo was killed by my son.'

Theme in Gooniyandi is, I have argued, associated with initial position in the clause. The information focus of an information unit is marked by tonic prominence in the corresponding tone unit; this focus is unmarked when tonic prominence falls on the final lexical item in the information unit. Thus, discontinuity provides a means of assigning unmarked focus to the Theme of a clause (McGregor 1997a: 96). This is the case in example (3.20), where the NP *wanyjirri jamarra* 'male river kangaroo', where this NP serves as both Theme (indexed by initial position) and unmarked information focus (marked by tonic prominence on the final lexical word – indicated by bolding of its initial syllable in (3.20)).

This strategy represents one way in which a Theme that is new and unpredictable can be introduced into the discourse. Typically, such Themes play relatively minor roles in the discourse, and retain thematic status for just a short while, as is the case for the kangaroo in (3.20), which plays no further significant role in the narrative. (Other strategies are typically invoked for the introduction of more significant Themes, including representation by an NP in its own separate intonation unit.)

The few exceptions in which the first discontinuous piece of the NP is not in initial position, or the second in final position, do not contradict my proposal. What precedes the first discontinuous piece is always a locative expression representing a spatial location for the situation, as in (3.21); this portion of the discontinuous NP thus remains Theme, in as much as it specifies the topical individual.

(3.21) *Jubilee maʔ googoomani warang-jiʔ   boolgaʔ Bred Gedil/*
     Jubilee [...]   cook   sit-3SG.NOM/PST+I old:man Fred Gedil
     'At Jubilee there was an old cook, Fred Gedil.'   Gooniyandi

What follows the second piece when it is not final is invariably a closed-class grammatical item. Final grammatical items do not serve as locus for unmarked focus; it is always the immediately preceding lexical item that serves this function. Hence in examples such as (3.22) the second discontinuous piece of the NP is unmarked focus.

(3.22) *ye   yaanya lamaj-jidi .   yoowooloo niyi-nhingi/*
     [...] other   pick.up-1EXC.NOM/3sgACC+DI man   that-ABL
     '... we picked up another Aboriginal man from there.'   Gooniyandi

As acknowledged above, there are some instances of apparent discontinuous NPs that do not satisfy the requirement that the two components fall into a single intonation contour; (3.23) is an example. In McGregor (1997a) I treated these as a separate type of discontinuous NP in which the second discontinuous piece is predicated of the first, attributing a property of it or identifying it. Although in examples like this the two nominals could comprise a single NP, I now believe that they do not: prosody is significant, and implies that the nominals do not in fact represent a single NP (see also Schultze-Berndt and Simard 2012). Rather, they represent either NPs in apposition, as in (3.24), or otherwise, as in (3.23), a nominal (*nyamani* 'big') in apposition with an NP (*wayandi* 'fire' – an NP since it serves in an experiential role in the clause, namely Undergoer). This reanalysis is consistent with the meaning conveyed by the construction.

(3.23) *wayandi jard-jidi/   nyamani/*   Gooniyandi
     fire   light-1EXC.NOM/3SG.ACC+DI big
     'We lit a fire, a big one.'

(3.24) *yoowarni-ngga-nyali gardiya/   laja-nga-ngarra/*   Gooniyandi
     one-ERG-REP   white:person ride-3SG.NOM/3sgACC/PST/A-1SG.OBL
     Ned Colin-ngga/
     Ned Collins-ERG
     'The same white person rode my horse for me, Ned Collins.'

3.3.2.2 NP fracturing

To wind up this section, I mention one further complication that arises in some languages. Here, while the pieces remain together, they show signs of status as separate units. Recall that in various languages of north-west Australia – for example, Gooniyandi, Nyulnyul, Warrwa, Ungarinyin – it is typical for a single instance of a case or number marking postposition to occur in syntagm with an NP. In a minority of instances, however, more than one postposition occurs in syntagm with what appears to be a single NP, as in (3.25) and (3.26).[5]

(3.25) *yoowooloo-ngga ngoorroo-ngga ngaarri yiganyi*   Gooniyandi
     man-ERG   that-ERG   stone   uncertain
     doow-nga-ngarra
     take-3SG.NOM/3SG.ACC/PST/A-1SG.OBL
     'Maybe it's that man who took my money.'

(3.26) *djaḷ   ine-men-an yer   walaŋg-aŋ*   Nyulnyul
     jarl   i-ni-m-in-ang-irr   walangk-ang
     pierce 3NOM-CM-put-IMP-APP-3AUG.ACC spear-INS
     warindjer-aŋ.
     warinjirr-ang
     one-INS
     'He speared them with his spear.' (More accurately, 'He speared them with one spear.') (Nekes and Worms 2006: 308)

I am aware of no research on this phenomenon – which I refer to as *phrase fracturing* (McGregor 1989b) – in any language other than Gooniyandi. Other nearby languages I worked on subsequently, including Nyulnyul and Warrwa, were virtually moribund, and there is no reliable information on the phenomenon in actual usage. As with discontinuous NPs, fractured NPs in Gooniyandi are subject to some strong constraints:

a. A single clause does not usually contain more than one instance of a fractured NP; there are just a few exceptions in the corpus.

b. Fractured NPs almost always occur at the beginning of a clause; occasionally they occur clause finally. Very rarely they occur elsewhere, in which case the more outer material occurs on a separate intonation contour.

c. Fractured NPs occur on a single intonation unit, which usually contains other units as well; potential instances of fractured phrases that occur on separate intonation units are actually separate NPs in apposition with one another.

d. Fractured NPs consist of just two words; when an apparent fractured NP consists of more than two words, there is reason to believe that these words comprise more than a single NP. For example, the prosody in (3.27) indicates that there are two NPs in apposition at the beginning of the clause, the first of which comprises two words that form a fractured NP.

(3.27) **niyi-ngga yoowooloo-ngga/ ruburn**   *mik-ngga*   Gooniyandi
     that-ERG man-ERG   Roebourne Mick-ERG
     mila-nga/
     see-3SG.NOM/3SG.ACC/PST/A
     'It was that man, Roebourne Mick, who was looking at him.'

As in (3.27) an initial fractured phrase involves two peaks of prosodic prominence in a single intonation unit. If the intonation unit also contains other material, as in (3.28), these other units are not accorded prosodic prominence.

(3.28) *thaarri*   **nganyi-ngga**   *gard-looni/*   Gooniyandi
mistakenly.believe 1SG.CRD-ERG hit-1SG.NOM/3SG.ACC+BINI
ngoorroo-ngga   **yaanya-ngga** *gard-bini/*
that-ERG   other-ERG   hit-3SG.NOM/3SG.ACC+BINI
'It was mistakenly believed that I had hit him, but it was really that other person who hit him.'

McGregor (1989b) argues that the two nominals in examples like (3.25)–(3.28) form a single NP in the sense that the words serve in the same grammatical relations to one another as they would within NPs – thus in (3.25) the demonstrative serves to modify the referent of the Entity nominal *yoowooloo* 'man', rather than to modify its reference. A single conceptual entity is construed. At the same time the presence of the separate intonation peaks on each of the items of the NP is highly marked, and is presupposition invoking. The remainder of the clause is typically presupposed. Thus, the construction codes a meaning similar to a cleft construction, as indicated by the free translations. This construction contrasts semantically with expressions involving two NPs in apposition, as in (3.29). Here the NPs construe different conceptual entities, which are asserted to be referentially identical; such clauses do not express a cleft meaning.

(3.29) *Ned **Colin**/*   *ngarragi **jockey**/* *... **la**ja-nga-ngarra/*   Gooniyandi
Ned Collins 1SG.OBL jockey   ride-3sgNOM/3SG.ACC/PST/A-1SG.OBL
ngarragi   **ya**warda/
1SG.OBL   horse
'Ned Collins, my jockey, rode my horse for me.'

Prosodic considerations are central to the identification of discontinuous and fractured NPs. Indeed, NP fracturing can be defined more generally in terms of the presence of more than one prosodic peak in the intonation contour of the NP than by means of the presence of more than a single instance of a case marking postposition. Fracturing is possible for not just phrases with case markers, but for NPs without them.

3.4 Concluding Remarks

The main purpose of this chapter is to argue in favour of the universality of a rank of phrasal units in human languages, and in particular for the universality of the NP. This is regardless of the existence or otherwise of a distinct noun or nominal part of speech. Given the paucity of data on many languages, it is, of course, impossible to argue the case convincingly. My strategy has been to examine a few Australian languages that fit the prototypes of languages with so-called 'flat' (non-hierarchical) clause structure – sometimes dubbed non-configurational languages – and argue that in these languages there is good reason to believe that a unit of the NP type exists. My hypothesis is that with more complete usage-based descriptions of other alleged 'non-configurational' languages it will emerge that the same holds for them.

I have suggested that the NP is a richly structured unit, that in terms of its grammatical organization shares features in common with clauses. Both show four-dimensional structuring in accordance with four grammatical-semiotic types; contra Hallidayan SFL the semiotics are not confused or intermingled at the rank of phrase. This chapter has only scratched the surface of the complexities of NP structure cross-linguistically. We have focused on simple NPs, and only touched in passing on complex structures involving relative clauses and other embedded units such as possessive phrases.

Another feature of the approach taken in this chapter is worth drawing attention to again in concluding the discussion of the NP. This is the notion that word order variation in the NP does not always correlate with distinct grammatical functions: distinct syntagmatic relations cannot be distinguished merely on the basis of different patterns in the ordering of units. Factors such as weight and (conceptual) unity may be relevant to the ordering of units, and need to be acknowledged in Neo-Firthian approachs.

The argument for the existence of NPs is not an argument against the existence of 'appositional' structures involving nominals. As we have seen, in some languages there are appositional constructions that comprise coordinated nominals and classificatory collocations of nominals; these constructions may fill roles in NPs. Moreover, NPs themselves may enter into appositional relations with one another; an NP may even enter into an appositional relation with a nominal. We have only touched on these phenomena in passing, in discussing discontinuity and fracturing. The theory of dependency assumed here – distinguishing two dimensions, parataxis vs hypotaxis and extension vs elaboration vs enhancement – is up to the task of describing and accounting for these appositional constructions. Apposition as a grammatical relation, however, demands further attention.

Chapter 4

Complex Sentence Constructions

4.1 Introduction

This section introduces the topic of complex sentence constructions by providing a very brief and selective overview of the literature. First, we provide (§4.1.1) a synopsis of some of the main characteristics of the general typological approach to complex sentences. Following this (§4.1.2) we look at some of the main features of Neo-Firthian approaches. Other functional and usage-based theories have, of course, made important contributions to the study of complex sentences, including: West Coast Functional Grammar (e.g. Talmy 1978), Functional Grammar (Dik 1997b), Functional Discourse Grammar (Hengeveld and Mackenzie 2008), Cognitive Grammar (e.g. Langacker 2008), and Role and Reference Grammar (Foley and Van Valin 1984). For reasons of space discussion of these approaches is not included.

4.1.1 A Brief Overview of Typologies of Complex Sentences

In Chapter 2 we saw the centrality of the clause in grammar and typology reflected in its rich and varied structure. Looking upwards we find a correspondingly rich and diverse range of grammatical structures and relations that clauses may enter into, further underlining the centrality of the clause. These structures and relations have also been of great interest to typologists. There is a substantial typological literature treating these phenomena in particular languages and cross-linguistically, including collections of articles such as Tomlin (1987); Haiman and Thompson (1988); Austin (1988); Shopen (1985, 2007); and contributions to journals and edited volumes on diverse topics, too numerous to list here. Textbooks on typology usually include something on the topic, for example, Comrie (1989: chapter 7); Velupillai (2012: chapter 11); Moravcsik (2013: 231–236).

Again, typological studies have been on the whole avowedly atheoretical, and often give the impression of suspicion of theory. They tend to assume 'received' theoretical notions – including those of traditional grammar – eschewing problematization of the grammatical relations and structures assumed to be involved. Semantic and pragmatic considerations tend to take second place to issues of form, and the categories are often comparative rather than descriptive or emic (§1.2.4.2).

In the typological and general descriptive literature a fundamental distinction is habitually drawn between coordination and subordination of clauses in complex sentences.

Coordination is presumably the most common way of combining clauses into larger units, and it seems likely that all languages admit this means of forming complex sentences. In coordination the clauses are of the same relative status, for instance, both are free clauses in *the farmer kissed the duckling and the duckling kissed the farmer back*. Coordinate relations typically distinguished include conjunction, disjunction, adversative conjunction, and causal conjunction. One of the cross-linguistic differences in coordination concerns the way in which coordination is indicated. Some languages employ linkers marking the relation between the clauses, as in English, with *and*, *or*, and *but*. In some languages the normal, perhaps only, strategy is juxtaposition of the clauses without the use of a linker. This is the case, for instance, in Gooniyandi, where juxtaposition is the only strategy available;[1] in Nyulnyul there is a linker *aa* 'and', though it is not commonly used, and juxtaposition is the preferred option. Languages differ in terms of where the linkers are placed (e.g. between the clauses, preceding or following one or both of the clauses). Another difference between languages concerns how information shared between coordinated clauses is dealt with, whether and under what conditions ellipsis is possible. For instance, in English, NP ellipsis is generally possible only when the NPs in both clauses are coreferential and both serve as subjects. In Gooniyandi, by contrast, the same grammatical role need not necessarily be served in the conjuncts for NP ellipsis to occur. See further Payne (1985); Mithun (1988); and Haspelmath (2007) for typological treatments of clause coordination.

Subordination is usually less frequent than coordination in usage; it is perhaps also universal, though there are alleged exceptions such as Pirahã (isolate, Amazonia) (Everett 2005: 629). In subordination the clauses have a different status: one is generally free in the sense that it could occur independently, while the other clause typically does not enjoy freedom of occurrence (there are some qualifications on this – see §4.5). For example, in *when the light turns yellow you may proceed with caution* the first clause *(when) the light turns yellow* does not have the potential of free occurrence, while the second clause *you may proceed with caution* does. Coordination and subordination are usually presumed to exhaustively cover the domain of complex sentences.

A range of types of subordinate clause are distinguished and discussed fairly extensively in the typological literature, including adverbial clauses, relative clauses and complement clauses. In what follows we briefly introduce these types and mention some of the main features by which they have been typologized.

Adverbial clauses modify another clause by providing contextual or circumstantial information, background against which the free clause is foregrounded, as in *when he arrived I left*. They are attested in languages from around the world, and include subtypes such as temporal, locational, manner, purpose, cause, circumstance, simultaneous, conditional, concessive, additive, absolute and substitutive (Thompson, Longacre and Hwang 2007). Whether these subtypes represent distinct constructions is an empirical question that needs to be addressed separately for each language. So also is the exhaustiveness of the above set of subtypes.

Adverbial constructions can be typologized formally in terms of the means of indicating the subordinate status of the adverbial clause and/or the grammatical relation the clause enters into. Common means of marking include by a subordinating morpheme, by a verb inflection, and/or by a marked word order. For instance, in various languages case markers are employed to mark certain types of adverbial clause. The case markers employed in this context are often a proper subset of the case markers in the language, and they do not necessarily make the same semantic contrasts as on nominal units. In some languages a dedicated marker is employed to indicate the subordinate status of the clause. Verbal inflectional categories such as marked moods like subjunctive or irrealis sometimes indicate certain types of adverbial clauses (Merlan 1981; McGregor 1988; Verstraete 2005b). In some languages word order differs in adverbial clauses (or subordinate clauses generally) and main clauses.

A question that has attracted a considerable amount of attention concerns relations between fillers of roles in the adverbial and main clauses, and whether there are restrictions on them. Different configurations of reference relations sometimes correspond to different subordinate clauses types. For instance, in some languages different types of purposive clause are distinguishable depending on whether the main and adverbial clauses share the same 'subject' or not.

Relative clauses have been particularly extensively investigated (e.g. Hale 1976; Keenan and Comrie 1977; Keenan 1985; Andrews 2007; LaPolla 2008; Lacroix 2009 to mention but a few treatments), and are a popular topic in typological textbooks – each of the three textbooks mentioned above discusses them. Relative clauses provide additional modifying information about the referent of an NP that serves a role in another clause. (This is a very approximate characterization, not a definition; see further e.g. Andrews 2007.) In English and various other languages a grammatical contrast can be drawn between restrictive or defining relative clauses and non-restrictive or non-defining relative clauses. A restrictive relative clause restricts the range of potential referents of the NP, as illustrated by the clause *who kissed the duckling* in *the farmer who kissed the duckling is feeding the chickens.* A non-restrictive relative clause adds descriptive information about the referent without narrowing the reference down to a particular entity, as in *the farmer, who kissed the duckling, is feeding the chickens.* Not all languages draw a grammatical contrast between these two types, and a single construction may function as both defining and non-defining in a language, for example Japanese (Kuno 1973: 235).

Relative clauses have been typologized on four main dimensions (Andrews 2007: 207). One is the relation between the relative clause and the NP it relates to in the main clause, for instance, whether or not it embedded in that NP. Given his rejection of the NP in Warlpiri and various other Australian languages it is unsurprising that Hale (1976) argues that relative clauses in these languages are adjoined to the main clause, not embedded in NPs (see further §4.3.3 below).

A second dimension concerns how the relativized entity is specified in the relative clause: whether or not there is some overt expression denoting it, and if so what, and whether there are constraints on where that expression may occur in the relative clause. For instance, in English there may be overt expression of the NP in the form of a relative pronoun *who*, *which* or *that*; this typically occurs in initial position in the relative clause.

Third, there may be constraints on the grammatical role of the NP in the relative clause itself. Keenan and Comrie (1977) proposed an Accessibility Hierarchy that encapsulates implicational relations concerning the grammatical roles that may be served by the NP specifying the relativized entity in the relative clause – or the grammatical role that would be served by this NP if it could occur in the relative clause. This universal hierarchy, shown in (4.1), indicates that if a relativized NP can serve in a given role in the relative clause, it can also serve in all roles to the left. This hierarchy has guided a good deal of typological research, and has been tested on a number of languages; the general consensus is that it bears up well, though there are potential counter-examples. In the present context I mention just one objection: none of these grammatical relations are proven universals.

(4.1)   subject > direct object > indirect object > oblique > genitive > object of comparison

Finally, there is the question of the nature of the relative clause itself, whether it is marked in some way, distinguishing it formally from the corresponding free clause that would express the same content. At least some types of relative clause in some languages (e.g. Gooniyandi and Reta (Papuan, Indonesia) – Willemsen in preparation) are formally indistinguishable from ordinary free clauses.

In complementation as it is generally conceptualized, one clause serves as an argument within another, referred to as the matrix (Noonan 2007: 52).[2] For instance, in (4.2) the initial *that* clause – it is claimed – serves as subject of the matrix clause with the verb *surprise*, while in (4.3), the *that* clause serves as object of the clause of belief. A language may show several distinct complement types. For instance, English has both finite (examples (4.2) and (4.3)) and non-finite complements, as in *the farmer's kissing of the duckling was noticed by all*. Complement constructions vary cross-linguistically and within a language on a number of other parameters, including the nature of the marking of the complement type, the grammatical characteristics of the complement clause (not just finite vs non-finite, but also subtypes), the semantic properties of complements and the semantic contrasts among the types, and the semantic categories of the matrix clauses (e.g. denoting situations of utterance, thought, desire, manipulation, permission, perception, etc.).

(4.2)   *That you cannot solve such a simple problem surprises me*

(4.3)   *I don't believe that the farmer kissed the duckling*

The universality of complement constructions is disputed. Dixon (2006) argues that Dyirbal has no true complements in the sense of clauses serving in argument roles in some matrix clauses. Dixon speaks instead of strategies for communicating the meanings expressed in other languages by means of complement clauses, by, for example, purposive clauses and relative clauses. His account, however, fails to go beyond morphological marking.

Within linguistic typology clause combining is often conceptualized as a continuum and/or a set of interacting continua pertaining to different dimensions of variation of complex sentences, such as the degree of explicitness of marking, the degree of interaction among the clauses (e.g. the extent to which they maintain their boundaries and do not interdigitate), the degree of downgrading of the subordinate clause (e.g. whether it is downgraded to an NP), and so forth (Lehmann 1988; Thompson, Longacre and Hwang 2007: 237–238; see also Foley and Van Valin 1984: chapter 6).

While some of the dimensions just mentioned may be gradable – for example, the degree of explicitness of marking and the separateness of the clauses – it is not at all clear that all are. For instance, in what sense can the 'downgrading' of a clause be placed in a meaningful way on a continuum? Worse, the syntactic relation between the clauses is often left weakly specified; it is usually assumed to be a dependency relation, either parataxis or hypotaxis. Thus, subordinate constructions are often assumed to invariably involve a head clause (or phrase) and a dependent clause. However, there are many problems with the notion of dependency, and different criteria for the identification of headship frequently do not agree (e.g. Zwicky 1985; Hudson 1987; Bauer 1990; Corbett, Fraser and McGlashan 1993). It is not always obvious that a subordinate clause is dependent on a main head clause or some unit in it. In complementation, for example, does the complement clause serve as a dependent of the matrix, as well as in an argument role? And if it exclusively serves an argument role, how can complementation be put on the same continuum as parataxis and hypotaxis?

These problems hark back to the general criticisms outlined in §1.2.4 of typology as it is currently practised. A viable typology needs to be concerned with exactly what units enter into the grammatical relations in complex sentence, the nature of these relations, and the complex sentence construction types distinguished in a language. It needs, that is, to be more concerned with the complex sentence categories of particular languages, and to use these as the comparanda. The typology of complex sentences must be enriched by attending to the emically significant grammatical relations and constructions.

4.1.2 Neo-Firthian Accounts of the Grammar of Complex Sentences

Halliday (1985: 192–251) presents extensive discussion of clause complex types in English.[3] He advocates an analysis of these constructions involving relations from the logical semiotic. Two dimensions are proposed for these logical relations. One dimension is taxis, in which a distinction is drawn between parataxis (equal status) and hypotaxis (unequal status, where one clause can be identified as head the other as modifier). The other is a system of 'logico-semantic' relations, also binary, distinguishing expansion from projection. In expansion one clause expands on another by elaborating it (expressing it in other words), extending it (adding to it), or enhancing it (embellishing on it). In projection one clause is projected through another which either represents it as a wording (giving reported speech) or an idea (reported thought).

This scheme provides a typology of relations between clauses that form complexes in which the clauses are effectively separate entities, neither entering into a grammatical relation within the other or a part of the other. The latter structures do exist, for instance, for relative clauses, as in (4.4). However, these involve rankshifting of one of the clauses, which serves as a unit within (a part of) the other: here *who is taking the pictures* fills a role in the NP with *girl* as head. The rankshifted clause in Halliday's analysis serves as a postmodifier of the head (Halliday 1985: 221), and the same three fundamental logico-semantic relations of extension identified in clause complexes are identified in these rankshifted structures. As distinct from a clause complex, the entire structure is that of a single clause.

(4.4)   *Do you know the girl who is taking the pictures?*

Halliday's scheme was proposed specifically for English. It has been applied to a small selection of other languages, including Finnish (Shore 1992), Gooniyandi (McGregor 1990a), Pitjantjatjara (Rose 2001), Mandarin Chinese (Xiaoqing 1986) and French (Caffarel 1996). No typological investigation of clause complexes I am aware of has employed the SFL framework. It seems safe to say that SFL practitioners believe that the scheme could be deployed in typological investigations, and currently a comparative SFL investigation of 'projection' in English, Spanish, Dagaare, Hindi, Arabic, and Japanese is underway (https://www.researchgate.net/project/Projection-in-several-languages – accessed 23 March 2020).

Hallidayan SFL inspired another Neo-Firthian approach to complex sentence constructions, that of SG (McGregor 1994a, 1997b), where the term *complex sentence* refers to any sentence that comprises more than a single clause, regardless of the type of construction formed. Thus, (4.4) is a complex sentence, even though it is not a clause complex in the Hallidayan sense. On the other hand, serial verb constructions (e.g. Durie 1997; Bisang 2009) and complex predicates (Alsina, Bresnan and Sells 1997; Amberber, Baker and Harvey 2010) are excluded since they comprise single clauses.

SG focuses attention on grammatical relations between clauses and other clauses or units that they enter into combination with, rather than with types of complex sentence construction per se. It proposes that these relations can be of any of the three semiotic components that are inherently associated with structures, namely experiential, logical and interpersonal (see §1.1.3).[4] These relations may obtain between a pair of clauses, or between a clause and some unit that forms a part of another clause, such as a word in an NP. Experiential relations obtain when one clause serves a grammatical role in another clause as a functioning part of the whole (these are discussed in §4.2 below). Logical relations exist when one clause enters into a relation of dependency (part-part) with some other grammatical unit (see §4.3). Interpersonal relations are conjugational relations, where both units relate to one another as wholes (see §4.4). This approach permits an overall more economical theory, one in which the relations clauses enter into are not special, but fundamentally the same as grammatical relations found between other types of linguistic unit, for example NPs. The theory is a typological one that proposes a universal scheme for grammatical relations involving a whole clause and something else.

A rather different Neo-Firthian approach is that of Verstraete (2007), which typologizes clauses according to their interpersonal potentials in complex sentence types. Verstraete identifies three parameters of variation: (a) modality – the epistemic or deontic line on the clause; (b) speech function – the assignment of interactional responsibility for the modal line; and (c) scope – the domains over which modality and speech function operate. The different values these parameters take define different complex sentence types, according to whether or not both clauses have a speech functional or modality value and, if these are lacking in one clause, whether or not the interpersonal resources of the other clause have scope over that clause. A coordinated clause will have its own independent values for modality and speech function, whereas subordinate clauses lack speech function values, and perhaps also modality as well; a subordinate clause may also fall within the modality and speech function choices of the clause to which it is subordinated. Although proposed specifically for English adverbial clauses, Verstraete (2007: 287–291) remarks on extensions to a wider range of complex sentence types and to linguistic typology.

In what follows we overview the SG typology of complex sentence constructions, discussing relations of each of the three semiotic types in order. Before beginning, however, it is worth highlighting some differences between the SG approach and the other two Neo-Firthian approaches.

In contrast with SFL, which presumes that only relations of the logical type may exist between a clause and another unit, SG presumes that clauses may enter into grammatical relations of all four semiotic types with other clauses or units. Thus, the SFL treatment of reported speech and thought treats the relation between the clause of speech or thought and the reported clause as a dependency relation, and proposes a special type of dependency relation for this, projection, a relation that is peculiar to clause complexes. There is, however, no evidence that a dependency relation exists between the two clauses, as argued in McGregor (1990b, 1994b); see also Vandelanotte (2009); Spronck and Nikitina (2019). The SG account argues that reported speech and thought involve an interpersonal relation between the reported and reporting clause.

The treatment of some types of embedded clause is also different. According to Halliday (1985: 225–226; 1994: 248–250) the embedded initial clauses of [*eating poison mushrooms*] *killed him* and [*worrying over what happened*] *sent him to an early grave* are in a dependency relation to an omitted head in an NP. This analysis appears to be forced by the strictures of the theory, and has no apparent foundation in linguistic reality. The SG approach permits the embedded clause to serve in the experiential relations of Actor and Agent within the larger clause structure directly.

The primary difference from the Verstraete (2007) approach is the focus of attention on syntagmatic relations in the SG model as against the respective interpersonal natures of the clauses that are combined in Verstraete's model. This does not represent a fundamental theoretical difference. Rather, the two approaches complement one another, and the SG account needs to be enriched by attention to the internal nature of the clauses in combination. This clearly interacts with the syntagmatic dimension, although these are orthogonal dimensions. For practical reasons of space it is impossible to develop this aspect of the story here.

4.2 Experiential Relations Involving Clauses

In this type of complex sentence one clause fulfils an experiential role within the other. This is typically a role that would normally be realized by an NP (see Chapter 2); the secondary clause thus acts as though it were a nominal. Such clauses are usually formally marked, and are often referred to as nominalizations. I avoid use of the term here because it is not clear that such clauses are necessarily nominal in nature: the fact that they behave in certain respects like nominal words or phrases does not make them nominals categorically. These complex sentence types satisfy the received definition of complement construction, though they are not usually treated under this rubric.

Headless relative clauses are relative clauses that do not serve as dependents on a nominal within an NP (see §4.3.2.2), but rather have no nominal head, as in English examples such as *whoever solves the problem will win a prize, I'll take whichever you don't want* and *I don't approve of what she does to her employees*. Headless relative clauses represent one type of clause that may serve in an experiential role in another clause (though they may have other uses as well).

It is sometimes suggested that the *wh*-word in examples such as the above serves as the head of an NP, on which the relative clause is dependent (e.g. Bresnan and Grimshaw 1978; Halliday 1985: 222). It is not clear, however, that these constructions are headed: the relative clause in *whoever solves the problem will win a prize* cannot be replaced by *whoever*. Moreover, there are languages such as Navajo – see example (4.5) – in which headless relative clauses involve no element that might plausibly serve as head.

> (4.5)   *Kinłání-góó*   *deeyáh-ígíí*   *bééhonisin*   Navajo
>   Flagstaff-ALL   3SG.go-REL.NPST   3SG.ACC.IMP.1SG.NOM.know
>   'I know the person who is going to Flagstaff.' (cited in Andrews 2007: 214)

Navajo is also said to have internally headed relative clauses, as in (4.6). It is questionable, however, whether in examples such as this the NP specifying the entity relativized on is really the head of the relative clause. It may simply be represented in that clause, in this instance as an Actor (see also Dryer 2007: 201). The fact that the NP *ashkii* 'boy' may instead appear in the main clause of speech further attests to the analysis that this relative clause is headless, and that the NP relativized on may appear in either clause, or neither. In other words (4.5) and (4.6) may differ simply in whether or not the Actor is ellipsed, and have nothing to do with headedness.

(4.6) *tl'éédą́ą́*   *ashkii* *ałhą́ą́'-ą́ą́*   *yádoołtih*   Navajo
      last:night boy   3SG.IMP.snore-REL.PST FUT.3SG.speak
      'The boy who was snoring last night will speak.' (cited in Andrews 2007: 212)

Another type of construction in which a clause serves in an experiential role in another clause is what Halliday (1985: 225) refers to as *acts*, as in the above examples *eating poison mushrooms killed him* and *worrying over what happened sent him to an early grave*. As remarked above, I see no compelling reason to postulate an ellipsed head noun – such as *act*, as in *the act of eating poison mushrooms killed him* – in order to treat these non-finite clauses as dependents within NPs. Furthermore, while such an analysis is conceivable for English, it is not feasible for some languages. For instance, in Nyulnyul there is no generic nominal that might serve as head of the non-finite clause in (4.7). There can be no reason to suppose that the non-finite clause *marriny* 'going' is in a syntagmatic relation to a nominal; this clause evidently fulfils the Agent role in the main clause.

(4.7) *bulj*   *nga-n-ji*   *marriny-in* *ngay*   Nyulnyul
      tired 1MIN.NOM-CM-say go-ERG   1MIN.CRD
      'I'm tired from walking.'

There are few possibilities for embedding of non-finite clauses in experiential roles in other clauses in Nyulnyul; the main clause is always medio-active, as in (4.7) (see §2.3.2 and McGregor 1999b). The non-finite clause thus serves in a core role (Agent), but not simultaneously in a nuclear role (see §2.3.2 on 'core' and 'nucleus'). By contrast, English permits a non-finite act-specifying clause to enter more comprehensively into the experiential structure of another clause, indeed into its nucleus. The extent to which non-finite clauses specifying acts can enter into the experiential structure of a finite clause is a dimension on which these constructions might be typologized.

4.3 Logical Relations: Dependency

Complex sentences in which one clause is in a dependency relation to another, or part of another, form a particularly rich range of construction types both within and across languages. They may be categorized according to the nature of the dependency relation and the units that are connected by that relation. For dependency relations the scheme proposed by Halliday (1985) is adopted here, with some reservations (one of Halliday's types, projection, is excluded – see Table 1.1 and §4.4). This scheme distinguishes two dimensions of variation: (i) parataxis vs hypotaxis, and (ii) extension vs elaboration vs enhancement. For the second dimension, the nature of the units in the dependency relation, there are also two major possibilities: (a) they are both clauses; (b) one unit is a clause, the other is a subclausal unit. The following subsections overview the main possibilities according to these two dimensions, dealing first with parataxis (§4.3.1) then with hypotaxis (§4.3.2).

4.3.1 Parataxis

4.3.1.1 Interclausal parataxis

In parataxis the two units are of equal value grammatically, and the construction is exocentric: the whole does not have the distribution of either of its parts. The construction has no head; it is symmetric. Complex sentences comprising paratactically related clauses are probably universal.

One type of paratactic relation that has been quite well studied in the descriptive and typological literature is coordination (see e.g. Payne 1985; Mithun 1988; Haspelmath 2004, 2007; Velupillai 2012: 307–315 – though these are not restricted to coordination of clauses; most grammars treat clause coordination to some extent). Coordination is a type of extension.[5] Two primary types are identifiable, conjunction ('and'), as in (4.8), and disjunction ('or'), as in (4.9). Further subtypes can be identified in some languages, including (among others) adversative and emphatic coordination.

> (4.8) *eu   munu namaloku go   eu   sale   poogi*
>   they drink kava   and   they dance   night
>   'They drank kava, and they danced at night.' (Mithun 1988: 348)
>
>   Nguna (Austronesian, Vanuatu)

> (4.9) *wǒmen zài zhèli chī huòzhe chī fàndiàn   dōu xing*   Mandarin Chinese
>   we   at   here   eat or   eat restaurant all OK
>   'We can either eat here or eat out.' (Li and Thompson 1981: 654)

Two issues have been prominent in the literature on coordination: whether the interclausal relation is marked by a conjunctive element, and if so, its nature and use; and the sharing of units between the clauses.

In elaboration one of the clauses provides supplementary additional information on the other, restating it in different words or providing it with another designation. These relations have not been investigated very extensively in the typological or descriptive literature. For Gooniyandi I have proposed three subtypes (McGregor 1990a: 426–427): exposition (restatement in other words), completion (provision of fuller details) and clarification (provision of additional information by way of explanation). These are illustrated in the following three examples, respectively. As these examples show, there is no explicit marker of the interclausal relation. There is, however, some evidence that elaboration is emically distinct from extension in Gooniyandi (McGregor 1997b: 196–198).

(4.10) *bala-wa*   *tharra niyi*   Gooniyandi
   send-2SG.NOM/3SG.ACC/FUT/A dog that
   joorra-ma
   chase-2SG.NOM/3SG.ACC/FUT/MI
   'Send the dog away; chase it.'

(4.11) *niyaji ral-wirra-yi*   *boonbooloo*   Gooniyandi
   this pluck-3PL.NOM/3SG.ACC/A-DU feather
   ral-wirra-yi
   pluck-3PL.NOM/3SG.ACC/A-DU
   'They two plucked it; they plucked out the feathers.'

(4.12) *ngidi-ngga*   *gad-jinmarni*   *nganyi*   Gooniyandi
   1PL.EXC.CRD-ERG separate-1PL.EXC.NOM/MARNI 1SG.CRD
   baboorroonggoo *ward-ngi* *niyi* *thaanoonggoo* *ward-ji*
   down   go-1SG.NOM/I 3SG.CRD up   go-3SG.NOM/I
   'We separated; I went up, he went down.'

In enhancement one clause embellishes on another, providing information on the circumstances of occurrence of the situation specified by the other. This may be in terms of features such as: time (as in *they plucked out the feathers and then put the bird in the fire*), place (e.g. *the seed fell and there grew an apple tree*), manner (e.g. *take it by the long end and in that way it will be easier to control*) or cause/condition (e.g. *she didn't want to discuss it any further, so she said nothing*; and *she said nothing, for she didn't want to discuss it any further*). This is not a full listing of the possibilities for English or any other language. Coordinated clauses can often be interpreted as connected by such relations of enhancement. For instance, (4.8) admits a simultaneous time interpretation, and less likely a sequential interpretation. Again, the status of these as separate enhancing constructions needs to be addressed separately for each expression type in any language.

4.3.1.2 Intraclausal parataxis

One environment in which a clause enters into a paratactic relation with a unit in another clause is where a relative clause identifies the referent of an NP in a relational clause, as in (4.13) and (4.14).[6] As for identifying relational clauses generally, the order of the two units may be reversed, albeit in the case of (4.13) with a change from *that* to *there*. The relative clause then construes that which is identified. In *what you see is what you get* both paratactically related units are relative clauses.

(4.13) *That is where it all began*

(4.14) *Tomorrow is when the answer will be revealed*

A relative clause may also construe a second order entity that is then attributed on, as in *what you have done is quite gross.*

Relations of enhancement and extension can also be found in relational clauses involving relative clauses. For example, in (4.15) the relative clause specifies a location for the glasses; it is in an enhancing relation to the initial NP – compare *your glasses are in the woodshed.* In (4.16) the relative clause specifies something that is a possession of the speaker; this is an extending relation, as argued in McGregor (1997b: 152–154) – compare *I have a bicycle.*

(4.15) *Your glasses are where you left them*

(4.16) *I have what you obviously crave so very much*

In English various non-defining relative clause types may also be in paratactic relations with NPs, as illustrated by examples (4.17)–(4.19). Here the relative clause does not form a phrasal unit with the NP it is syntagmatically related to. Rather, the two units form an endocentric construction with the relative clause in apposition with the NP. Such non-defining relative clauses differ prosodically from defining relative clauses, which do form NP units with what they enter into syntagmatic relations with (see further Halliday 1985: 205–206).

(4.17) *The mouse, who seemed to be a person of authority among them, called out*

(4.18) *They sold it to their neighbours, whose dog barks all night*

(4.19) *Next we went to Wensleydale, where the infamous plastic cheese is made*

Non-defining relative clauses such as (4.17) elaborate on the NP they enter into the paratactic relation with: they provide an alternative designation of the referent. The referent in (4.17) is both a mouse and a person of authority. The two designations are asserted to be coreferential. In the case of (4.18) the relative clause does not provide an alternative designation of the neighbours, but rather specifies a possession – they have a dog that barks all night. This is a subtype of the relation of extension. In (4.19) the relative clause enhances on the place, specifying it via an event that happens there. The relativized NPs plus non-defining relative clauses in these examples are syntagmatically identical with NP complexes, as in, respectively, *the mouse, their leader; their neighbours, with the barking dog;* and *Wensleydale, near Hawes.* (Recall that PPs are considered to be subtypes of NPs – see §3.1.1.)

The treatment of this section glosses over many complications, and does not pretend to be a full account of parataxis in complex sentences in English or any other language. I have not, for instance, taken into account the formal properties of the clause paratactically extending on the other. The above examples are all instances of finite clauses; however, non-finite clauses may also enter into paratactic relations with other clauses or NPs in other clauses. Most obviously a pair of non-finite clauses can be coordinated, as in, for example, *as well as cooking your meals and washing up after you, do you also expect me to clean up your room?* And a non-finite clause in English can enter into a paratactic relation with an NP in relational clauses (e.g. *kissing ducklings is a reprehensible act, a toothbrush is for cleaning teeth*) and in appositional constructions with NPs (e.g. *it's Murdoch's invention, to detect blood*).

4.3.2 Hypotaxis

4.3.2.1 *Interclausal hypotaxis*

In interclausal hypotaxis the two clauses are of unequal status, one being the head, the other a dependent on it. The construction is endocentric, with one clause showing the same distribution as the entire construction. It seems likely that most, if not all, languages admit hypotactic relations between clauses, though in terms of discourse usage hypotaxis is generally less frequent than parataxis in many languages. Usually there is some formal indicator of the marked status of the dependent clause in the shape of a morpheme indexing its dependent status, a marked verb form, or marked word order. The head clause may also be marked in some way, though this is less common and is normally accompanied by simultaneous marking of the dependent clause. This is illustrated by the English *if-then* conditional, in which the *if*-marking of the dependent clause is obligatory, while the *then*-marking of the head clause is optional.

Extension, elaboration and enhancement are found in hypotactic combinations of clauses. But whereas extension represents the prototypical paratactic relation between clauses, enhancement represents the prototype for hypotaxis; this is where the grammar tends to be richest. In what follows we briefly discuss these three types in order.

In hypotactic extension the dependent clause adds to, provides an alternative for, or replaces the head clause. The first two clauses of the second sentence in the previous paragraph – *But whereas extension represents the prototypical paratactic relation between clauses, enhancement represents the prototype for hypotaxis* – is an example. Here the two clauses are related by adversative addition, with the first clause, the dependent clause, adding to the second. Hypotactic alternation can be expressed in English by a type of conditional construction: *if you haven't eaten it, then it must be in the fridge*, the hypotactic equivalent of *either you've eaten it or it's in the fridge*. In hypotactic replacement the head clause indicates an event that replaces that specified by the dependent clause, as in *instead of just sitting there you might contribute something to the discussion*.

In hypotactic elaboration the dependent clause provides further elaborative commentary on the head clause. This is illustrated by one type of non-defining relative clauses in English, in which the relative clause is in a dependency relation to another clause, not an NP. This is illustrated by (4.20).

(4.20) *They were trapped in the lift for hours, which annoyed everyone greatly*

Hypotactic enhancement gives us a range of subordinate clause types generally referred to as adverbial clauses. These have been extensively studied in the typological literature (e.g. Hengeveld 1996; Thompson, Longacre and Hwang 2007; and various contributions in Haiman and Thompson 1988; Austin 1988; Tomlin 1987) as well as the descriptive literature (most grammars deal with them). A wide range of enhancement types can be distinguished etically, in terms of the meaning relation between the two clauses, including at least the following – which can be further divided into (etic) subtypes:

> temporal: contemporaneous, subsequent, previous
> spatial
> manner: means ('by means of'), comparison ('like')
> purpose
> apprehensional (a sort of negative purposive in terms of meaning; 'lest')
> reason
> conditional: real, unreal (hypothetical, counterfactual, predictive)
> concessive (a sort of counterexpectation conditional: the consequence holds contrary to
>   expectations)
> causal

As Thompson, Longacre and Hwang (2007: 243) observe, in the first three types the dependent clause may be replaced by single words, often adverbials, while for the remainder single word replacement is not usually possible. Consistent with this, in some languages the first three meanings are expressed by relative clauses that are dependent on an NP in the primary clause rather than on the primary clause itself.

As indicated above there is a range of formal means by which dependent clauses may be indexed, including by a special morpheme (such as a free word, a clitic, an affix, that may have some other usage as well, e.g. as a case marker), a verb form (e.g. a participial or infinitival form, a particular mood like subjunctive), or marked clausal structure (such as marked word order, presence/absence of certain structural elements, etc.). There may be separate formal markers in a language that distinguish at least some of the types discussed above. These formal markers are an obvious dimension for typologizing dependent clauses.

In some languages a single form marks just the dependent status of a clause, without precisely specifying the meaning relation. In such circumstances the question arises as to whether or not there is a single polysemous dependent clause type with meanings distinguished by context and/or pragmatic implicatures. This is not an easy issue to resolve.

4.3.2.2 *Intraclausal hypotaxis*

Here the dependent clause enters into a syntagmatic relation with a nominal or NP within another clause, forming an NP unit with that nominal or NP. The dependent clause is embedded in an NP, which it forms a part of. The dependent clause delimits the reference the NP it is embedded in in relation to its role in the situation that dependent clause specifies. These are defining or restrictive relative clauses, as in (4.21) and (4.22).

(4.21)   *The book I bought from Amazon should have arrived yesterday*

(4.22)   *That is the person who built the shack by the creek*

In examples (4.21) and (4.22) the relative clause enters into an elaborating relation with the nominal it is dependent on, specifically, the relation of attribution. The relative clause effectively serves the same function in the NP as an adjective would in a language such as English; see also note 15.

A relative clause may also enhance or extend on the head nominal. Enhancing relative clauses provide circumstantial modification of the head nominal, for example in terms of time (e.g. *the day when the sun stopped shining*) and place (e.g. *the town where I lived as a child*). An example of an extending defining relative clause is (4.23): here reference is made to the persons who have the barking dog. They are characterized in terms of their possession of this dog.

(4.23)   *They spoke to the neighbours whose dog barks all night*

Possession is probably the only relation of extension found in defining relative clauses in English (Halliday 1985: 222). However, in a language with so-called inclusory conjunction – where one conjunct specifies the entire set, the others, some of its members, as in, for example, *we including you* with the meaning 'me and you (and possibly others)' (see e.g. Haspelmath 2007: 33–35) – a relative clause in an additive relation to its head might be possible. This is illustrated by example (4.24). (We leave aside for now the question of whether this really is a relative clause construction – see next section.)

(4.24)   *gardiya-yoorroo*   *bagi-la-woorroo-yoo*   *goornboo*   Gooniyandi
          white.person-DU   lie-FCT-3PL.NOM/I-DU   woman
          niyaji-ngga   *ngang-ngindi*   *nganyi*
          this-ERG   give-1SG.ACC/3SG.NOM/DI   1SG.CRD
          'The woman who lives with the white man gave it to me.'

As mentioned in §4.1.1 a good deal of attention has been accorded in the descriptive and typological literature to the role of the referent of the NP relativized on in the relative clause. The main concern of this section, the type of relation between the relative clause and its head, is effectively with the same issue, albeit from a different perspective. Elaboration, extension and enhancement relations depend on the relation that the expression denoting the thing relativized on bears in the relative clause (or would bear if present). Specifically, the three relations correlate with the following roles for the relativized entity in the relative clause, respectively: an argument role, a relation within a superordinate NP, or a dependency relation.

4.3.3 Further Remarks

In this section we have presented a scheme for dependency relations that clauses may enter into with other clauses or (nominal) units within other clauses. Many issues have been ignored, including the formal nature of the clauses in the dependency relation. The emic status of the various types of syntagmatic relations identified is an issue that needs to be addressed separately for each language: many of the types and associated meanings we have identified may well be etically but not emically distinct. Aside from this, there is the question of constructions: which of the phenomena we have discussed represent separate constructions in a language? Can we make generalizations about which might fall together as etic subtypes of a single construction? These are some of the questions that a Neo-Firthian approach raises for description and typology.

To wind up the discussion of dependency, I raise one additional set of problems for the SG scheme. These concern the nature of the unit that a clause enters into a dependency relation with. On the one hand, it may be that both possibilities discussed above – a full clause and a nominal/NP – are not available in a given language; on the other hand, there may be other types of unit that a clause may be in a dependency relation with.

For some Australian languages it has been suggested that clauses may enter into dependency relations with other clauses, but not with nominals or NPs. There would be, that is, no relative clauses that form syntagms with nominals or NPs. Relative clauses would necessarily be adjoined: they enter into a syntagmatic relation with another clause, rather than an NP within it (see further Hale 1976; Andrews 2007: 214–217).[2] For instance, in Warlpiri the relative clause does not necessarily appear next to the NP relativized on, and it is argued that they do not form a single grammatical unit together. The relative clause always either precedes (example (4.25)) or follows (example (4.26)) the other clause; it is never interpolated within it. Furthermore, when the two clauses share the same tense the subordinate clause admits a temporal interpretation.

(4.25)   *nyuntulu-rlu*   *kuja-npa*   *wawirri*   *parntu-rnu* *ngajulu-rlu*   Warlpiri
         2SG-ERG   REL-2SG.NOM kangaroo spear-PST 1SG-ERG
         kapi-rna   *purra-mi*
         FUT-1SG.NOM   cook-NPST
         'I will cook the kangaroo you speared.'

(4.26)   *ngajulu-rlu*   *kapi-rna*   *wawirri*   *purra-mi*   *kuja-npa*   Warlpiri
        1SG-ERG   FUT-1SG.NOM kangaroo cook-NPST REL-2SG.NOM
        parntu-rnu *nyuntulu-rlu*
        spear-PST   2SG-ERG
        'I will cook the kangaroo you speared.'

In Gooniyandi not only is there no unequivocal evidence that a finite clause can form a syntagm with an NP, but there is no segmental marker of relative clause status. What translates as a relative clause in English always admits other interpretations as well. Thus, for instance, (4.27) and (4.28) naturally translate as relative clauses. However, in (4.27) the two finite clauses appear to be in a paratactic relation, and the meaning relation between them might be simply a type of addition: 'He ambushed two white men; (and) they were coming along in a wagon'. In the case of (4.28) the putative relative clause appears to be in a hypotactic relation to the second clause. The adverbial clause interpretation 'when you told me the words the other day, I forgot them' cannot be ruled out, even if in this case it seems somewhat implausible.

(4.27)   *yawan-bina*   *garndiwirri* *wagon-ngarri* *gardiya*
        slaughter-3SG.NOM/3PL.ACC/A two   wagon-COM   white:person
        ward-birri   Gooniyandi
        go-3PL.NOM/I
        'He ambushed two white men (who were) coming along in a wagon.'

(4.28)   *jamoondoo*   *goowaj-gila-nggi-ngarragi*   *niyaji*   Gooniyandi
        other:day   tell-FCT-2SG.NOM/I-1SG.OBL this
        thangarndi   *nyin-limi*
        word   forget-1SG.NOM/3SG.ACC/MI
        'I forgot the words you told me the other day.'

Confronted with facts such as these, Australianists have generally taken the view that there is a single construction which may admit different (etic) interpretations, and that the relative clause is adjoined to the other clause – and hence enters into a syntagmatic relation with a clause rather than an NP. However, it is possible that the relative interpretation corresponds with a different structure, in which the clause enters into a syntagmatic relation of parataxis or hypotaxis with an NP in the other clause. It is possible in this scenario that the NP and syntagmatically related clause do not form an NP unit together, and the structure is not embedding. Instead the clause may be in an appositional relation to an NP. I have previously suggested that this is the case in Gooniyandi (McGregor 1988: 59–60; 1990a: 444–448). The evidence is admittedly inconclusive. It is, however, striking that in putative relative clause constructions the NP relativized on is almost always at the boundary of the clauses, and hence, as in the examples above, also adjacent to the relative clause. Exceptions exist, as in (4.29), but these do not argue conclusively against the possibility that the NP (*niyi tharra* 'that dog') and clause (*jamoondoo nganyi wirdginbinirni* 'it tried to bite me the other day') are in a dependency relation – discontinuous apposition of NPs is possible in the language (McGregor 1997a). Perhaps prosodic evidence could resolve the problem, but this remains to be investigated.

> (4.29) *yaningi   moongaya niyi   tharra mila-la   jamoondoo*
> today   morning   that   dog   see-1SG.NOM/3SG.ACC/A   other:day
> *nganyi   wird-ginbini-rni*   Gooniyandi
> 1SG.CRD   bite-3SG.NOM/1SG.ACC/IRR/BINI-POT
> 'This morning I saw that dog that tried to bite me the other day.'

In some instances it seems that a clause may enter into a syntagmatic relation with something other than another clause or nominal/NP. In examples such as (4.30)–(4.32) the adverbial clause does not enhance on the head clause; it does not specify a circumstance for the occurrence of the head clause situation. In the case of (4.30) the person's car still being in a particular place is not the cause of the person being at home. Rather, her car still being there represents the reason why the speaker makes the claim that she is at home. The dependent clause provides the evidential basis for asserting the main clause.

> (4.30)   *She is at home because her car is still there*

> (4.31)   *If you are interested Crabtree survived the shoot-out*

> (4.32)   *As you must be aware the university is no longer hiring new personnel*

The adverbial clause in such examples plausibly enters into a syntagmatic relation with an interpersonal component of the main clause, the high-level illocutionary operator, in these instances the declarative mood marker (which of course is not even realized by a segmental morpheme). This parallels the usage of adverbials such as *frankly*, *honestly*, *bluntly* and the like (Dik 1989: 258–261; McGregor 1997b: 220). There is evidence that these are constructionally distinct from ordinary adverbial clauses.

4.4 Interpersonal Relations

In this section we turn to complex sentence types in which one clause relates to another clause via an interpersonal relation. Three distinct types of interpersonal relations potentially apply between clauses: framing, scope and tagging. These relations may also obtain between clause and a unit belonging to another clause, often an NP. We treat these three relations in order in the following subsections. Complex sentences involving the relations of framing and scope correspond by and large with the traditional category of clause complementation. Most types of complement clause thus do not involve one clause serving in an argument role in another; rather one clause, the matrix clause, specifies how the other clause should be taken interactively (McGregor 2008a).

4.4.1 Framing

The terms *reported speech* and *reported thought* refer to the phenomenon in which a stretch of wording is employed to represent the utterances or thoughts of some individual, who they are attributed to. For instance, in *they told me I would find you asleep* and *I thought I would find you asleep* the words *I would find you asleep* represent respectively an utterance allegedly directed to the present speaker by some group of persons and a thought entertained at some point of time by the speaker. This representation is, of course, always approximate: an utterance token is unique, and another token of the same type can never be absolutely identical with it. Moreover, the degree to which the representation resembles the reality can range from quite similar (if, for instance, they had said 'You will find him asleep' or the speaker had thought the words 'I will find him asleep') to very different (e.g. if they had said 'he is probably snoring his head off', or if my thoughts had been purely visual). The crucial point is that there is a referent (real or imaginary), and this is in the first place an utterance or thought. Of course, some situation or relation in the real or an imaginary world will often also be construed, though indirectly – and one is not necessarily construed, as in, for example, *I thought 'ugh!'*.

The referent of the reported words – an utterance or thought – is demonstrated or depicted by those reported words, which construct them by providing a possible linguistic shape for them (Clark and Gerrig 1990: 764; McGregor 1994b: 77; 1997b: 253; Clark 2016).[8] The reported words depict their referent utterance or thought much as a person might depict via their own actions the walking style of another person or a gorilla, or a painting or photograph depicts its referent. Put in other words, what is involved in reporting is imitation: the reported words or thoughts imitate the words or thoughts spoken or entertained in another context.

It seems likely that all languages have grammatical constructions dedicated to the expression of reported speech and thoughts (e.g. Spronck and Nikitina 2019). Some attempts have been made to provide a more precise definition of these constructions, specifying criteria that must be met for a construction to be a reported speech or thought construction in a given language (e.g. Güldemann 2008; Spronck and Nikitina 2019). Such attempts are in line with the approach to typology advocated in this book, namely to use emic categories in languages as the comparanda. It is proposed that two criteria must be met:

(i) the expression must be a multi-clausal construction, i.e. a grammatical sign in the given language; and

(ii) this construction must specify that a certain stretch of wording depicts or demonstrates another wording or potential wording.

(i) restricts the domain to complex sentence constructions. Constructions consisting of a single clause and a hearsay marker are excluded since they do not comprise complex sentences. They also fail to meet (ii) – they specify the evidential basis for the claim made by the clause, rather than demonstrate another utterance (McGregor 2019b: 209).

There may be various expression types that are deployed by speakers of a language in the construal of a stretch of wording as a demonstration without representing constructions or signalling the demonstration status of the wording. These could include gestures or marked prosody. In writing, strategies such as indentation and use of quotation marks may be employed. The existence of such alternative phenomena in a language – and cross-linguistically – is of typological and theoretical interest; see also Spronck and Nikitina (2019: 142). However, this does not undermine the hypothesis that all languages have complex sentence constructions dedicated to the reporting of speech and thoughts and satisfying (i) and (ii).

4.4.1.1 *Reported speech*

Reported speech constructions are complex sentence constructions involving at least one clause that demonstrates an utterance and one clause that specifies the speech situation in which the demonstrated utterance allegedly occurred. This is illustrated in the Megeb Dargwa (Northeast Caucasian, Dagestan) example (4.33), where the first clause describes the speech event in which the utterance demonstrated by the second clause allegedly occurred.

(4.33) *malla-rasbadi-j-ʔini* *ʔ-ib,* *ħa-la* *kʼunkʼul-li-ʔini*
Molla-Nasreddin-OBJ-ERG say:PF-PST 2SG-ERG cauldron-OBJ-ERG
b-aqʼ-ib-il *kʼunkʼur-gʷa* *iš* Megeb Dargwa
N-make:PF-PART cauldron-FOC this
'Molla Nasreddin said: "This is a cauldron born by your cauldron".' (cited in Spronck and Nikitina 2019: 124)

According to one line of thought, constructions such as (4.33) are complement constructions in which the reported clause serves in an argument role – an object – in the clause of speech. There is little support for this: the reported clause shows little in common grammatically with objects, even in languages like Latin in which the reported utterance typically takes grammatical marking associated with objects (McGregor 1994b, 1997b: 258). Another line of thought takes the relation between the clauses to be a dependency one. As seen in Table 1.1 and §4.1.2 this is Halliday's position: the reported clause is in a dependency relation of either parataxis or hypotaxis with the reporting clause, and involves the special type of logical relation referred to as projection. McGregor (1994b) argues against this analysis also, and shows that the relation between the clause of speech and the reported clause cannot be one of dependency (see also Vandelanotte 2009: 19–57; Spronck and Nikitina 2019: 124–125).

I have proposed instead (McGregor 1994b, 1997b: 253) that the interclausal relation is one of FRAMING: the reporting clause of speech frames the reported speech clause, specifying its status as a demonstration. This term invokes the metaphor of a frame around a picture, which likewise sets the picture off from its surroundings, indicating its special semiotic status, more specifically how it is to be taken interactively. Framing is a relation belonging to the grammar of the interpersonal. This model accounts for various features of reported speech constructions, including the range of choices for the deictic centres (McGregor 1997b: 254–255), and for the widely recognized correlations between reported speech constructions and modal phenomena such as evidentiality and epistemic modality. It also accounts for the well-known distancing effect of reported speech, whereby reported speech constructions serve to distance the speaker (of the complex sentence itself) from the reported utterance (e.g. Güldemann 2008: 6; 2012: 118; McGregor 2019b: 210–211).

Reported speech constructions differ both within and across languages. Traditionally a distinction is drawn between direct and indirect speech; the former allegedly reproduces the wording of the quoted utterance exactly, the latter reproduces it approximately, representing its meaning. This view, as many commentators have observed, is untenable. Rather, demonstration of an utterance ranges along a scale from greater to lesser faithfulness to the imitated utterance with respect to certain features. Relevant to the contrast between direct and indirect speech is what happens to deictic and modal categories in the reported utterance. In direct speech they are in accordance with the utterance reported on in its context of occurrence; in indirect speech they are in accordance with the speech situation in which the complex sentence was uttered. Other dimensions of faithfulness – for example, lexical choice, choice of grammatical construction – are irrelevant to this contrast.

Languages differ in terms of whether they show different constructions for direct and indirect reporting of speech. Some languages apparently have just a single construction, which in terms of its formal properties most resembles direct speech of languages such as English (e.g. Rumsey 1990). Shifting grammatical categories are mostly presented from the perspective of the reported speech situation; they are demonstrated more faithfully. It seems probable that all languages have a complex sentence type that demonstrates these categories as per the reported speech situation.

Many languages make two or more contrasts, distinguishing direct and indirect quotes, and possibly other types as well, such as free indirect speech (Bally 1912; Vološinov 1973; Vandelanotte 2009). Indirect speech constructions differ cross-linguistically in terms of the way shifting categories are treated: which are represented from the centre of the reported speech situation, and which from the centre of the reporting speech situation (Li 1986; de Roeck 1994)? It seems that pronominal categories are usually with respect to the reporting situation, though there is cross-linguistic (and intralinguistic) variation in the treatment of spatial and temporal deictic and modal categories (de Roeck 1994). Some may be presented from the perspective of the reporting situation, some from the reported. Sometimes a choice may be avoided entirely: representation of the reported clause by a non-finite clause may permit avoidance of a modal perspective, as in Latin (Lyons 1968: 174). If other reported speech constructions are distinguished, they differ in terms of their treatment of these shifting categories.

As mentioned above, it seems that direct representation of reported speech is universal in the sense that all languages have a reported speech construction in which the deictic and modal categories are (mostly) represented in accordance with the reported speech situation. In various languages of Africa and elsewhere a special set of logophoric pronouns are employed in reported speech constructions (and usually also reported thoughts). These pronouns specifically indicate that the centre for person deixis is the reported speech situation. In Goemai (Afro-asiatic, Nigeria), for instance, there is a set of first and second person logophoric pronouns that indicate speaker and hearer of the reported utterance; third persons in that speech situation are represented by ordinary non-logophoric pronouns (Hellwig 2006: 219). In (4.34) the logophoric pronoun *ji* indexes the speaker of the reported speech; this is a different form to the ordinary first-person singular pronoun *hen* '1SG'. However, other deictic categories such as time are represented from the perspective of the reported speaker: the temporal deictic expression *m-b'itlung* 'LOC-morning' is in accordance with the temporal origin of the quoted utterance.

(4.34) *dyen*   *k'wal* *yin* *d'in*   *ji*   *wul*   Goemai
        PST.YEST   talk SAY PST.CLOSE SG.M.LOG.SP arrive
        m-b'itlung
        LOC-morning
        '(He₁) said yesterday that he₁ arrived earlier today (i.e. he arrived yesterday from the perspective of the current speaker).' (Hellwig 2006: 219)

It seems that Goemai also has an indirect reported speech strategy (not treated as such by Hellwig 2006: 219). The same logophoric system of person reference is employed, but other shifting categories are represented from the perspective of the reporting utterance. Thus, in (4.35) the yesterday past in the quoted utterance is in accordance with the speech situation of the entire sentence.

(4.35) *ni*   *kut*   *goepe* *dyen*   *ji*   *wul*   Goemai
        3SG talk THAT PST.YEST SG.M.LOG.SP arrive
        'He₁ said that he₁ had arrived yesterday.' (Hellwig 2006: 212)

In languages where a contrast between direct and indirect reporting of speech is maintained direct reporting is normally the unmarked member of the pair. This is manifested in token frequency, at least in some languages. For instance, in Gooniyandi reported speech is overwhelmingly frequently represented directly, as in (4.36). However, speech is occasionally reported indirectly, as shown by example (4.37).

(4.36) *nginyji-ga   joorra-wa-woo /*   Gooniyandi
2SG.CRD-ERG chase-2SG.NOM/3SG.ACC/A-EXC
miga-yinmi-nhi   garndiwirri-ngga /
say-1PL.EXC.NOM/MI-3SG.OBL   two-ERG
'"You chase [the kangaroos]!" we two told him.'

(4.37) *yan.gin-ba   ngoonyi-yirra ward-giri*   Gooniyandi
ask-2SG.NOM/3SG.ACC/A   where-ALL   go-3SG.NOM/PRS/I
'Ask him where he is going.'

In keeping with the greater faithfulness of demonstration in direct than indirect speech reports, direct speech is associated with greater distancing from the reported utterance than indirect speech.[9] In Gooniyandi indirect speech highlights the relevance of some aspect of the reported utterance to the present speech situation, and thus presents the reported utterance more from the perspective of the reporting speech situation. It is strongly associated with four circumstances (McGregor 1990a: 418–420).

First, if the speaker and/or hearer in the present speech situation (i.e. of the complex sentence) are also interactants in the events of the reported speech utterance, indirect report is preferred: that is, there is a preference to use first and second person categories for the present speaker and hearer, rather than to use the third person category. This is somewhat more general than the phenomenon Evans (2013) dubs 'second person magnetism': the dispreference for third person reference applies to the speaker as well as hearer.

Second, indirect reporting is more likely if the reported utterance requests information that the present speaker also wishes communicated to themselves, as in (4.38) – see also (4.37).

(4.38) *ngoorroo-ngga   yoowooloo yiniga-mi-nganggi*   Gooniyandi
that-ERG   man   do:thusly-3SG.NOM/3SG.ACC/MI-2SG.OBL
ngoonyi-yirra   ward-giri
where-ALL   go-3SG.NOM/PRS/I
'Where did that man tell you he's going?'

Third, if the reported utterance expresses a command the present speaker wishes relayed (usually by the present addressee) to some third party, indirect speech is preferred, as in (4.39).

(4.39) *jag-ma-nhi   ward-ja-wi   niyaji*   Gooniyandi
tell-2SG.NOM/MA-3SG.OBL   go-SUB-3SG.NOM/FUT/I   this
bala-wa
send-2SG.NOM/3SG.ACC/A
'Tell him to go; send him away.'

Fourth, there is a dispreference to use the second person pronoun in reference to a kinsperson in an avoidance relation to the present speaker. If such a person is referred to in a quote, there is a preference to use the third person category – and thus indirect speech when they are the addressee of the utterance.

The above discussion does not argue for a continuum between direct and indirect speech. Rather, the contrast, if it is maintained in a language, is a discrete one, perhaps binary, perhaps ternary, perhaps quaternary, perhaps more. It is an empirical question for each language how many different reported speech constructions exist; each of these is a discrete unit, a construction. Scalarity comes into the picture only indirectly, when we compare the constructions cross-linguistically in terms of variables that can be placed on a scale (of sorts), such as the number of deictic or modal categories that are centred on the reported versus reporting speech situation.

4.4.1.2 *Reported thought*

It seems likely that all languages also have means of reporting thoughts, complex sentences in which one or more clauses report the contents of a thought, and another clause specifies the thought situation in which it occurred. Again, as in reported speech, the reported clauses demonstrate the thought by (re)enacting it in words; the clause of thought frames these words, specifying their marked semiotic status as a demonstration. This is illustrated by the Nkore-Kiga (Niger-Congo, Uganda) example (4.40), where the first clause specifies a type of thought process (remembering), and the second clause re-enacts the contents of that thought process in words.

> (4.40) *b-a-ijuka*   *ku*   *y-aa-gambire ekyo*   Nkore-Kiga
> they-TP-remember   COMP   he-RP-say   that
> 'They remembered that he had said so.' (Taylor 1985: 17)

The grammatical relation between the reported and the reporting clauses in reported thought is arguably the same as between the reported and reporting clauses in reported speech, namely framing. The difference concerns what is demonstrated by the framed utterance, a thought or an utterance. Whether complex sentence constructions reporting thoughts and complex sentence constructions reporting speech are emically distinct or are merely different possible etic interpretations of a single construction type is a question that must be addressed separately for each language. This is one dimension on which reported expressions might be typologized. The difficulty, however, is that the descriptive question of construction status has not been addressed in very many languages, rendering such a typology impossible for the foreseeable future.

In reported thought different modes of representation may be possible, including direct and indirect, possibly along with others. These modes of representation differ cross-linguistically also in terms of the treatment of deictic and modal categories. In some languages it seems that there is a preference for indirect reporting of thoughts, or at least that indirect reporting is more common for thoughts than speech.

The reporting clause may, as in (4.40), specifically indicate the status of the demonstration as a thought. However, in a number of Australian (and other) languages a single generic verb – admitting senses 'say', 'think', 'do' – is employed in framing both thoughts and speech.[10] This is the case in Gooniyandi (McGregor 1990a), Ungarinyin (Rumsey 1990; Spronck 2015) and Nyulnyul (McGregor 2012a). For instance, Nyulnyul example (4.41) also admits the interpretation '"I will spear them," he said'.

(4.41) *djaḷ   ŋang-am   yer,*   Nyulnyul
        jarl   nga-n-ka-m-irr
        pierce   1MIN.NOM-CM-FUT-put-3AUG.ACC
        in-djan-djer
        i-n-j-an-jirr
        3NOM-CM-say-IMP-3AUG.OBL
        '"I will spear them," he thought.' (Nekes and Worms 2006: 309)

Although Gooniyandi, Ungarinyin and Nyulnyul have a range of verbs of thought, these are not normally used in complex sentences reporting thoughts. Aside from the generic 'say, think, do' verb, reporting clauses of thought normally employ verbs of perception, most commonly the 'see' verb. This extended usage of verbs of perception is not uncommon cross-linguistically.

Some languages have separate complex sentence constructions that express restricted types of reported thoughts. Here I mention two that are found in some languages of north-west Australia (and elsewhere). One of these is dedicated to the representation of mistaken beliefs, as shown by example (4.42). The separate constructional status of these in Ungarinyin is supported by the compositional unpredictability of the meaning. Similar constructions are found in Gooniyandi and Warrwa.

(4.42) *goanna-karra   nga-ma-ra   nya-langkun kuno*   Ungarinyin
        goanna-maybe   1SG-do-PST   3F.SG-head N_W-DIST
        'I thought it was a goanna's head over there (but I turned out to be wrong).' (Spronck 2015: 178)

The other construction demonstrates desires or wishes. This is illustrated by the Warrwa example (4.43), where the projected desire is enacted in terms of a possible wording in the mind of the person. McGregor (2007a) argues for the separate construction status of this mode of expression in Warrwa. Various other nearby languages show a similar construction, including Bunuba (Rumsey 2000) and various Worrorran languages (e.g. Ungarinyin and Worrorra).

(4.43) *baalu / baalu lakarr ka-na-ngka-yi   ø-ja-n /*   Warrwa
        tree   tree   climb   1NOM.FUT-CM-FUT-say   3MIN.NOM-say-PRS
        'He wants to climb up the tree.'

4.4.2 Scope

A syntagmatic relation of SCOPE holds between clauses when one clause modulates another clause in terms of how it is to be taken interactively. The former clause provides as it were a modal 'slant' on the latter in a similar way to negative particles, epistemic modifiers (e.g. *maybe, probably*), deontic modifiers (e.g. *must*), illocutionary modifiers (such as interrogative markers, as found in languages such as Mandarin Chinese and Warrwa), and so on. For example, in (4.44) the first clause expresses the speaker's evaluation of the likelihood of the proposition 'he'll come', while in (4.45) the first clause expresses the attitude of the girls to the imagined situation of their dancing, that they find it desirable.[11]

> (4.44) *tá   amhras orm   an   dtiocfadh sé*   Irish
>   COP   doubt   on:me INT   come.FUT   he
>   'I doubt if he'll come.' (Noonan 2007: 126)

> (4.45) *de   zarap   zem yi   degoe n-marap   gya*   Goemai
>   SO.THAT   girls(PL) like SUBORD PURP   PURP-step(PL) performance
>   '(...) so the girls wanted to dance' (Hellwig 2006: 210)

Framing and scope are different syntagmatic relations of the interpersonal type. Which relation is involved in a particular instance cannot be simply read from the lexical features of the outer clause or the apparent meaning of the construction. Not all instances of putative reported speech or thought involve the framing relation, or count as reported speech or thought constructions. Vandelanotte (2009) identifies a category of distancing indirect speech, as illustrated by examples (4.46) and (4.47), which he argues is emically distinct from free indirect speech. As he argues, the syntagmatic relation is one of scope; the inner clause is not framed as a demonstration.

> (4.46) *John will be late, he said.* (Reinhart 1975: 136)

> (4.47) *He mailed you earlier today, he said, so please do answer him.* (Genuine e-mail example, cited in Vandelanotte 2004: 496)

Similarly, in reported thoughts such as *I don't believe that pudding will ever be cooked* the proposition expressed by the inner clause, 'that pudding will be cooked', is modalized by the outer clause of thought. It does not demonstrate a thought, and the two clauses are related by a scopal relation (see further McGregor 2008a: 38–39; Vandelanotte 2009: 314, who argue that these are structurally distinct from framing constructions).

These and other non-framing types of reported speech and thought have been fairly extensively studied in theoretical and stylistic studies of English. Typological investigations have largely ignored such constructions in their treatment of reported speech and thought. Doubtless this is largely because descriptions of languages other than the major ones rarely deal with these phenomena, which may not be frequent in usage or at the forefront of the minds of fieldworkers as targets of elicitation. Potential candidates for such constructions do exist, however, as shown by the following Nyulnyul example from a lengthy narrative (McGregor 2012b: 711–734).

(4.48) *yarrad-mad-mad /*   *kinyingk-mad /* *burrb /* *liyan /*   Nyulnyul
         1AUG.CRD-EMP-EMP DEF-EMP   dance   like

         mi-na-m   *akal /*   *mi-n-di-jarrad /*
         2MIN.NOM-CM-put   and   2MIN.NOM-CM-say-1AUG.OBL

         '"We did! You wanted it because you wanted to dance, so you told us!"'

For communicative and cognitive complement constructions the syntagmatic rela-tions involved may be either framing or scope, and languages differ in terms of their treatment of particular instances. Thus, as we have seen (§4.4.1.2), desiderative comple-ments in Warrwa and some nearby languages involve framing, whereas in Goemai and many other languages the relation is scope: the outer clause has scope over the situation specified by the inner clause, and indicates the attitude of the thinkers specified in the outer clause to the situation.

Some languages also have complex sentence constructions in which the outer clause modifies the status of the inner clause in terms of its truth value or some other modal category, as in, for example, *it is not the case that John will be late* and *it is possible that John will be late*. In some languages a complement construction is the preferred or only mode of expressing negation. This is apparently the case in Fijian (Austronesian, Fiji), as shown by (4.49).

(4.49) *ena   sega   ni   lako   ko   koya*   Fijian
         FUT   NEG   COMP   go   ART   he
         'He won't go.' (cited in Noonan 2007: 144)

Manipulative complements such as causatives (as in *the police forced the trackers to follow his dripping blood until nightfall*) and permissives (as in *the police let the trackers follow his dripping blood until nightfall*) also arguably involve the interclausal relation of scope in languages like English (McGregor 2008a: 39–45). In some languages, for exam-ple Gooniyandi, by contrast, these meanings are expressed by framing constructions, as illustrated by the following example.

(4.50) *bala-ji-la*   *wayandi*   Gooniyandi
         send-IT-1SG.NOM/3SG.ACC/A fire

         gaj-ba-ngangi
         cut-FUT/2SG.NOM/3SG.ACC/A-1&2OBL

         'I sent him (saying) "Cut firewood for us!"', 'I sent him to cut firewood for us.' Or 'I made him cut firewood for us.'

Whether or not these represent a separate construction type in the language or are merely variant contextual interpretations of a single reported speech construction type is uncertain – though I suspect the latter for Gooniyandi.

This brief section has only scratched the surface of scoping clause complexes, and has not addressed the question of what subset of construction types usually treated under the heading of complementation are amenable to this analysis. I have not, for instance, addressed the question of the analysis of perceptual complements such as *he saw the girls dancing* or conjunctive complements (Noonan 2007: 144–145).

A number of dimensions of cross-linguistic variation in complement constructions have been identified in the literature (e.g. Noonan 2007), including: whether or not a complementizer is employed, what sort of unit that complementizer might be, the nature of the inner clause (whether it is a full finite clause, an infinitival or nominalized clause, or whatever), whether there are restrictions on reference relations among any of the arguments, whether and under what circumstances ellipsis of an argument in the inner clause is possible (so-called 'equi-deletion'), or under what conditions, if at all, it is possible for an argument or other unit of the inner clause to be represented in the outer clause ('raising').

It is not that these are unimportant or uninteresting descriptive and typological issues. Rather, the point is that there are other questions of equal or greater significance, in particular the interclausal relationship and the range of construction types distinguished and their grammatical properties. These also represent dimensions of typological variation of complement constructions.

4.4.3 Tagging

Whereas in framing and scope there is an outer and inner clause, in tagging neither syntagmatically related clause encompasses the other. Instead, one clause (the tagging clause) is attached to another clause (the stem), which it modalizes. Some languages show very restricted tagging constructions in which a particle representing a minor clause is tagged to another clause, as in Walmajarri (Pama-Nyungan, Australia) example (4.51).[12]

    (4.51)   *ngurti pa wulyu, payi*   Walmajarri
               car   it   good   OK
               'The car is good, isn't it?' (Hudson et al. 1978: 93)

Some languages admit tagging of reduced and possibly modified versions of the stem clause. English has a number of tags in which the tagged clause is in interrogative mood, and normally consists of just an auxiliary together with a pronominal cross-referencing the subject of the stem clause, and optionally a negative marker. There are tagged clauses with the same polarity as the stem clause, as in *you saw her yesterday, did you?* and tagged clauses with the reverse polarity, as in *you saw her yesterday, didn't you?* Declarative and imperative clauses admit both same and reverse polarity tags for both positive and negative stem clauses. However, only positive interrogative and exclamative stems admit tags, and these must be same and reverse polarity respectively (McGregor 1995a, 1995b, 1997b: 245).

I have argued that the syntagmatic relation between the stem and tagged clauses is an interpersonal one, and have proposed meanings for some tag types in English, central to which are: (i) modalization of the stem clause in terms of presuppositions and expectations and/evaluations of truth or falsity; and (ii) (intensified) response soliciting (McGregor 1995b, 1995a, 1997b: 244–249).

The formal properties and meanings of tags in English have been quite extensively treated in the literature, from a range of grammatical perspectives, not just formal but also functional-interactional (Hasan 1996; Kimps and Davidse 2008; Kimps, Davidse and Cornillie 2014; Kimps, Davidse and O'Grady 2019) and sociolinguistic (e.g. Holmes 1986). Less is known about tags in other languages: grammatical descriptions rarely discuss these phenomena. Their existence or otherwise in many languages is impossible to ascertain with certainty – absence of evidence for their existence is not evidence of their absence. For instance, in some languages it may be that no genuine tagging constructions exist, and the types of meanings typically expressed by tagging are expressed by modal particles or enclitics that cannot serve as separate minor clauses. This is a matter for further empirical investigation. A comprehensive typological study awaits more information from a wider variety of languages.

4.5 Insubordination and Defenestration

The evocative label *insubordination* has been given to the phenomenon, quite widespread in languages of the world, whereby a clause that is formally indexed as bound – or subordinate – conventionally occurs independently, in the absence of an expected main clause.[13] For instance, conditional protasis clauses in English, which are bound, sometimes appear without head clauses, as in for example, *if we could have some silence please*, used by a teacher to quieten a noisy class. Excluded from insubordination is the situation in which a head clause is ellipsed when it presents information that is presumed given or predictable. In insubordination no such given clause is available that could serve as the head: in the above example there is no apodosis clause that could be filled in from knowledge available in the speech interaction.

Insubordination has not been extensively studied in the descriptive literature, and relatively few grammars make mention of the phenomenon. Recently, however, it has attracted some attention – for example, Evans (2007); Evans and Watanabe (2016b); D'Hertefelt (2015); D'Hertefelt and Verstraete (2014); Verstraete, D'Hertefelt and Van linden (2012). The following presents an indication of how insubordination can be treated in a Neo-Firthian approach, rather than a typology of insubordination.

McGregor (2017a: 205–209) proposes that insubordination involves refunctioning of the bound clause as a free clause. Effectively, a clause that is specified as not expressing its own speech function and/or modality (Verstraete 2007) is used as though it does express a speech functional value of its own. Thus, our previous example *if we could have some silence please*, which formally has no separate speech function of its own, is employed as though it does, here as a polite request. This refunctioning of the bound clause satisfies the conditions for interpersonal grammar (see §1.1.3), and this is consistent with the range of interpersonal meanings that are habitually expressed by insubordination (see Mithun 2008: 72; Evans 2009: 11; Evans and Watanabe 2016a; Gras 2016; Verstraete, D'Hertefelt and Van linden 2012; McGregor 2017a: 206–209).

A comparable – though even more poorly studied – phenomenon can be found in the domain of interpersonally related clauses, where a clause of reported speech occurs without a matrix clause that frames it or has scope over it. I am not referring to the rather common phenomenon, attested in many languages, of ellipsis of the framing clause of speech. Nothing special is involved in ellipsis of clauses of speech that requires the identification of a distinct and separate phenomenon: it can be accounted for in terms of ellipsis generally – i.e. in relation to the givenness of the information presented. For instance, in reported dialogues in narrative framing clauses of speech are frequently omitted, being predictable from the turn-taking nature of dialogue (see Spronck 2017 and many other references).

Rather, what we are concerned with are instances in which – as in insubordination – a reported speech clause is used as though it were not an instance of reported speech: it is refunctioned as something else, an utterance of the present speaker. Following Spronck (2015, 2017) I refer to this phenomenon as *defenestration*.[14] Consider (4.52), addressed to me by a woman on a hiking track in the UK. I was sitting beside the track eating lunch with my wife, who was holding an iPhone. The woman's dog came up to us, and sniffed at my backpack.

(4.52)   *Take a picture of me*

Two features of this utterance index it as a defenestration. First, it was uttered on a marked prosodic contour, in a higher register than expected, in the manner of a reported utterance. Second, the imperative form is quite contextually inappropriate to the request of a photograph: one does not utter such directives to strangers one meets on walking tracks. Much more interactive preparatory work is necessary, and if a clause referring to the situation of taking a photograph is employed, it is never (in my experience) in an unmodulated imperative. All interactants instantly understood (4.52) as the imputed words of the dog, the centre for person deixis the *me* in the utterance, provoking laughter all around.

Defenestration is not uncommon in signage, and I have recently observed a number of instances in the UK as well as in Denmark; see Wales (2013); Pascual (2014: 4) for

Figure 4.1 A notice in the toilet of a carriage in a ScotRail train (author's photograph, 2018)

further examples, including in Dutch and Anglo-Saxon (Old English). Often an institution or company deploys an inanimate object such as a product as their mouthpiece for speaking to the public, as shown in Figure 4.1 (see McGregor 2019b: 213–214 for discussion); also popular is for religious organizations to employ God as their mouthpiece.

I have proposed (McGregor 2019b) that defenestration is an interpersonal phenomenon in the same way as insubordination, and codes an interpersonal meaning. In the case of (4.52) it represents an attempt to defuse a situation of potential conflict and serves as the woman's excuse for her dog's inappropriate, perhaps menacing, behaviour. Rather than directly uttering an excuse, she uses the dog as her mouthpiece, resituating the excuse as though instigated by the dog – it is as though the dog were saying 'please excuse my coming up so close to you, it is only because I want you to take a picture of me, being such a nice dog'.

4.6 Concluding Remarks

To present a Neo-Firthian typology of complex sentences is well beyond present prospects. There is simply insufficient descriptive data available from a range of languages.

At present the best that can be done is to present an outline of a Neo-Firthian approach, and hint at how this might be deployed in a typology – and more fundamentally in the description of complex sentences in particular languages. The approach advocated here has something to offer in terms of the rich theoretical architecture it provides for the analysis of complex sentences in terms of syntagmatic relations, and the attention to meaning. At the same time it is acknowledged that the approach is highly demanding analytically: sorting out emic categories of complex sentences – separating them from etic ones – in any language is a non-trivial task. And to effect this for a representative sample of languages would take many years, if not decades.

The present approach focuses on the syntagmatic relations a clause may enter into with another clause or part thereof. This needs to be augmented by more careful attention to the grammatical features of the clauses in these syntagmatic relations. It seems to me that the approach of Verstraete (2007) is likely to be effective: it is set at the right level of generality for an emic typology, with its focus on modal potentials of the syntagmatically connected clauses, rather than on issues of mere form.

Finally, it is worth remarking that the theoretical machinery developed in this chapter for describing complex sentences is not peculiar to these constructions. One advantage of the present approach is that it does not require dedicated machinery peculiar to complex sentences. Other types of grammatical unit, such as nominals and NPs (as well as perhaps verbs and VPs) may also serve in syntagmatic relations of the same general types. The domain of complex sentences happens to be one in which the syntagmatic possibilities are particularly rich, due in part to the rich set of interpersonal choices available at the level of the clause, many of which are not available at phrase level.

Chapter 5

Optional Case Marking

Whereas the previous three chapters deal with topics that have attracted considerable interest among both typologists and Neo-Firthian linguists, the case studies of this chapter and the next concern grammatical phenomena that have attracted little interest among either, even though they are far from being linguistic raria. I attempt to provide theoretically informed typologies grounded in Neo-Firthian linguistics. For both studies I provide explicit recognition criteria. This does not mean that the criteria are theory neutral, or that they always provide a binary yes-no answer. Different theoretical premises will lead to different interpretations and contextualizations of the criteria, and there are admittedly cases where the criteria proposed do not yield clear decisions, even with a single theory, as well as cases where they yield decisions that conflict with our intuitions.

5.1 Introduction

5.1.1 Definition of Optional Case Marking

The term *optional* is used in a wide range of different senses in linguistics (McGregor 2013c: 1149–1151). A case marker might be said to be optional in a variety of different circumstances. For instance, in describing the morphological structure of nouns in a language it might be said that case markers are optional, permitting an economic structural description such as N-(number marker)-(case marker). It might alternatively be said that a case marker is optional in that its presence or absence on a nominal in a clause token does not affect grammaticality, or that the presence and non-presence of the case marker are in free variation.

The first of these senses is grammatically uninteresting: optionality is merely an economic strategy in formulation. The third notion might well be non-existent: along with many others I take the view that completely free variation does not occur in languages. The second notion gets us closer to something usable, but still admits too many disparate phenomena. For instance, one might imagine a language with an ergative marker that could appear or not on the NP specifying the eater in a clause of eating that lacked an NP specifying the thing eaten, without any effect on grammaticality or gross meaning. However, if it turned out in this language that the two possibilities correlate with different constructions, the former with a transitive clause, the latter with an intransitive one, then one might object to this as a genuine case of optionality: the ergative is present exclusively in transitive clauses, absent exclusively in intransitive ones. The grammatical construction demands either the ergative or its absence.

To exclude these the following definition is proposed of optionality in general, regardless of the particular type of linguistic unit involved (McGregor 2013c: 1152):

> (5.1) An element is optional in a given construction if, in a specifiable set of linguistic circumstances:
> i. it may be present or absent in tokens of the construction; and
> ii. its presence or absence does not affect the grammatical structure: the construction remains unchanged as a linguistic sign regardless of whether or not the element is present.

Alternatively, ii. could be rephrased as iii., where we focus on grammatical relations rather than constructions.

> iii. its presence or absence does not affect the grammatical relation borne by the unit in the construction that is marked by the element when it is present.

The reference to construction tokens in the definition is essential. This is because otherwise – if the item in question, the putative optional item, were to occur or not occur in a construction type – it is possible that its presence and absence might be in complementary distribution according to inessential grammatical features of the units comprising the constructions. Such a situation would arise in a particular language where non-pronominal Agents of transitive clauses are marked by the ergative marker, but pronominal ones are not (recall §1.2.2.3). However, such an ergative marker is not aptly described as optional since its presence or absence is grammatically predictable.

An optional case marker is thus a case marking morpheme that may be either present or absent on an NP in a given clause token without affecting the grammatical role borne by that NP – or the clausal construction itself. For instance, in Shua the accusative case marking postposition *ʔà* – which alternates with a suffix *à* and low tone and lengthening of the final vowel of the marked nominal – is optional in certain contexts on Undergoer NPs. This is shown by examples (5.2) and (5.3), without and with the accusative marker on the Undergoer NP, *tii zibira-na* 'my clothes'. The experiential meaning of the two clause tokens is identical, as is the grammatical role borne by the initial NP.

> (5.2) *tii*   *zibira-na*   *ǀui*   *ǁ'aː-ha*   Shua
> 1SG.OBL   clothes-PL   one   wash-PST
> 'She washed only my clothes.'

> (5.3) *tii*   *zibira-na*   *ʔà*   *ǀui*   *ǁ'aː-ha*   Shua
> 1SG.OBL   clothes-PL   ACC   one   wash-PST
> 'She washed only my clothes.'

(5.1) excludes a number of phenomena from optional case marking that might potentially be treated as instances. For instance, the preposition *to* in English is not optional on NPs specifying recipients in ditransitive clauses in pairs such as *She gave the clock to me* and *She gave me the clock*. These two clauses are tokens of distinct constructions, and the *to* preposition cannot be omitted in the first token while maintaining the same construction.

As the present chapter will reveal, optional case marking is not uncommon in the world's languages. Until recently, however, it has enjoyed little prominence in linguistic theory, description or typology. Since 2000 there has been a significant increase in publications on the phenomenon in particular languages (see McGregor and Verstraete 2010; Chelliah and Hyslop 2011; Chappell and Verstraete 2019 and the references therein, and further references below), as well as attempts to account for it theoretically and to develop a typology (e.g. McGregor 2010, 2013c).

In this chapter we focus attention on optional case marking of NPs serving in core roles (as per §2.3.2). NPs in other grammatical roles may also be optionally case marked. However, such situations have not been studied to the same extent as core roles, and are ignored here.

5.1.2 A Semiotic Theory of Optional Case Marking

The most common explanation for optional case marking in linguistic typology and descriptive linguistics is couched in the S, A, O theory and alignment (see §2.2). It builds on the underlying notion that alignment is a means of distinguishing the roles in transitive clauses, which it extends to specific tokens. Thus, it proposes disambiguation – the need to distinguish A and O in particular transitive clause tokens – as fundamental. Advocates of this explanation include, among many others, Comrie (1978); Cook (1988: 87); Dixon (1979: 73; 1994); Geytenbeek and Geytenbeek (1971: 13); Haiman (1979: 59); LaPolla (1992, 1995); Taylor (1970: 30); Walsh (1976); Williams (1980: 94); Evans (2003: 139). As Dixon (1979: 73) puts it (speaking of optional ergative marking of Agents generally), '[the ergative marker is] normally used only when the identity of the A NP cannot be inferred from any other grammatical or semantic information in the sentence'. Knowledge of the world is also frequently invoked in this account: for instance, the fact that animates are more likely to act on inanimates than the reverse.

I have observed in various places (e.g. McGregor 2010: 1618–1619) that this explanation is inadequate, and has not been convincingly argued for in any language. Evidence from various languages attests to the occurrence of optional ergative or accusative markers in circumstances in which there is no likelihood of any confusion as to the respective roles of NPs in a transitive clause, as shown by Yuwaalaraay (Pama-Nyungan, Australia) example (5.4).

(5.4)   *bulaarr-u rdayn-du   rdinggaa   rdaldarna*   Yuwaalaraay
           two-ERG   man-ERG   meat.ABS eat.PROG.PRS
           'Two men are eating meat.' (Williams 1980: 36)

Examples such as this show that the discriminatory function cannot account for all instances of the presence of optional case markers. The theory may have some explanatory value in accounting for absences of optional case marker. In languages with optional case marking of core roles the ergative or accusative marker are generally omitted only when there is no real possibility of confusion as to which NP fills which role. Occasional exceptions are, however, remarked on in the literature. For instance, in the case of Khwe (Khoe-Kwadi, Botswana) example (5.5) it would seem that there is a genuine possibility of confusion as to who is acting on who – the addressee standing up would seem to be equally a precondition for their taking the speaker and for the speaker taking them. Nonetheless, no instance of the accusative marker *(ʔ)à* is present.

(5.5)	*tàn*	*tî*	*tcá*	*tí*	*ú*	Khwe
	stand:up	then	2SG.M	1SG	bring	

'Stand up, then I may take you.' (Kilian-Hatz 2013: 373)

Lidz (2011: 54–59) provides a careful evaluation of the discriminative function as an explanation of the presence versus absence of the ergative marker in Yongning Na (Mosuo) (Tibeto-Burman, China). She shows that the presence of the ergative marker does not always resolve potential alternative interpretations, when abstracted from context. Furthermore, the ergative marker appears in contexts in which there is no real likelihood of confusion as to the respective roles of NPs.

Two explanations for the occurrence or not of optional case markers commonly invoked concern so-called 'semantic' factors such as agentivity, volitionality, control, power, patientitivity, and affectedness (e.g. Anderson and Wade 1988; Foley 2000: 374; Coupe 2007: 157), and 'pragmatic' factors such as focus and topic (e.g. Givón 1995; Lambrecht 1994; Aikhenvald 1994: 211–212; Quesada 1999; Saxena n.d.). In many languages both types of factor are relevant: optional ergative case markers sometimes invoke notions of volitionally, and sometimes appear in contrastive contexts. This is the case for instance in Gooniyandi and Warrwa (e.g. McGregor 1998, 2006a), among many other languages.

Rather than merely listing the range of polysemies of the use or non-use of the case markers, McGregor (2010, 2013c) proposes a semiotic theory that attempts to generalize on the above observations, and recast them into a unified framework. Fundamental to this theory are two notions.

First, a distinction must be drawn between meanings that are coded by a linguistic category or choice and meanings that are acquired from context or inferred via pragmatic implicatures.

Second, it is necessary to draw a distinction in optional case marking systems between the meanings of the grammatical roles that are marked by the case markers, the meanings of the case markers themselves as morphemes, and meanings associated with their uses and/or non-uses. Thus, there are three loci for coded meanings in optional case marking systems, and correspondingly three separate components of meaning to be distinguished. The grammatical roles are experiential ones, and express experiential meaning (see Chapter 2). As to the case markers, these code as morphemes abstract meanings that do not necessarily fall into a single semiotic type (§1.1.3). Finally, the meanings coded by their usage or non-usage is invariably interpersonal (McGregor 2010: 1622–1628; 2013c: 1156–1160).

Specifically, this interpersonal meaning concerns joint attention, the sharing of the attentional resources of interactants within a shared interactional frame, the joint-attentional frame (Tomasello and Farrar 1986; Tomasello 2003, 2014). The use and/or non-use of a case marker concerns the integration of information of a particular type into the joint-attentional frame: whether or not this information is accorded particular attention within the frame, or whether or not it is presumed present and thus assigned to the background. There is a non-arbitrary association of these meanings with usage phenomena, as shown in (5.6).

> (5.6) use   [±prominent]
>   non-use [±backgrounded]

According to this proposal, both use and non-use of a case marker may potentially code a meaning; this will be the meaning activated by the positive value of the feature, either making something prominent or assigning it to the background. Usage of a case marker serves to make some meaning prominent, assuming it codes any meaning. That is, it emphasizes some component of the expressed meaning (see §5.3 for indication of the range of meaning components that might be emphasized), drawing particular attention to it, thus placing it at the centre of attention – putting it in centre stage. A certain component of meaning is highlighted, and brought into relief against other phenomena in the joint-attentional frame.

By contrast, if non-use codes a meaning, this will be to background a component of meaning, placing it outside of the domain of that which is attended to. The meaning component is assigned to the periphery of the joint-attentional frame, to where it is not active, but remains readily activated. It thus becomes part of what is presumed by the speech interactants, who need not pay any special attention to it. Backgrounding is thus akin to greying a component of meaning or putting it into fine print. Effectively, this is information that can be ignored without affecting the message communicated, because it is assumed by the interactants. But it is still present and available for immediate attention should this be demanded.

Example (5.6) also allows that either use or non-use may select the minus value, in which case no specific meaning is expressed. Sometimes just one of the contrasting choices, use versus non-use, conveys a meaning, while the other choice is neutral or unmarked: attention is neither drawn to something, nor is that item of information assigned to the background. It is also possible that neither choice may code a meaning, both being neutral with respect to attentional resources. The fact that usage and/or non-usage does not code a meaning does not mean that the choice to use or not use the morpheme is completely meaningless, or randomly distributed. Instead of being coded, meanings may be derived by pragmatic inferencing (see §5.3.1.1 for some discussion).

A non-linguistic illustration may be useful at this point. A police car has a set of flashing blue lights and a siren, both of which may be optionally turned on or left off (the normal or unmarked state). When turned on, they draw attention to the vehicle, warning others to exercise caution as the vehicle is not bound by all of the rules of the road; there is a directive that other vehicles should move out of the way. This meaning is evidently interactional and imperative. The representational meaning 'engaged in police business' is highlighted, and other drivers are expected to adjust their driving accordingly. By contrast, the non-use of flashing lights and siren conveys no information, and no directive is communicated; attention is not drawn to the vehicle (beyond what is drawn to it by having the markings of a police vehicle). The representational meaning 'engaged in police business' is not activated, and other drivers are not expected to modify their driving by moving out of the way – and nor, of course, should they completely ignore the vehicle! In this system use of the optional feature codes a meaning, whereas its non-use codes no meaning, and is semantically neutral. However, even though non-use of the lights and siren do not code a meaning, other drivers might well imbue it with meaning, and (in certain circumstances) infer, for example, 'just cruising'.

Two qualifications are in order. First, [prominent] and [backgrounded] are not antonyms. Backgrounding involves more than just making something non-prominent: it also puts that item outside of the attentional domain, although it is still available for attention to be readily turned to it. Likewise, making something prominent involves more than not backgrounding it; the information is also brought into relief within the joint-attentional frame.

Second, [+prominent] corresponds to the notions of figure in the figure-ground dyad (e.g., Talmy 1978; Townsend and Bever 1977; Reid 1980), i.e. foregrounding (Hopper 1979), and trajector in the trajector-landmark dyad (Langacker 1987). The term 'prominent' adds something to these notions by invoking the interpersonal dimension of joint attention and the semiotic activity of assigning something to the centre of the joint-attentional frame. In a similar way, [+backgrounded] cannot be identified with the features ground and landmark in the above equipollent oppositions, and the two privative oppositions [±prominent] and [±backgrounded] cannot be replaced by a single equipollent opposition prominent-backgrounded.

Given the two privative features [±prominent] and [±backgrounded], there are four possibilities for the contrast between using and not using an optional case marker in any language, as shown in Table 5.1. The above discussed system of flashing lights and siren on police cars is of Type 2 in Table 5.1: their use tells other drivers something; their non-use tells them nothing.

Table 5.1 Feature values that may be associated with use and non-use of a case marker

	1	2	3	4
use	coded meaning +prominent	coded meaning +prominent	no coded meaning −prominent	no coded meaning −prominent
non-use	coded meaning +backgrounded	no coded meaning −backgrounded	coded meaning +backgrounded	no coded meaning −backgrounded

Optionality is an expression type satisfying the characteristics of an interpersonal grammatical phenomenon (see §1.1.3 and Table 1.1). The proposed associations between 'forms' (use and non-use) and meanings are evidently motivated, and do not show proto-typical Saussurean arbitrariness. The contrary scenario, in which non-use conveyed prominence, and use indicated backgrounding would be counterintuitive. It would be comparable to finding a society in which police sirens were turned on in order to make the vehicle inconspicuous, and switched off to draw attention to them!

This approach has some important descriptive and analytical implications. It is an empirical question for any language whether or not both usage and non-usage of a case marker code a meaning – or, put differently, whether or not an explanation needs to be sought for both its usage and its non-usage. This is contrary to the usual presumption that usage and non-usage express antonymic meanings or are motivated by contrasting factors (e.g. Dixon 1979, 1994; Coupe 2007: 157; Anderson and Wade 1988; Foley 2000: 374 and many others on optional case markers, and Bolinger 1972; Yaguchi 2001; Jaeger 2006, 2010 on the optional *that* complementizer in English).

Following from this is a methodological consideration. A consequence of the different types of paradigmatic opposition between use and non-use is that corresponding differ-ences are expected in the relative frequencies of usage and non-usage. If both use and non-use code a meaning, and are in equipollent opposition, it is to be expected that their token frequencies will be similar. If only one codes a meaning, then we expect to find that there will be a marked difference in token frequency associated with use and non-use, the marked meaning being associated with the less frequent choice. For the remain-ing scenario, where neither conveys semantic meaning, it is again expected that token frequencies of use and non-use would be about equal. Given these associations, we can turn things around to give us a strategy for making an initial hypothesis concerning the meanings of usage versus non-usage. If there is a marked token-frequency differential, it is reasonable to expect one member of the pair expresses a positive semantic mean-ing, the other being unmarked. If there is no marked differential in token frequency, we expect either that both are semantically meaningful or neither is; these situations are difficult to distinguish. Ultimately, the frequency correlations are at best indicative; one needs to explore the actual situation carefully to ensure that the expectations are indeed fulfilled.

5.2 Asymmetries in Case Systems and Case Marking

Optionality of case markers is a type of asymmetry in case marking; there are various other types of case marking asymmetry, as shown in Table 5.2 (an elaboration of the typology proposed in McGregor 2010: 1613). These are, I would argue, both formally and semiotically (emically) distinct. In what follows I situate optional case marking with respect to these other types of asymmetry.

Table 5.2 Typology of asymmetries in case marking

		Lexically or grammatically conditioned	Not lexically or grammatically conditioned; 'free' variation
Accidental identity of form		Syncretism	
Different case systems		Split Case Marking	
Different marking of the same grammatical relation	two different case markers	Differential Case Marking	Adversative Case Marking
	one case marker and nothing	Conditional Case Marking	Optional Case Marking

The second and third columns distinguish asymmetries that are lexically or grammatically conditioned from those that are not. In the former lexical or grammatical features predict the differences in case marking. Three main types are distinguished: syncretism, split case marking and different marking of the same grammatical relation.

Syncretism refers to circumstances in which two separate cases that are typically accorded different markings in a language are formally identical for certain lexical items, and these lexical items do not form a predictable set.[1] For instance, in Latin dative and ablative cases are syncretic in the o-declension, the membership of which is lexically conditioned; in other declensions they are distinct. Syncretic forms are always conditioned.

Split case marking refers to the situation in which nominals serving in the same grammatical relations in a language are marked according to different case systems depending on the lexical or grammatical environment. These were briefly discussed on pp. 19–20 above. Whereas in syncretism the same case marking system applies to all nominals, in split case marking systems there are distinct systems of case marking, such as ergative and accusative. In practice it is not always clear where the boundary between the two occurs, and differences of opinion may exist. Thus, Goddard (1982) proposes that what is normally treated as split case marking in Australian languages is really case syncretism. In my view, however, where the case marking system is predictable grammatically, it is preferable to analyse these as split case marking systems.

The final row of Table 5.2 turns from case marking systems to the case markers themselves and their distribution: whether or not the choice of case marker is lexically and/or grammatically predictable.[2] It should be noted that differential and Conditional Case Marking systems are effectively the same phenomena as Split Case Marking systems, viewed from different angles: either the case marking forms themselves in the first two cases, or the case marking systems in the third case. From the perspective of the forms there are two distinct possibilities, which are obscured when viewed from the system perspective.

The same contrasts are drawn in the final row of Table 5.2 for each of the two final columns: (a) a choice between two different case markers (Differential Case Marking and Adversative Case Marking) and (b) a choice between a case marker and nothing (Conditional Case Marking and Optional Case Marking). (a) and (b) show different semiotic potentials, as will be seen below.

In (a) two different case markers mark the same grammatical relation, either in specifiable circumstances or not. Both possibilities are illustrated by Kuku Yalanji (Pama-Nyungan, Australia) where there are two distinct ergative case markers comprising different sets of allomorphs (Patz 2002), as well as two parallel sets for dative, locative, and ablative cases. One allomorph set takes the shape *-(V)ngkV*; the other, *-(V)bu ~ -njV ~ -dV*, where V is determined by vowel harmony (Patz 2002: 47). Pronouns, human nouns, and the interrogative 'who' take only allomorphs from the former set; the interrogative 'what' and nominals denoting plants and tools take just the latter set of allomorphs. The allomorph sets represent two distinct ergative morphemes since nominals occupying intermediate positions on the animacy hierarchy take allomorphs from both sets. The choice is meaningful: an allomorph of the first set indicates that the Agent is potent (conceived of as acting under its own volition or energy-source), whereas allomorphs from the second set indicate neutral agents. For NPs in the intermediate positions on the animacy scale there is a system of Adversative Case Marking in which the choice of ergative morpheme conveys a meaning that is dependent on the added non-grammatical meaning of the ergative markers. For other NP types the system is one of Differential Case Marking.

In some languages a marker of a different grammatical relation is deployed instead of the standard marker of that relation. For instance, in Jaminjung the ablative case marker can be used instead of the ergative marker on an Agent NP. This marked choice assigns particular focus to the Agent (Schultze-Berndt 2000: 168). In Agul (North Caucasian, Southern Dagestan and Russia) and Lezgian (North Caucasian, Azerbaijan) ergative marking of the Agent alternates with adelative marking, the latter indicating an involuntary Agent (Malchukov and de Swart 2009: 352–353; Haspelmath 1993).

In (b) the presence or absence of a given case marker is either conditioned or not (in which case (5.1) is satisfied, giving an Optional Case Marking system). In Israeli

(Modern Hebrew) definite Undergoer NPs are marked by the accusative (*et*), but other Undergoers are unmarked. The distribution of this preposition is conditioned by grammatical characteristics of the NP: pronouns, personal names, and definite nouns marked by the definite prefix *ha-* take the accusative marker; other nouns do not (Zuckermann 2006, Ghil'ad Zuckermann pers. comm.). Israeli thus shows a system of Conditional Case Marking.

To wind up this discussion, it should be noted that where the choice is conditioned by lexical or grammatical features and is thus predictable – i.e. the middle column of Table 5.2 – speakers do not have any real choice. Whatever option they select is imposed by the circumstances. Usage of a marker cannot convey any meaning in contrast with non-usage or usage of something else. The form and its usage do not represent separate loci for meaning contrasts, as in Optional Case Marking systems (§5.1.2). It is only in systems where the choices are not conditioned by external considerations – the third column of Table 5.2 – that speakers are confronted with a genuine and meaningful choice. In §5.1.2 it was proposed that in Optional Case Marking systems the meaning contrast between the two options concerns the domain of the interpersonal semiotic, specifically joint attention. On the other hand, the semantic differences between the contrasting forms in Adversative Case Marking systems need not necessarily concern joint attention, but may relate to differences in the semantics of the case markers.

5.3 Optional Case Marking of Core Roles in a Typological Perspective

Our concern in this chapter is with optional case marking of NPs serving in core grammatical roles in situation clauses. Our primary focus is on optional ergative and accusative marking of Agent and Undergoer NPs; these are dealt with in the following two subsections, respectively.

Other grammatical roles may also be optionally case marked. A few marked nominative languages (§1.2.2.3) – for example, Saisiyat (Austronesian, Taiwan – Hsieh and Huang 2006), Tubu (Nilo-Saharan, Chad – König 2008a: 40) and Gimira (Afro-Asiatic, Ethiopia – Breeze 1990: 30, cited in Iggesen 2004: 610–611) – permit optional nominative case marking of Actor NPs. Other unusual types include (though some of these are contentious): optional ergative marking of Undergoers (e.g. Fore (Papuan, Papua New Guinea) – Scott 1986: 171), optional accusative marking of Actors of some intransitive clause types (e.g. Amharic (Afro-Asiatic, Ethiopia) – Amberber 2000: 325; 2009: 750, 753–754 and Khwe – Kilian-Hatz 2008: 56), and, in some active languages, optional agentive marking of Agent NPs in transitive and active intransitive clauses (as in Tlingit (Na-Dene, Alaska) – Naish 1979: 29, 68, cited in Iggesen 2004: 621). Optional absolutive marking of Medium NPs is very poorly attested, and the only clear instance I am aware of occurs in Kabardian (Circassian, North Caucasus), where it seems to be restricted to proper nouns (Kumakhov, Vamling and Kumakhova 1996). This is doubtless a consequence of the rarity of ergative systems in which the absolutive is marked.

5.3.1 Optional Ergative Case Marking

Optional ergative case marking of Agent NPs is not a marginal phenomenon in ergative languages. Over one hundred languages show optional ergative marking, amounting to an estimated 10% of ergative languages (McGregor 2010: 1616); McGregor (2010: 1629–1632) provides a partial listing. Optional ergative languages cluster in two geographical regions, Australia–Papua New Guinea and northern India–Nepal–Tibet–western China, areas that are hotspots for ergative case marking (McGregor 2010: 1616). Many languages from the Pama-Nyungan family, non-Pama-Nyungan families and Papuan families in the former region, and both Tibeto-Burman and Indo-Aryan languages in the latter region show optional ergative case marking. Indeed, according to LaPolla (1995), ergative marking in Tibeto-Burman is prototypically optional.

5.3.1.1 Distribution of optional ergative case marking according to grammatical environment

In some languages optional ergative case marking seems to be entirely general, across all grammatical environments: that is, the Agent role is optionally marked by the ergative marker irrespective of the environment, including such features as animacy of the filler of the role, tense, aspect and mood, and other features that are known to affect case marking. This is the case for Gooniyandi and Warrwa. However, this does not mean that these features are irrelevant to the presence of the ergative case marker. In both languages, for instance, inanimate Agents are almost always marked by the ergative, while animate Agents are less frequently ergatively marked.

Somewhat more frequently, optional ergative case marking is restricted to certain grammatical environments, and the marker is either obligatory or precluded elsewhere. Thus, ergative case marking has been reported to be obligatory for inanimate Agents, and optional for animate Agents in various languages, including, for example, Umpithamu (Verstraete 2010) and Tujia (Tibeto-Burman, China) (Lu et al. 2019). In a number of languages optional ergative case marking is distributed according to Silverstein's hierarchy, as shown in Figure 5.1. Obligatory ergative case marking begins (if it exists) at the

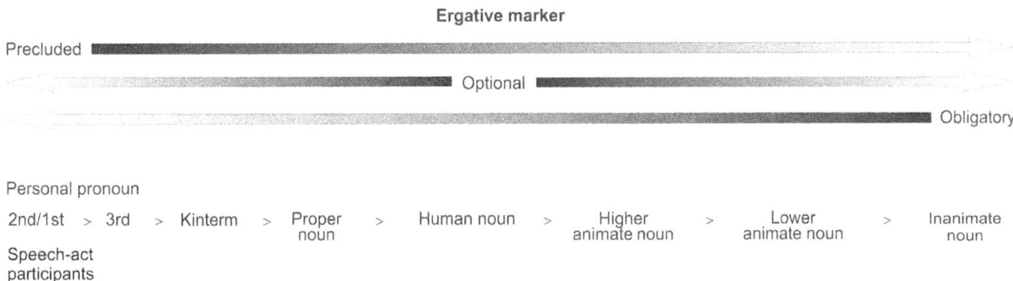

Figure 5.1 Distribution of optional ergative case marking according to Silverstein's hierarchy (building on McGregor 2010: 1617)

far right of the hierarchy, extending leftwards; if ergative marking is precluded any-where, it is at the far left, extending rightwards. Optional ergative marking (if it exists in a language) tends to be found in the intermediate domains, thence in a region extending leftwards and/or rightwards. Silverstein's hierarchy also accounts for frequency of use of an optional ergative marker: within the region in which optionality is possible, token frequency of usage tends to increase in the rightward direction.[3]

Other factors that are known to be relevant to the distribution of ergative case marking in split systems are also relevant to the distribution of optional ergative case marking in some languages. Tense, mood and aspect are sometimes relevant. In Nepali (Indo-European, Nepal), for instance, the ergative is optional on animate Agent NPs in imperfective aspect, though it is obligatory in perfectives (Li 2007: 1465–1466); in Tibetan (Tibeto-Burman, Tibet) the ergative is obligatory on Agent NPs in the perfec-tive, but optional in the imperfective (DeLancey 1985, 2006; Tournadre 1995: 265). In Tujia the ergative is optional in both perfectives and imperfectives; however, its usage is more frequent in perfectives than imperfectives (Lu et al. 2019: 51).

In some languages optional ergative marking is restricted to certain grammatical constructions. In Tsez (North-east Caucasian, Dagestan) it is restricted to a certain periphrastic construction; elsewhere ergative case marking of Agent NPs is obliga-tory (Comrie 2000). In Enga (Papuan, Papua New Guinea) optional marking of Agent NPs seems to be possible only in clauses of thought and speech that frame complement clauses (Li and Lang 1979: 320–321).

Optional ergative marking is sometimes lexically and/or semantically distributed. In Newari (Tibeto-Burman, Nepal) the Agent of a highly transitive verb such as 'kill' is obligatorily marked in the ergative in the inchoative construction ('begin to'). However, ergative marking of the Agent of a less transitive verb such as 'eat' is optional in this construction (Givón 1985: 98).

5.3.1.2 *A typology of optional ergative case marking of Agent NPs*

Table 5.1 distinguishes four possibilities for coding of meanings by the use and/or non-use of the ergative case marker on Agent NPs. Each of these possibilities is attested, thus providing a broad typology of optional ergative case marking systems. Before dis-cussing this typology, it is important to say something about the two attentional features, prominent and backgrounded, in relation to optional ergative case marking. There are two primary considerations relevant to according prominence to, or backgrounding an NP in the role of Agent:

a. Referential status concerns the identity of the entity filling the Agent
    role, and whether or not that entity is expected in that grammatical
    role. Expectedness can relate to broad discourse level considerations, or
    to more local ones. An example of a discourse level consideration is the
    Expected Actor Principle, according to which in narrative episodes the

protagonist is – once it is established – the expected Actor of all situation clauses (McGregor 1998, 2006a), including in all transitive clauses, where it is simultaneously the Agent. At the local level are phenomena such as (contrastive) focus, where one referent is brought into relief against other possible contenders for the role, and accorded special attention.

b. The degree of agentivity or potency of the Agent entity may be remarkable, and worthy of special attention (highlighting) or not (backgrounding). Agentivity or potency can concern internal considerations such as the degree of intentionality, deliberateness and control of the Agent, and degree of activity of the event (how much energy or intelligence is required to effect it). They can alternatively invoke external considerations such as the degree of impact of the Agent on the Undergoer – i.e. the affectedness of the Undergoer.

Languages differ in regard to the features that are relevant to the assignment of prominence or backgrounding to Agents via use versus non-use of ergative markers. A considerable number of languages admit both types of features. This is the case, for instance, in languages such as Gooniyandi (McGregor 1989a, 1992a, 1998), Warrwa (McGregor 2006a), Dalabon (Gunwinjguan, Australia) (Luk and Ponsonnet 2019) and Tujia (Lu et al. 2019): use and/or non-use of the ergative marker is sometimes motivated by referential considerations, sometimes by considerations of agentivity – and sometimes both.

For instance, consider examples (5.7) and (5.8) from Gooniyandi, a language of Type 3 (Table 5.1), in which non-use of the ergative marker codes meaning, but use does not. In both of these examples the Agent NP of a transitive clause is unmarked by the ergative postposition. Example (5.7) comes from a narrative describing a man going hunting; by this point in the story he is the established protagonist and hence the expected Actor of the clause; accordingly, his identity is backgrounded, even though he is surely a potent Agent, having just successfully speared a kangaroo. Example (5.8) is very unusual in that it is the only example in my entire narrative corpus in which an inanimate Agent NP is not marked by the ergative. Because of its inanimacy and because the rain is not the episode protagonist, it is highly unexpected as Agent, and thus one would not expect it to be backgrounded by non-use of the ergative. However, the reason for backgrounding it is apparent in the narrative itself, where we are told in the next sentence that there was only a sprinkling of rain, which had no effect on following the person's tracks. This inanimate Agent is of minimal potency.

<pre>
(5.7)   niyi   laandi nyag-bini /   Gooniyandi
        3SG.CRD   up   pierce-3SG.ACC/3SG.NOM/BINI
        'He speared it up there.'
</pre>

(5.8) *thinga gilba-yidi-yi /*   *gamba /*   Gooniyandi
       foot   find-1EXC.NOM/3SG.ACC/DI-DU water

       yilij-jina   *garr*   *garrwaroo /*
       rain-1EXC.ACC/3SG.NOM/A after... afternoon

       'We found his tracks, but it rained on us that afternoon.'

In Tujia and Dalabon (probably Type 1 languages) it seems that the ergative marker is employed both to draw particular attention to the agency of an Agent and to foreground it in its discourse context, when it is unexpected as an Agent (Lu et al. 2019; Luk and Ponsonnet 2019).

In some languages, however, it seems that only referential considerations or only considerations of potency are relevant to the occurrence or not of an optional ergative marker. A number of investigators have suggested that use of an optional ergative case marker in a certain language assigns particular focus to the Agent referent, bringing its identity into relief. For example, in Tariana (Maipurean, Brazil) the ergative case marker is rarely used, but when it is employed it accords particular focus or prominence to the Agent (Aikhenvald 1994: 211–212). Example (5.9) describes the sudden appearance of an evil spirit that changes the course of events.

(5.9) *diha ñamu-ne*   *ikułi di-aphua-ka*   Tariana
       he   evil.spirit-ERG crab   3SG.NF-immerse.after-DECL

       ne-hyu-kade-pidana
       NEG-appear-NEG-PART

       'The evil spirit immersed after a crab and didn't reappear.' (Aikhenvald 1994: 211–212)

Similarly, in Bribri and Cabécar (both Chibchan, Costa Rica) presence of the ergative marker highlights importance and relative salience of the Agent, while its absence is associated with topic continuity (Quesada 1999), and thus with backgrounding. The situation in some Papuan languages seems comparable. In Dani use of the ergative case marker is associated with focus or counter-expectation, as shown by (5.10), which describes the unusual situation of a python eating a man (Bromley 1981; Foley 2000: 375). Usually men eat pythons, and thus the ergative marker is not used in (5.11).

(5.10) *ap   palu-nen   na-sikh-e*   Dani
        man   python-ERG   eat-RP-3SG.NOM

        'The python ate the man.'

(5.11) *ap   palu   na-sikh-e*   Dani
        man   python   eat-RP-3SG.NOM

        'The man ate the python.'

By contrast, according to Anderson and Wade (1988); Foley (2000: 374), in Folopa (Papuan, Papua New Guinea) control is the primary factor in the decision to use or not use the ergative case marker: ergative marking of an Agent NP foregrounds wilful agentivity while omission of marker downplays individual will. Similarly, Coupe (2007: 156–160) argues that in Mongsen Ao (Tibeto-Burman, Nagaland) wilfulness, volitionality, and self-motivation of the Agent condition ergative marking of Agent NPs, while Agents acting in accordance with social expectations will not be marked by the ergative. For example, (5.12) describes a neutral situation in which the chickens are eating paddy they have been fed, whereas (5.13) invokes the nuance that they are wilfully stealing it.

(5.12) *a-hən*   *a-ʧak*   *ʧaʔ-ə̀ɹ-ù?*   Mongsen Ao
NRL-chicken   NRL-paddy   consume-PRS-DECL
'The chickens are eating paddy.' (Coupe 2007: 157)

(5.13) *a-hən*   *nə*   *a-ʧak*   *ʧaʔ-ə̀ɹ-ù?*   Mongsen Ao
NRL-chicken   ERG   NRL-paddy   consume-PRS-DECL
'The chickens are eating paddy.' (Coupe 2007: 157)

The theory of optional case marking outlined in §5.1.2 thus provides a general account of the phenomenon that permits explanation of the situations in specific languages through differences in what speakers choose to make prominent or background (referent status or agentivity), and the motivations for doing so (what motivates the expectations, e.g. whether the global or the local domain in a narrative). Considerations of joint attention provide a general account, beyond the specifics of particular languages. This gives a window on the cross-linguistic variation in optional ergative case marking.

Let us now look at examples of each of the four types of optional case marking system identified in Table 5.1.

The first type is exemplified by Mongsen Ao, where both usage and non-usage of the ergative on an Agent NP are reported to be meaningful (Coupe 2007: 157; 2011). The situation in Tujia (Lu et al. 2019) is apparently the same. Consistent with this, usage and non-usage are approximately equally frequent in discourse in these languages.

Examples of languages with the second type of system – in which use of the ergative makes the Agent prominent, and non-use codes no meaning – include Umpithamu (Verstraete 2010), Kâte (Papuan, Papua New Guinea) (Suter 2010; Edgar Suter pers. comm.), and Dalabon (Luk and Ponsonnet 2019). In Central Tibetan, in the imperfective aspect use of the ergative marker seems to be associated with contrastive focus (Tournadre 1991, 1995, 1996). In these languages usage of the ergative is infrequent compared with its non-use, which is the norm, and marks no particular meaning. In Dalabon, for instance, less than a third of Agent NPs in transitive clauses are marked by the ergative (Luk and Ponsonnet 2019). Relative frequency does not always correlate with semantic markedness, however. In Umpithamu just under two thirds of Agent NPs in transitive clauses are marked by the ergative, though use of the marker conveys a contrastive meaning, non-use no meaning (Verstraete 2010).

Languages of the third type, in which use of the ergative conveys no meaning and non-use does, include Warrwa (McGregor 2006a, 2010) and Gooniyandi (McGregor 2010). In these languages non-use of the ergative postposition is rare, with less than 20% of Agent NPs in transitive clauses being unmarked by this morpheme. In Central Tibetan ergative marking of Agent NPs is almost obligatory in the perfective aspect, and presumably carries no meaning; non-use appears to be restricted to conditions of high topicalization of the Agent (Tournadre 1995: 265), and thus may be associated with its backgrounding.

The fourth type of situation shown in Table 5.1 is one in which no meaning is coded by either the usage or the non-usage of the ergative marker in a language. This does not mean that usage and non-usage are in completely free variation, and are used randomly by speakers. Rather, it means that specific meanings are not invariably or inherently associated with usage or non-usage. Samoan (Austronesian, Samoa) possibly illustrates such a system. According to Ochs (1982, 1988: 86–104), ergative marking is a sociolinguistic variable: frequency patterns in its usage correlate with and index sociolinguistic factors including age, gender, and social distance between interlocutors (Ochs 1988: 88). The frequency of use of the ergative marker in environments in which it is optional (i.e. on post-verbal Agents) ranges from lows of 17% (for men) and 20% (for women) in intimate settings with family members to highs of 75% (men) and 46% (women) in formal speech with non-family (Ochs 1988: 93). From Ochs' descriptions it seems to be just the overall patterns of usage or non-usage that are meaningful; particular instances of use or non-use would seem to convey no specific meanings.

Another possibility for a situation of the fourth type is that usage and non-usage are pragmatically conditioned. Neither codes a specific meaning, but some meaning may be implicated by Gricean maxims, relevance theory or Levinsonian heuristics (Levinson 2000). For instance, non-use of the ergative marker might, by application of the Q-principle (the maxim of quantity) – what is saliently not said is not so (Levinson 2000) – implicate that the fuller statement, which includes the ergative marker, is denied. Omission of the ergative marker might thus implicate 'not an Agent'. However, the referent clearly is an Agent, by virtue of its grammatical representation. It cannot be the fact that the NP fills that particular grammatical role that is denied; what might be plausibly denied is that it is an agent in the lexical sense of the word. Thus, it could be inferred that the Agent is weak in agentivity. It is difficult to see, however, how the referential senses associated with non-use of the ergative marker might be explained by pragmatic implicatures in languages like Gooniyandi and Warrwa.

Alternatively, by invoking the M-principle (corresponding to Grice's first and fourth maxims of manner) – roughly, 'what is said in an abnormal way, isn't normal; or marked message indicates marked situation' (Levinson 2000) – use of a formal marker might implicate that the situation is non-normal or non-stereotypical. One possibility is that a high degree of agentivity is implicated. Another is that the situation is marked in regard to the identity of the Agent – it is not an expected one. Referential senses associated with use of the ergative are thus amenable to explanation in the pragmatic approach.

These situations in which meanings are pragmatically associated with use and/or non-use of an optional ergative marker are difficult to distinguish from the situation in which their meanings are coded. The main cue is defeasibility. If the meanings are implicated, then they should be defeasible, though they should not be if they are coded. I have argued (McGregor 2005, 2006a) that the pragmatic account is inconsistent with the non-defeasibility of the meaning associated with non-use of the ergative marker in Gooniyandi and Warrwa.

To wind up this discussion I draw attention to two significant points. First, the typology of Table 5.1 applies to systems of optional ergative case marking. It does not typologize languages: a given language may have more than one system of optional ergative case marking, which may be of different types, as we saw above for Central Tibetan.

Second, the four types of system distinguished in Table 5.1 correspond to oppositions of very different natures. Type 1 systems involve an equipollent opposition between prominence and backgrounding. In Types 2 and 3 one feature is marked and takes a positive value, while the other is unmarked and conveys no meaning. The values of [+prominent] and [+backgrounded] in Type 2 and 3 systems differ from those of [prominent] and [backgrounded] in Type 1 systems. Presumably the positive valued features will contrast more sharply with no meanings than will the equipollent ones with one another. And indeed there seems to be some evidence that this is so. Thus, [+prominent] in Umpithamu appears to convey a more contrastive sense than does [prominent] in Mongsen Ao. Finally, Type 4 contrasts two unmarked choices, and effectively means no choice in the semantic sense. We return to these observations in §5.4.

5.3.1.3 *Optional ergative case marking of Actors in intransitive clauses*

In a fair number of ergative languages the ergative case marker admits occasional presence on Actor NPs in intransitive clauses; see McGregor (2007c: 219) for a partial listing (the past decade has seen a number of additions). This usage of the ergative marker is always quite rare and infrequent, since otherwise the morpheme would be a nominative marker. In Gooniyandi and Warrwa the ergative marker occurs on fewer than 5% of (overt) Actor NPs in intransitive clauses (McGregor 1998: 502; 2007c: 206). Luk and Ponsonnet (2019: 307) report for Dalabon just 24 tokens of the ergative marker on Actor NPs in some thousands of intransitive clauses in their corpus.

Only Type 2 and 4 systems are possible: usage of an optional ergative marking of Actor NPs in intransitive clauses must mark [+prominent] while its non-usage conveys no meaning, or, if not, neither use nor non-use may code a meaning. The other two possibilities, types 1 and 3, are inconsistent with the status of the morpheme as an ergative marker. In what follows I overview a small selection of type 2 systems; further examples and discussion can be found in McGregor (2007c: 219–222). Whether Type 4 systems exist is uncertain: they are difficult to distinguish from Type 2 systems. If they do exist, use of the ergative in an intransitive clause would represent a marked fuller expression than its non-use, and thus that the referent situation – and thus presumably that the Actor – is non-normal or non-stereotypical.

McGregor (2007c) argues that in Warrwa intransitive clauses the system is Type 2, and that the feature [+prominent] involves both agentivity and referential unexpectedness of the Actor.[4] In some languages it seems that agentivity of the Actor is the primary consideration. For instance, it has been reported that in Hindi-Urdu (Indo-European, India-Pakistan) ergative marking of Actor NPs indicates prominent or strong agentivity or deliberateness (Enfield, Kelly and Sprenger 2004: 101). Similarly, in Mongsen Ao, the Actor's control and deliberateness in performing the event is the most salient consideration according to Coupe (2007). Thus, (5.14) contrasts with (5.15) and (5.16) in terms of deliberateness. The inclusion of the converb *asáʔ* 'be deliberate' guarantees the use of the ergative marker, as in example (5.15); in its absence the ergative marker can still be used, as in (5.16).

(5.14) *nì   akhət*
      1SG   cough.PST
      'I coughed.' (Coupe 2007: 160)

Mongsen Ao

(5.15) *nì   nə   asáʔ-əkə   akhət*
      1SG   ERG   be.deliberate-SIM   cough.PST
      'I deliberately coughed.' (Coupe 2007: 161)

Mongsen Ao

(5.16) *nì   nə   akhət*
      1SG   ERG   cough.PST
      'I coughed.' (i.e. on purpose, to get your attention) (Coupe 2007: 161)

Mongsen Ao

Optional ergative marking of intransitive Actors in Mongsen Ao is not across the board. Rather, it is restricted to particular types of intransitive clauses: to clauses of speech, clauses of motion, and intransitive clauses denoting activities like coughing that are typically uncontrolled but admit deliberate control by a human.

Referential unexpectedness seems to be the crucial feature in some languages. Suter (2010) reports that the use of the ergative enclitic on Actor NPs in Kâte is contrastive, as illustrated by example (5.17); it conveys nothing about the potency of the referent as an agent. It seems that the prominence accorded by the ergative marker on an Actor in Kâte is somewhat stronger than in Warrwa, where contrastiveness is not indexed.

(5.17) *â   australia-zi   mâreŋ juwickec   irec   woraŋ fuŋ-ko   Kâte*
      and   Australians-ERG   land   down.there from.there mango base-LOC
      kec   irec   hâmo-mbiŋ.   ŋic-zi   amerika   â   australia
      lo!   from.there die-RP.3.PL   man-ERG   Americans and Australians

hâmo-mbiŋ.
die-RP.3.PL
'The Australians died over there where you can see the mango tree. American and Australian men died.'

A further indication of the focal value of the Kâte ergative marker is the rare use of the marker on Undergoer NPs in transitive clause (Suter 2010). This is not attested in many other ergative languages.

Finally, I draw attention to a common phenomenon in optional ergative marking of Actor NPs: the prospective use of the marker, presaging subsequent agentivity of the Actor – the present Actor will be an Agent in a closely following transitive clause. This usage is found in a number of Australian languages, including Warrwa (as in (5.18)), Gooniyandi, Dalabon, Ngaanyatjara, and Guugu Yimithirr (Pama-Nyungan), as well as the Papuan languages Kâte and Siane.

(5.18) *yiri-nma   inyja   ø-ngi-rnda-n   baawa yaarr*   Warrwa
woman-fERG walkabout 3MIN.NOM-NFUT-go-PRS child pull
ø-na-ng-ka-n-ø
3MIN.NOM-CM-EN-carry-PRS-3MIN.ACC
'The woman is going along dragging the child.'

5.3.2 Optional Accusative Case Marking

Like optional ergative case marking, optional accusative case marking of Undergoer NPs is not a grammatical oddity. It is attested, for instance, in some grammatical environments in a range of languages from many different families spread around the world, including all continents. The following is a small selection of likely candidates:[5]

Africa   Afro-Asiatic: Gurage, Dullay, Kefa (König 2008a: 227) and Gimira (König 2008a: 228); Khoe-Kwadi: Khwe (Kilian-Hatz 2008: 63), Shua (McGregor 2018a), Ts'ixa (Fehn 2014), Tyiretyire (McGregor 2018a), !Ora (Haacke 2013: 341); Nilo-Saharan: Tubu (König 2008a: 39–40)

Americas Muskogean: Koasati (Kimball 1991: 333–336); Uto-Aztecan: Cupeño (Hill 2005); Arawakan: Tariana (Aikhenvald 1994); Puinavean: Dâw (Martins and Martins 1999)

Australia Pama-Nyungan: Mpakwithi Anguthimri (Crowley 1981: 163–164), Dharumbal (Terrill 2002: 31–32), Duungidjawu (Wurm 1976; Kite and Wurm 2004: 26–27), Dyirbal (Dixon 1983: 457), Nhanda (Blevins 2001: 49–50), Nyawaygi (Dixon 1983: 457), Southern Paakantyi (Hercus 1982: 58–59), Uradhi (Crowley 1983: 308, 336, 353), Warrgamay (Dixon 1981: 32), Western Arrernte (Wilkins 1989: 12), Yidiny (Dixon 1977: 150–151)

Eurasia   Austroasiatic: Korku (Kittilä and Malchukov 2009: 551); Indo-European: Hindi-Urdu (Mohanan 1994: 87–88), Romanian (Mardale 2010: 5); Tibeto-Burman: Manipuri (Bhat and Ningomba 1997: 140); and the possible isolates Japanese (Fujii and Ono 2000; Minashima 2001; Fry 2003) and Korean (Lee 2007: 1466–1468).

Optional accusative marking shares general features in common with optional ergative marking, including patterns of distribution within the grammar and meanings. Differences lie primarily in the details, as will be seen in the ensuing discussion, which begins with grammatical distribution then addresses semantics.

5.3.2.1 *Grammatical distribution of optional accusative case marking*

Optional accusative marking is not usually across the board, but rather restricted to certain grammatical environments. In some languages it is dependent on the nature of the Undergoer NP, and distributed according to Silverstein's hierarchy. This appears to be the case in Shua, as shown in Figure 5.2.

As shown, accusative marking is either obligatory or almost so at the upper end of the hierarchy. It is obligatory for all pronouns – except for the third person singular common gender pronoun (which typically refers to inanimates) – and for personal names as well as NPs that include a person-gender-marker. (PGN markers in Shua effectively mark just human NPs or personify lower order animates.) At the opposite end of the hierarchy the accusative marker is effectively precluded from NPs that specify masses or non-individuated entities.

Optional accusative case marking is found between these two extremes, on NPs specifying human referents, animates and inanimates that are individuated and are not masses. The frequency of use of the marker on these NPs is overall lowish, and decreases with decreasing animacy. At the same time, speakers become less willing to accept use of the accusative marker as animacy decreases.

The situation in related languages appears to be somewhat different, at least these few languages where optional accusative marking has been discussed in sufficient depth.

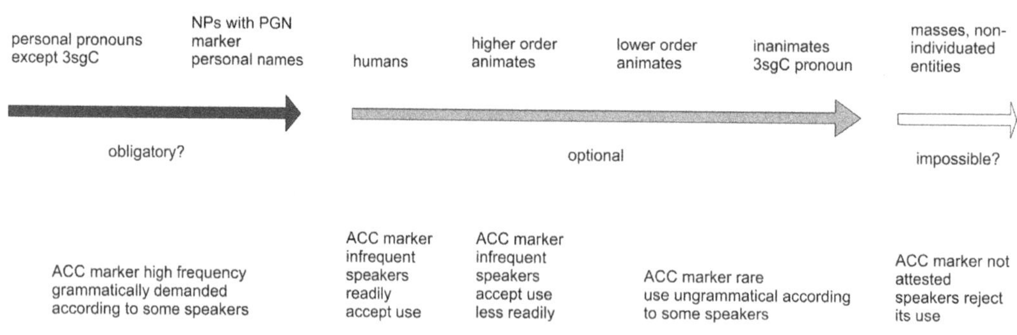

Figure 5.2 Distribution of accusative marking in Shua according to NP type

In Ts'ixa it seems that definiteness and word order constrain optional accusative case marking. According to Fehn (2014: 231) for definite NPs accusative marking is obligatory in the two most frequent word orders, Agent-Undergoer-Event and Agent-Event-Undergoer, and is optional in the marked case of Undergoer-Agent-Event. For indefinite NPs by contrast accusative marking is precluded in Agent-Event-Undergoer order, optional in Agent-Undergoer-Event and Undergoer-Agent-Event orders.

The situation for Khwe is not entirely clear from the descriptions of Kilian-Hatz (2008, 2013). However, it seems that definiteness is a major consideration, and that accusative marking of Undergoer NPs is obligatory for personal names and almost obligatory for other definite lexical NPs. Contrary to Silverstein's hierarchy, it is optional for pronouns and for indefinite NPs.

5.3.2.2 *Semantics of optional accusative case marking*

The theory of optionality outlined in §5.1.2 accounts for optional accusative case marking (McGregor 2010: 1626–1627; 2013c: 1174–1175). Usage of an accusative case marker may be associated with prominence, its non-usage with backgrounding as per Table 5.1, though conclusive examples of all four types are not available.

Furthermore, it seems that appropriately modified versions of the two considerations identified in §5.3.1.2 are relevant to decisions to make an Undergoer prominent or to background it. These are (a) the identity of the Undergoer referent, whether or not it is expected as filler of that role, and (b) its degree of affectedness or patientivity.

Japanese appears to exemplify a Type 2 language, where usage of the accusative marker assigns prominence to the Undergoer, while non-usage is the unmarked and most frequent option (Fujii and Ono 2000; Fry 2003: 99) and conveys no inherent meaning. Thus, Kurumada and Jaeger (2012) argue that use of the accusative marker correlates with the unexpectedness of the Undergoer; Fry (2003) makes a similar observation that use of the accusative marker is associated with discourse-salient Undergoers, and Undergoers whose identification requires additional cognitive processing. Korean appears to be similar (Lee 2007: 1466–1468).

Cupeño may show a Type 2 system for inanimate Undergoers (which are usually not marked by the accusative) and a Type 3 system for animate Undergoers (where presence of the accusative is the norm). According to Hill (2005) inanimate Undergoers tend to be marked by the accusative in positions of high narrative tension; for animate Undergoers things are not clear from the description in Hill (2005).

Type 2 systems can also be found in Khoe languages. It seems that in Ts'ixa presence of the accusative postposition in circumstances in which it is optional assigns focus to the Undergoer (Fehn 2014: 230; McGregor 2018a: 259–260). For instance, the presence of the accusative marker on the Undergoer NP in (5.19) assigns selective focus to it. By contrast, the accusative marker is not employed in (5.20), and the lion is neither foregrounded nor backgrounded.

(5.19) xaḿ=mà   ʔà   ʔé.ǁù   ǀ'ũ̋-á-tá   Ts'ixa
       lion=3SG.M.II ACC 3PL.M kill-J-SDPST
       'They killed the lion (and not something else).' (Fehn 2014: 229)

(5.20) xaḿ=mà   ʔé.ǁù   ǀ'ũ̋-á-tá   Ts'ixa
       lion=3SG.M.II 3PL.M kill-J-SDPST
       'They killed the lion.' (Fehn 2014: 229)

Likewise, in Shua in the mid region of Figure 5.2 where the accusative marker is optional and infrequent its use assigns prominence to the Undergoer. In contrast with Ts'ixa however, as well as referential considerations, considerations of the degree of patientivity of the Undergoer are also germane. Example (5.21) illustrates the first type of consideration. This example comes from a description of a drawing in the wordless picture book *A boy, a dog, and a frog* (Mayer 1967) which depicts the boy netting his dog in a fishing net. The preceding drawings construct a story in which it is expected that the boy will net the frog; the identity of the object referent is thus unexpected.

(5.21) aba: ʔa   ema   ǁam-rekareka   Shua
       dog   ACC 3SG.M hit-maybe
       'Maybe he is hitting the dog.'

Occasionally the accusative marker is associated with contrastive focus on the filler of the Undergoer role, as in (5.22). However, speakers are less happy with such contrastive examples for Undergoers at the lower end of the animacy hierarchy than for human referents.

(5.22) ta: aka ke   lori ʔa   mũ: ta: aka sekuskara   ʔa   Shua
       1SG PST IMP truck ACC see 1SG PST donkey.cart ACC
       mũ:-ta
       see-NEG
       'I saw the truck, not the donkey cart.'

Example (5.23) shows use of the accusative on an Undergoer that is particularly patientive: the tent has been completely destroyed. Here the Undergoer is affected to a higher degree than might be expected – it is not just knocked down, but completely wrecked. (Considerations of Undergoer identity are irrelevant here.)

(5.23) hẽ:xo: ʔa   tu:-a-ta   tu: ka:ro ka   tante ʔa   Shua
       this   LOC rain-J-PST rain hail   INS tent   ACC
       bo:ru-hu-a-ha
       hole-CAUS-J-PST
       'The rain that rained here with hail tore the tent to shreds.'

Type 3 systems are also attested in Khoe languages. I have argued (McGregor 2018a: 262–263) that such a system is found in Khwe on specific Undergoers, on which NPs the accusative marker is almost always present, and thus unlikely to convey a meaning. Only non-use of the marker conveys a meaning: it backgrounds the Undergoer. In examples such as (5.24), then, the absence of the *(ʔ)à* on the Undergoer NP of the second clause backgrounds it: the genet is the primary discourse topic, and thus may be presumed as part of the common ground at that point in the interaction.

(5.24) *tínù   córò-mà-à*   ‖*gàa-khòè-djì*   *n|góá-à-tè*   Khwe
then   rock:monitor-3SG.M-ACC   female-person-3PL.F   cook-J-PRS
kx'á-khòè-‖è   *tcámba-mà*   *n|góá-à-tè*
male-person-1PL.M   genet-3SG.M   cook-J-PRS
'Then the women are cooking the rock monitor, and we men are cooking the genet.'
(Kilian-Hatz 2008: 62)

I suspect the situation for PGN marked NPs in Shua is similar: for such NPs accusative marking is the norm, its absence rare. However, this hypothesis remains to be substantiated. Indeed, the theory of optional marking is in need of extensive and intensive testing for the accusative case.

5.4 Optionality in a Wider Grammatical Context

The approach to optional case marking advocated in this chapter differs from other approaches in linguistic typology and theory. In particular, it presumes that optional case marking is never entirely random and meaningless: usage and non-usage of case markers are never in complete free variation. It further presumes a difference between semantic and pragmatic meaning according to whether or not the meaning is coded or inferred by pragmatic implicatures or heuristics. Hence not just morphemes but also their usage/non-usage may be the loci of coded meaning. Separating these two loci and the meanings that are associated with each is an essential first step in an investigation of optional case marking.

The theory of optional case marking outlined in §5.1.2 is an instance of a more general theory of optional marking of grammatical relations and categories. This theory proposes that a coding association may exist between abstract (non-morphological, non-segmental) 'forms' – specifically usage and/or non-usage – and meanings relating to the domain of joint expectations as per (5.6). If such codings exist, they are motivated: use invokes greater attention, non-use lesser attention. Optional grammatical marking thus always codes meaning of the interpersonal type, assuming it codes any meaning. The locus of coding of the interpersonal meaning is in the system of optionality; it is not the optional grammatical morphemes themselves that code this type of interpersonal meaning.

The theory permits a quaternary typology of optional marking systems in terms of the possible coded meanings associated with usage and non-usage of a grammatical marker. McGregor (2013c) tests the theory in other domains, including the optional *that* complementizer of English, optional definiteness markers in Tirax, and optional person and number markers in Cupeño. The results are promising, and the approach throws new light on the well-studied domain of optional *that*. In each of these domains the attention of investigators has focused on systems in which meaning is coded somewhere. Systems in which no meaning is coded, and all meaning is inferred, are mentioned only in passing. They are in need of serious attention in linguistic typology and description. The issue is not whether a semantic versus pragmatic account of optional marking is viable in general, but rather which works in a particular grammatical environment in a particular language. And to determine which is no easy task.

The theory acknowledges cross-linguistic variation in terms of the construal of the features [prominent] and [backgrounded]. It proposes that two considerations are particularly relevant to optional case marking, and limit the variation, namely the issue of the identity of the filler of the given grammatical role, and the degree to which the filler of a role shows the features prototypical of that role. These considerations account for a wide range of typological variation among languages. However, they are specific to optional case marking, and are not relevant to optional complementizers or definiteness markers.

The features [prominent] and [backgrounded] are not characteristics of the linguistic or extralinguistic context of a token, and cannot be read off from the context. Choices made by speakers construe these features. Nevertheless, it is to be expected that speakers will choose to make something prominent or to background it depending on contextual considerations. Thus, statistical correlations can be expected between usage and/or non-usage of an optional grammatical marker and quantifiable contextual variables such as first mention, previously mentioned, production difficulty (indexed by speech rate, disfluencies, and pauses), information value (measured in information-theoretic terms), and the like. Statistical patterns are therefore of importance to the present theory of optionality. However, they are not considered to be the ultimate goal of investigations of optionality: more important is what lies behind the statistical patterns. Of primary significance are those instances which do not fit the patterns. Rather than disregard these as minority exceptions to robust generalizations, they demand examination and, ultimately, explanation.

In the contrast between use and non-use of an optional element we have an opposition between something and nothing: in (5.3) there is an item of linguistic form that is missing from (5.2), and this is the salient difference between the two clauses. There is no reason in Shua to identify any linguistic form in (5.2) in the place corresponding to the place occupied by the accusative marker in (5.3). There is, that is, no reason to postulate a zero postposition on the Undergoer NP in (5.2) corresponding to the accusative postposition in (5.3); the NP is simply unmarked, a bare one. It follows that Haas' proposed reconceptualization of the notion of a zero morpheme as an 'operational zero' (1957: 42–43) – the operation of omission – is not viable. Optional grammatical marking fits the bill for an operation of omission, while the notion of zero morpheme is inapplicable.

The nothing of form in an instance of non-use of an optional marker cannot be the signifier of a sign. The point of this chapter is that the operation of using some grammatical item can represent a form with an associated meaning. This opens the door to construal of non-use of that item as an item of linguistic form, just as the existence of a range of bound pronoun forms can yield the construal of a morphological nothing as a zero – and thus as a genuine linguistic sign. The principle is the same: filling in paradigmatic gaps. More generally, this is a reflection of a cognitive capacity of humans. As members of the symbolic species we are adept at construing not just presences, but also absences as signs, building on expectations.

Usage-based grammars by and large construe the interaction between grammar and usage diachronically (Hopper 1987; Bybee 2010): effectively, yesterday's usage is today's grammar. Usage remains on the perimeter of grammar. This remains so even in the few attempts that have been made to assign it a more central place. For example, Halliday has argued that usage probabilities are associated with choices in system networks (e.g. Halliday 2008, 2013); Schmid (2013) argues that grammatical knowledge includes knowledge of usage patterns, including frequency-related characteristics of grammatical patterns. The proposals of this chapter reveal that there is more to usage in grammar than mere frequency patterns. Usage can be a part of the grammatical system of a language, a part of the grammatical resources of the interpersonal semiotic.

The notion of choice plays a crucial role in SFL (e.g. Fontaine, Bartlett and O'Grady 2013), and is construed in terms of networks of options available at particular choice points. Where usage systems of grammatical units might be located is, however, unclear. Indeed, there is no obvious place for them: usage as such is not incorporated into the SFL model of grammar beyond probabilistic tags and realization statements attached to nodes. Clearly usage systems of optional case marking cannot share a locus with case markers of a language: they must be separate from the system of oppositions for inflectional cases or adpositions available at word or phrase level. It will hardly do to put them in some higher stratum: there is no reason why optionality does not belong to grammar per se.

Chapter 6

Verb Classification

Another relatively unknown and poorly studied domain in linguistic typology is the grammatical classification of verbal lexemes. This contrasts strikingly with the phenomenon of nominal classification (noun classes or genders, noun classifiers, numeral classifiers, etc.) which has attracted an enormous amount of attention in linguistic typology and descriptive linguistics. I have nothing new to contribute to the typology of noun classification systems, and hence this chapter focuses attention on the lesser-known domain of verb classification. However, granted that nominal classification is a relatively familiar topic in linguistics, it provides a useful way into the the phenomenon of grammatical classification and the less well-known domain of verb classification. Thus, we begin in §6.1.1 with an overview of the typology of nominal classification, which leads us naturally into an attempt to delimit the domain of grammatical classification (§6.1.2). The following three sections discuss verb classification systems in some detail. This chapter also explores the theoretical relevance and implications of the phenomenon of grammatical classification, suggesting ways in which it can be accounted for within a broad Neo-Firthian framework. I argue in particular that it implies the need for a theory of grammatical marking, and outline some features of such a theory.

6.1 The Phenomenon of Grammatical Classification

6.1.1 Preliminary Remarks

Noun classification systems have long held a great fascination for typologists as well as descriptivists, semanticists, pragmatists, psycholinguists, sociolinguists, discourse and text linguists, grammaticalization theorists, diachronic linguists and others. SFL has had little to say about noun classification, except for the type manifested in English in constructions such as *electric train, express train, espresso machine,* and the like ('subclassification' in the scheme presented below). This is surprising given the frequent nods towards Mandarin Chinese as an influence on the shape of SFL. Like many languages of the Sinosphere, Mandarin Chinese shows a system of numeral classification (Chappell 2015; Jian 2015); this is, however, treated as a system of 'measure' in the NP, its classificatory aspect being wholly ignored (e.g. Li 2017: 345–347, who indirectly hints at this aspect through use of the completely inappropriate and misleading term 'agree').

A range of types of noun classification systems are customarily distinguished, including: noun class or gender systems, noun classifier systems, numeral classifier systems, possessive classifier systems, verb classifier systems, deictic classifiers, and locative classifiers (see e.g. Allan 1977; Dixon 1986; Croft 1994; Craig 1986b; Senft 2000; Aikhenvald 2000). It is generally agreed that these types are not discrete, but represent prototypical categories within spaces of variation (e.g. Aikhenvald 2000: 13–14). There are systems that are difficult to assign to the types: the Ngan'gityemerri and Murrinh-Patha (both Southern Daly, Australia) systems lie on the border of noun class and noun classifier systems (Reid 1997; Walsh 1997). For the orientation of the reader, some of the basic features of the prototypes are overviewed in the following paragraphs.

Noun class or gender systems are perhaps the best known and most widely studied of nominal classification systems, being attested in many languages of Europe, including French, Italian, German, Danish, Swedish, Russian, among others, as well as languages of the African continent (famously Bantu languages), Australia, and the Americas. Noun class systems are characterized by agreement phenomena, by morphosyntactic markers that occur on other members of the noun phrase such as articles, demonstratives and adjectives, and/or on the verb; the marking is never exclusively located on the noun lexeme itself (Corbett 1991). The number of noun classes ranges from two to ten or twelve – at most there might be a couple of dozen. These are typically disjoint, or almost disjoint, and are usually exhaustive: all nouns are assigned to some class. Noun class systems are never completely arbitrary in terms of their membership; nor are they (ever?) completely regular. There is always some semantic basis to the assignment to classes.[1] Features such as animacy, sex, humanness, and sometimes shape and size are commonly pertinent, though not determinative. Sometimes there is also phonological motivation (e.g. nouns showing certain phonological shapes may tend to be assigned to the same class) or morphological motivation (e.g. nouns with a certain derivational affix may tend to be assigned to a certain class).

Noun classifier systems have a set of classifiers that collocate habitually with nouns in a language, assigning them to categories. These classifiers are typically free words with generic meanings such as 'tree', 'vegetable', 'person', 'vehicle', 'instrument', and the like. Noun classifiers are found in various Australian, Western Austronesian, Tai, and Mayan languages, and typically number from about a score to a hundred or so. The categories established by classifiers tend to overlap more than those of noun classes, and different noun classifiers may not uncommonly be used with the same noun to express different meanings. For instance, in Minangkabau (Austronesian, Sumatra), we find *batang limau* (tree lemon) 'lemon-tree', but *buah limau* (fruit lemon) 'lemon-fruit'. Whereas noun classes are typically exhaustive, noun classifiers do not necessarily accompany all nouns.

Numeral classifiers are morphemes that typically occur adjacent to numerals or quantifiers and categorize the quantified or counted noun (Grinevald 2000: 63–64; Aikhenvald 2000: 98), as shown by (6.1). Inventories of numeral classifying morphemes can number in the hundreds, though many of these may be infrequent in occurrence.

(6.1) *hkwei hnǎ kauñ*   Burmese (Tibeto-Burman, Myanmar)
       dog   two animal
       'two dogs' (Okell 1969: 209, cited in Enfield 2019: 145)

In some languages numeral classifiers also occur in other environments, such as when a noun occurs with a demonstrative, as in Mandarin Chinese (Jian 2015: 110–111). Numeral classifier systems are common in the languages of Asia, including Sinitic languages as well as Thai, Japanese, Korean, Dravidian, Indic, Turkic, and a number of Austronesian languages; they are also found in some Mayan languages, various languages of the north Amazon and a number of Niger-Congo languages of Africa (Kießling 2018).

It is customary to distinguish between two major types of numeral classifier, sortal classifiers and mensural classifiers.[2] Sortal classifiers indicate a property of the quantified nominal, as in (6.1). Mensural classifiers instead indicate something about the way in which the referent entity is measured, in the manner of English expressions such as *ten head of cattle*, *three packs of dogs* and *four stacks of dishes*. In numeral classifier systems not all nouns need take a numeral classifier, and it is common for a noun to collocate with different classifiers, the difference in classifier expressing a meaning difference. Often, as in Mandarin Chinese, there is a generic classifier that can collocate with many nouns, and can frequently replace a more specific classifier.

Possessive classifiers are typically employed when a noun occurs in a possessive construction. Three types are normally distinguished, according to what is categorized: possessum classifiers, possessor classifiers, and relation classifiers (Aikhenvald 2000: 125; 2006: 467). Possessum classifiers typically classify nouns in terms of physical properties such as animacy, size, structure and shape; such systems are found in a number of South American languages including Panare (Carib, Venezuela). Possessor classifiers classify possessor nouns in terms of animacy; these systems are found in very few languages, mostly of South America (e.g. Dâw and Makú (isolate, Brazil) languages).

Relation classifiers are generally considered to classify the nature of the possessive relation between the possessor and possessum in terms of how the possessum is handled or used – for example, whether eaten, drunk, worn, or used in some other way. These are largely restricted to alienable possession constructions. Systems of this type are found in many Austronesian languages, especially of the Oceanic subgroup, as well as a few languages of South America. This is a somewhat problematic category: if relational classifiers exclusively categorize the possessive relation itself, there would be no reason whatever to include them as a subtype of noun classification – Crowley (1995) takes this position for Paamese (Austronesian, Vanuatu). Assuming they categorize the possessum as well as the possessive relation itself, they would be comparable with function classifiers in noun classifier systems, that categorize nouns in terms of their uses. Lacking any agreed-to criteria for classification systems, the analytical issue is unanswerable; this is partly my motivation for identifying a set of necessary and sufficient criteria for grammatical classification systems – see §6.1.2 below.

The remaining three types of system are labelled according to the locus of the classifying morpheme. In so-called verb classifier systems (not to be confused with systems of verb classification discussed in this chapter) the classifier morpheme occurs in the verb, but what is classified is a clausal argument. Like the other systems discussed above, these are semantically based, invoking features such as animacy, shape, size, structure, and stance of the nominal argument. Such systems are found in a number of languages of North America and Papua New Guinea. In Cherokee (Iroquoian, USA) about forty verbs, mostly verbs of handling such as 'give', 'hold', 'handle', 'carry', 'hang up', and the like, take these classifiers (Blankenship 1997: 96). The Papuan languages Waris and Imonda have a system of classifier prefixes to certain verbs of handling, while Enga, Ku Waru (also Papuan) and Imonda deploy different existential and positional verbs according to the nature of the entity predicated on or located (Lang 1975; Merlan, Roberts and Rumsey 1997). A number of sign languages have what seem to be verb classifier systems, including ASL (American Sign Language), Auslan, BSL (British Sign Language) and DTS (Danish Sign Language), among others. For instance, in ASL many verbs of motion, handling and position involve special classifier handshapes, that indicate the salient shape or size of the positioned or moving object, or the handshape employed when handling it (Neidle and Nash 2015: 49–50).

Deictic and locative classifiers are uncommon, and are attested in just a few languages. Deictic classifiers obligatorily occur on deictic elements such as demonstratives and articles, and categorize the collocating noun in terms of shape, animacy and spatial position. Some languages of North America (including Siouan and Eskimo languages) and South America (Guaicuruan languages) have deictic classifiers. Locative classifiers occur in locative phrases, and are normally fused with an adposition. They typically classify the accompanying noun in terms of features including shape, dimensionality, and boundedness. Locative classifiers are best attested in South American languages, including Palikur (Arawakan, Brazil), Carib languages and Dâw.

6.1.2 Criteria for Grammatical Classification Systems

Given the extent of interest in noun classification it is surprising that the majority of investigators have been content to leave it undefined, and presume that noun classification systems wear their label on their sleeves so to say. Hence, well-known writers in this domain – for example, Allan (1977); Dixon (1982: 217–218; 1986); Craig (1986a, 1994), Grinevald (2000: 54); Silverstein (1986); Aikhenvald (2000, 2006) – assume the general domain is recognizable relatively unproblematically. Noun classification systems are effectively defined by extension, and criteria are invoked to distinguish among the subtypes. This extensional approach is unsatisfying in as much as it does not identify anything significant shared by classification systems or indeed any prototypes, but merely lists candidates.[3] In order to permit a typology of emic phenomena that are similar enough in terms of form and function to be treated under the label classification, McGregor (2002b) proposes a set of necessary and sufficient criteria.

To begin with, the domain of grammatical classification must be divided into two fundamentally different types, subclassification and superclassification (McGregor 2002b:

4–5). In systems of subclassification, the extensional domain of a lexical item is partitioned into a number of possibly overlapping categories. The above-mentioned system of English is a system of subclassification: terms such as *electric, express, steam, model*, and so on divide trains into subtypes. The subcategories are typically peculiar to each given lexeme. Systems of superclassification, by contrast, work in the opposite direction: the entirety of the lexicon of a given part of speech is partitioned into subsets. All or the majority of lexemes of the given part of speech are assigned to higher-order categories. Nouns in French are divided into two categories, masculine and feminine, in terms of their grammatical characteristics. In this chapter we focus almost exclusively on super-classification systems, with only brief mention of subclassification systems.

Common across systems of superclassification is that the lexicon of a certain part of speech is partitioned into subsets on the basis of forms habitually accompanying the lexemes in certain grammatical contexts. Different forms collocate with different sub-sets of lexemes. For example, nouns in Danish typically collocate with just one of the indefinite articles *en* and *et*, and the corresponding bound definite forms *-en* and *-et*. According to which of the pairs a noun collocates with it can be assigned to one of these subsets, which basically cover the entirety of the nominal domain, with a relatively small overlap. McGregor (2002b: 18–19) proposes a set of four criteria to encapsulate the above remarks; these are repeated in somewhat revised form in i.–iv. below. See also Gerner (2009: 705–709; 2014: 267–268); Janda et al. (2013: 185); Seifart (2018: 10).

i. Exhaustiveness: the domain (D) covered is the entirety or a substantial component of an open lexical class (P);

ii. Collocation: the items in the domain collocate – in well-defined grammatical environments – with members of another set of linguistic items M, such that: (a) all members of M can occur in collocation with some member of D; and (b) all items with this potential are included in M;

iii. Cardinality: the cardinality of M is greater than one, but significantly less than the cardinality of D; and

iv. Partitioning: members of M show differences in patterns of collocation with members of D; specifically, there must exist at least one pair $\{M_i, M_j\}$ for which the set of Ds they collocate with, $\{D_{i,1}, D_{i,2}, D_{i,3}, ...\}$ and $\{D_{j,1}, D_{j,2}, D_{j,3}, ...\}$, are significantly different.

Brief explanation of these conditions, and their significance, follows; see McGregor (2002b: 18–22) for more detailed discussion.

First, i. serves to restrict classification systems to those that are more or less exhaustive of the lexical content of a given open part of speech, while not excluding the possibility that a few lexemes may be excluded, and some from other parts of speech might be included. While we may talk of classification of smaller sets of lexemes the point of doing so diminishes as the sets reduce in cardinality. Thus, Hup, Yuhup (both Puinavean, Amazonia) and Apurinã (Arawakan, Amazonia) have systems of bound nouns that serve a classifying function, but are quite restricted in terms of the nouns they collocate with: in Hup, the system is virtually restricted to neologisms for non-native manufactured items (Epps 2011: 646–647). Because of the narrowness of application, Epps rightly does not consider this to be a system of nominal classification.

Conditions ii. and iii. concern the manner in which the set of lexical items of interest, D, is categorized. Specifically, ii. ensures that the categorization is effected by linguistic forms, members of a set M, that collocate with the members of D. This means that the items in M serve as markers of the categories. Our domain of interest is systems of overt classification, not covert ones in which the categories are established by reactances, as is the case for instance for the categorization of English verbs as per Levin (1993).[4] Conditions (a) and (b) in ii. ensure that we have the entire set of category markers.

The members of M will typically be linguistic units of a comparable type. However, no such stipulation is included because of languages such as Ngan'gityemerri (Reid 1997) in which the category markers include both bound morphemes and free lexemes. Indeed, not infrequently the Ms include both bound and free grammatical forms (as in Danish), even non-segmental fusional forms. Some caution is needed here, as it is possible that different types of M unit might impose different categorizations on D (e.g. Evans 1997).

The conditions in iii. and iv. serve to exclude cases in which collocating Ms define trivial or uninteresting partitionings of D. Condition iii. precludes cases in which either D is not divided up at all (just one member in M), or is divided into (almost) as many subsets as there are members in the set (where D and M are of roughly the same cardinality). Finally, iv. serves to ensure that the subsets in the partitioning of D do not overlap too much. The motivation is that if for instance each of the subsets differ only in a few elements, then most likely this is accidental, and the members of M in reality are unrestricted in terms of their collocations with members of D, and the exceptions are simply irregularities. This condition excludes, for instance, the categories defined by collocations with *a* and *the* in English: virtually all nominals collocate with both. On the other hand, this condition does allow for a number of markers to carve out identical subsets: there may be different markers of the same category.

Use of terms such as 'substantial', 'significantly less' and 'significantly different' in criteria i.–iv. allocate a degree of vagueness to the definitions. This is intentional and unavoidable. There will be cases where linguists might disagree on whether what we have in a particular instance is substantial or significant, and these will be cases where the system is on the borderline of a classification system. Whether or not it should be counted as a system of classification will depend on whether or not it is useful or in any way enlightening to treat it as one. For instance, such borderline systems that partially meet criteria i.–iv. may be relevant to the diachronic emergence or loss of a classification system; see Dammel and Kürschner (2018).

6.2 Systems of Verbal Classification

Systems commonly referred to as verb classifier systems (see above p. 135 and pp. 137–138) categorize nouns by morphemes whose locus is in the verb. By contrast, the systems discussed in this section categorize the lexemes of a verbal part of speech. That is to say *D* represents a significant subset of the set of lexical verbs of a language. Systems of verbal classification are not nearly as well known as systems of nominal classification, and the typological literature on them shades in comparison with that for nominal classification. For instance, WALS has four chapters dealing with systems of nominal classification, but none on verbal classification. Nonetheless, such systems are not uncommon in the world's languages, and are found in languages of diverse geographical and genetic provenances.

In what follows I present a typology of verb classification systems based on previous work by McGregor (2002b); McGregor, Schultze-Berndt and Wiebusch (2007) and Schultze-Berndt and Sagna (2010). This typology distinguishes five main types of verb classification system: verb classifier systems, numeral classifier systems, manner classifier systems, instrumental classifier systems, and verb class systems. These types are explained and discussed in the following subsections. For now, it is worth drawing attention to resemblances between this typology of verb classification systems and the typology of nominal classification systems presented in §6.1.1 above. These are summarized in Table 6.1.

Table 6.1 Correspondences among nominal and verbal systems of classification

Nominal classification system	Corresponding verbal classification system
noun classifier	verb classifier
numeral classifier	numeral classifier
noun class (gender)	verb class (conjugation)
possessive classifier	—
verb classifier	—
deictic classifier	—
locative classifier	—
—	manner classifier
—	instrumental classifier

As will become apparent in the subsequent discussion, the correspondences go deeper than the mere labels given. For now, I observe that verb classifier systems and noun classifier systems are alike in terms of their prototypical usage of lexical items as markers of the categories. Numeral classifier systems in both nominal and verbal domains are called into use when the relevant phenomena are quantified. Verb class systems show resemblances with noun class systems, including marking by dedicated grammatical morphemes, rather than by lexical items (as for classifier systems). These are the most grammaticalized of the systems. Correlations among the other categories of the typologies in the nominal and verbal domains are rather less clear-cut. These observations are not comprehensive: other significant connections can be drawn between the nominal and verbal categorization systems – see, for example, p. 148 below.

We discuss the five types in order in the following subsections. As in the case of nominal classification systems, the types are prototypes within a space of variation, and do not represent entirely discrete types.

6.2.1 Verb Classifier Systems

Verb classifier systems (not to be confused with verb classifier systems in the nominal domain) like the prototypical noun classifier system in that the classifying morphemes are generally lexical items, rather than purely grammatical items. They also resemble noun classifier systems in that the number of categories they distinguish tends to be in the order of ten or more, as against the smaller norm for verb class systems, which ranges from two to about half a dozen or so. These are tendencies, and there are borderline systems such as the Gooniyandi one (see below) in which the category markers are grammatical items, though they derive from lexical verbs.

Verb classifier systems are found in languages from across the world, including in Australia, Europe, the Indian subcontinent, Asia, Africa, North America and Amazonia. Two main types of morpheme serve as verbal classifiers: lexical verbs and lexical affixes. In what follows we overview both types.

6.2.1.1 *Lexical verbs as classifiers*

A number of languages from northern Australia show two distinct parts of speech corresponding to verbs of SAE languages, which I will here refer to as uninflecting verbs (that take no inflections) and inflecting verbs (that inflect for tense, mood and aspect, as well as, in many languages person and number of core arguments); see §1.2.2.2 and note 8 to Chapter 1. Uninflecting verbs usually occur in syntagms with inflecting verbs, which in most languages they precede, in what is sometimes called a compound verb construction.[5] Inflecting verbs, by contrast, generally have the potential of independent occurrence in simple verb constructions, though in some languages a few inflecting verbs are restricted to occurrence in compound verb constructions. Languages with these two parts of speech and two fundamentally different verbal constructions come from a number of non-Pama-Nyungan families of Australia (including Bunuban, Nyulnyulan, Worrorran, Jarrakan, Mirndi, Daly River families, East Arnhem, and possibly Gunwinyguan), as well as from Pama-Nyungan, and are spoken from the Pilbara, Dampier Land and the Kimberley regions of Western Australia across northern Australia and into Arnhem Land. Examples (6.2) and (6.3) illustrate compound verb constructions and simple verb constructions respectively in Miriwoong (Jarrakan).

(6.2) *dilyb   ge-ma-n-tha*   Miriwoong
       break   3SG.M.NOM-3SG.M.ACC-get-PST
       'He broke it off.' (Kofod 1978: 109)

(6.3) *nguwag   nyi-ni-ø-nyan*   *ngal-ayuga/*   Miriwoong
       not   3SG.F.NOM-sit-IRR-3SG.F.CNT   3SG.F-alone
       yawurrubtha   be-ni-ya-wun/
       all   3NSG.NOM-sit-RLS-3NSG.CNT
       'She was not sitting by herself. They were all sitting (there).' (Kofod 1978: 50)

McGregor (2002b) argues that compound verb constructions are the grammatical locus of verb classification in languages of northern Australia showing this construction; see also Schultze-Berndt (2000) on the Mirndi languages Jaminjung and Ngaliwurru, among others; Rumsey (1982: 115–120); Saunders (1997); and Silverstein (1986) on Worrorran languages, especially Ungarinyin and Worrorra; Green (1989: 315–389) and Reid (2000) on the Daly River languages Marrithiyel and Ngan'gityemerri. Specifically, the inflecting verb roots that can occur in compound verb constructions – which typically represent a subset of inflecting verbs numbering around a dozen to about a score – serve as the *M*s. In most languages the cardinality of *M* is less than a tenth of that of *D*, which is normally an open class with several hundred members. In Ungarinyin (Worrorran), for instance, just fourteen inflecting verb roots from a set of several hundred have the potential of use in compound verb constructions. The inflecting verb roots define categories of uninflecting verbs by virtue of their collocations with them; the *D*s are thus uninflecting verbs together with a smallish set of other lexemes that can also occur in compound verb constructions (usually including some nominals and possibly adverbials).

The *M*s partition the *D*s into a dozen to a score of subsets, depending on the language. These sets typically overlap somewhat, though they are by and large distinct from one another; condition iv. is thus satisfied. This is demonstrated by the situation in Nyulnyul, where ten inflecting verbs are productive in the sense that they each collocate with at least ten different uninflecting verbs. There is, however, little similarity in the sets of collocating inflecting verbs: the most similar sets show only about 0.1 (10%) overlap. (See further McGregor 2002b: 110.)

What makes these systems of verb classification interesting is that the categories defined by the collocations with inflecting verbs are not arbitrary, but are semantically based. Indeed, the semantic basis for the categories is remarkably similar across languages showing the systems. McGregor (2002b: 29–34, 101–147) argues that three features encapsulate the semantics of these systems:

–   Aktionsart – the aspectual character of the event, primarily whether it is telic or atelic, but also such temporal features as dynamic, momentatious and the like;

- valency – the valency value of the event in terms of its transitivity, largely construed in terms of the number of inherent arguments to the event;

- vectorial configuration – an abstract representation of the event in terms of action vectors that comprise it.

Table 6.2 provides a description of the meanings of each of the ten primary categories of Nyulnyul (i.e. those comprising at least ten members).

Table 6.2 Semantic characteristics of the ten primary categories in Nyulnyul. *Source:* McGregor (2012a: 450)

Valency	Telic	Atelic
1	-BARNJ 'exchange' [reflexive/reciprocal action]	
		-N 'be' [stative (non-dynamic)] -JID 'go' [activity progresses over time]
1/2	-J 'say, do' [dynamic activity]	
	-R 'pierce' [action taking place in a straight line, impacting on something at a point] -W 'give' [action directed outwards from actor, making contact with something] -NY 'get' [acquire or achieve an entity or condition by active means] -M 'put' [induce something to enter new state, condition, or location]	-KAL 'wander' [action not uniquely directed towards a specific goal] -K 'carry' [move something by constantly applied force to new location]

Four observations are pertinent at this point. First, two categories are unspecified for telicity, those marked by -BARNJ 'exchange' and -J 'say, do'. Second, although there are three categories that are specified as inherently monovalent, none is specified as inherently bivalent: the remaining seven categories are unspecified for valency. The -J 'say, do' category is thus quite general semantically, and specifies nothing more than that the event is dynamic. Third, within the categories defined by Aktionsart and valency distinctions are made according to vectorial configuration. For instance, -KAL 'wander' specifies a meandering action vector, not directed towards any particular goal, whereas for -K 'carry' – like the four 1/2 telic categories – the vector is directed. Fourth, although the lexical meanings of the inflecting verbs are not a part of the meanings of the categories they define in the compound verb construction, there are clear correlations between these meanings, reminiscent of the semantic bleaching often associated with grammaticalization. Thus, the atelic nature of the categories marked by N 'be' and -JID 'go' clearly relate to the atelicity of the lexical verbs; the fact that the former is a stative category while the latter is dynamic clearly follows as a consequence of their lexical meanings. Other more lexical components of the meanings of the inflecting verbs are bleached out.

The system of verb classification in the somewhat distantly related Nyulnyulan language Warrwa is very similar to the system for Nyulnyul, with many of the categories marked by cognate inflecting verbs (McGregor 2018b: 340). Further afield, the numbers of categories are somewhat more divergent, although they hover in the region of ten to twenty or so for the productive categories, and up to about fifty including the non-productive ones. The inflecting verbs that serve as markers also differ in form and meaning, though they are mostly basic verbs that one expects to be high in frequency of usage, including 'say, do', 'sit, be', 'stand', 'fall', 'become', 'go', 'carry', 'put', 'throw', 'catch, get', 'poke', 'give', and 'hit'. Not all of these are, of course, always employed as classifiers – for example, 'hit' is not used as a classifier in Nyulnyul.

Broadly speaking in languages with this style of verb classification uninflecting verbs collocate with between one and six or seven inflecting verb roots. For instance, in Nyulnyul the majority of uninflecting verbs (almost 80%) collocate with a single inflecting verb; about 14% collocate with two different inflecting verbs, 5% with three, and the remainder with four or five. Comparison of the alternative possibilities of classification for a given uninflecting verb brings out the semantic nature of the classification system more clearly than does a perusal of the range of uninflecting verbs that collocate with a given inflecting verb. This is revealed in the following alternative pairings of some of the more promiscuous uninflecting verbs with inflecting verbs.

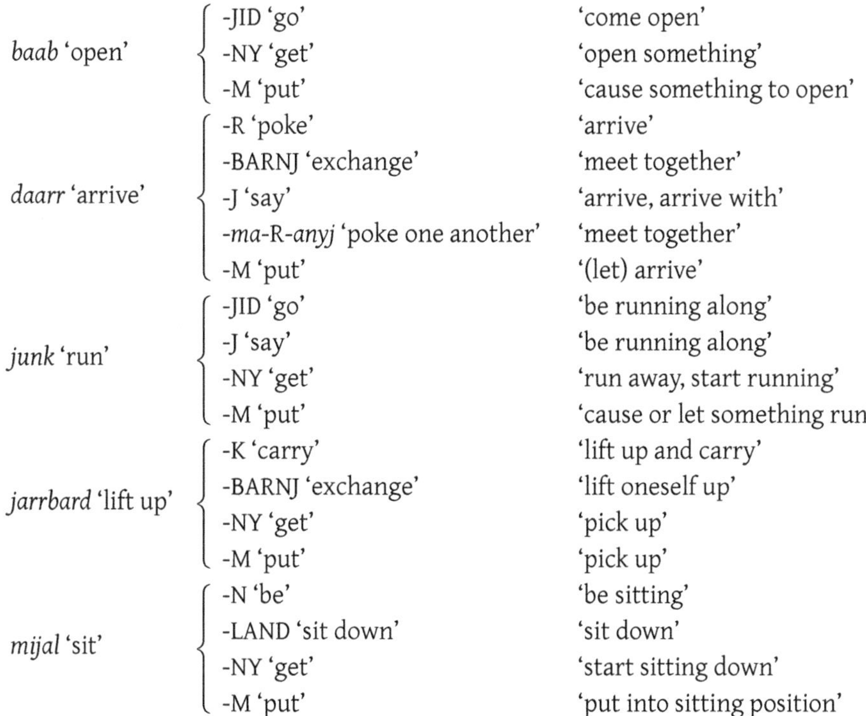

baab 'open'	-JID 'go'	'come open'
	-NY 'get'	'open something'
	-M 'put'	'cause something to open'
daarr 'arrive'	-R 'poke'	'arrive'
	-BARNJ 'exchange'	'meet together'
	-J 'say'	'arrive, arrive with'
	-ma-R-*anyj* 'poke one another'	'meet together'
	-M 'put'	'(let) arrive'
junk 'run'	-JID 'go'	'be running along'
	-J 'say'	'be running along'
	-NY 'get'	'run away, start running'
	-M 'put'	'cause or let something run'
jarrbard 'lift up'	-K 'carry'	'lift up and carry'
	-BARNJ 'exchange'	'lift oneself up'
	-NY 'get'	'pick up'
	-M 'put'	'pick up'
mijal 'sit'	-N 'be'	'be sitting'
	-LAND 'sit down'	'sit down'
	-NY 'get'	'start sitting down'
	-M 'put'	'put into sitting position'

Gooniyandi is exceptional for a language of the northern region in that it has just one verbal part of speech and a single finite verb construction type (McGregor 1990a: 190–227). There is evidence that this construction derives historically from a compound verb construction, which took over as the sole construction in the language, ousting the simple verb construction (McGregor 2002b). What was previously a pair of lexical items became a single lexeme, a single word both distributionally and lexically. The inflecting verbs lost their independence of occurrence, and became collocationally dependent on the erstwhile uninflecting verbs. They lost their status as lexical items, and became markers of verbal categories exclusively, pure classifiers.

McGregor (1990a: 557–572; 2002b: 41–100) provides detailed discussion of the system of classification, including its semantic basis. For present purposes it is sufficient to mention that the twelve categories are semantically motivated in terms of Aktionsart, valency and vectorial configuration. There are just a few instances in which a lexical verb in Gooniyandi seems to be assigned to an inappropriate category. The main offender is the verb *doow-* 'get', which is inexplicably assigned to an atelic category.[6] McGregor (2002b: 83–85) discusses some possible reasons for this, most of which invoke changes in the lexical semantics of the verb *doow-*. Perhaps irregularities began to creep into the system along with the increasing grammaticalization of the system – I am not aware of such blatant anomalies in the less grammaticalized Nyulnyulan systems.

Ngiyambaa (Pama-Nyungan) shows a system that is rather too restricted to call a verb classification system, but might be either the historical remnant of a previous one, or an incipient system. This system involves a compound verb construction consisting of a bound non-inflecting result-oriented modifier together with a bound inflection-taking verb root. The inflecting verb root apparently serves a categorizing function as in the systems just described for northern Australian languages, except that it categorizes a set of just eleven result-oriented modifiers, rather than an open class of lexical items. Given the small number of result-oriented bound modifiers, the system runs foul of criterion i., and is at best a very marginal classification system. As in verb category systems multiple classification is rife, and conveys predictable meaning differences. For instance, the result-oriented modifier *ga-* 'break' collocates with at least the following three bound verb roots: transitive -MA-*l*, intransitive -MA-*y*, and -DHI-*l* 'do with foot', with predictable meaning differences (Donaldson 1980: 220–221).

Outside of the Australian continent a few other systems of verb classification by means of lexical verbs are attested; some are mentioned below. I suspect that more such systems will emerge with more comprehensive descriptions of the world's languages.

Hindi-Urdu shows a system that closely resembles the type of system just described in Australia (Hook 1974; Agha 1994). Two lexical items are involved, a bare verb stem followed by an inflecting verb (variously referred to as an 'auxiliary', 'vector verb', 'operator', etc.) in what Hook (1974) refers to as a 'compound verb'. The inflecting verbs form a small class of between eight and fifty members (depending on source); Hook (1974: 119–120) distinguishes two dozen, most of which are reminiscent of the inflecting verbs in Australian compound verb constructions. Agha (1994) argues that the inflecting verbs function as classifiers, and partition the domain of bare verb stems into a number of semantically based categories. Aktionsart, valency and agentivity appear to be the primary semantic features distinguished (Hook 1974: 160; Agha 1994: 23).

In contrast with the Australian verb classification systems, in Hindi-Urdu it seems that compound verb constructions are in privative opposition with simple verb constructions such that the compound verb construction expresses completion of the event (Hook 1974: 314). For instance, the verb 'run' in a simple verb construction refers to the normal atelic process of running, whereas in a compound verb construction it construes a telic event such as running away. Put in other words, it is only when the verb shows the particular aspectual character of completion or telicity that it is classified. Again this is reminiscent of a recurrent feature of Australian systems: there are always more distinctions in the telic than the atelic categories – see Table 6.2.

In South America at least two languages are known to have verb classifier systems employing lexical verbs as classifiers: Tsafiki (Barbacoan, Ecuador) and Mosetén (Mosetenan, Bolivia). Both languages show two verbal parts of speech, an open class of uninflecting verbs and a smallish closed class of inflecting verbs, most of which have the potential of independent occurrence (Dickinson 2000: 28; Sakel 2007: 317, 325). Both languages also show a compound verb construction consisting of an uninflecting element in collocation with an inflecting verb (Dickinson 2000, 2003; Sakel 2006, 2007). In Mosetén eight inflecting verbs occur in compound verb constructions: *-i-* 'be, have', *-yi-* 'do, be', *-tyi-* 'put', *-jo-* 'become', *-ki-* 'be', *-ti-* 'do', *-wi-* 'see, hear' and *chhi-* 'move, have'. Most of these can also occur independently. Sakel (2006, 2007) argues that they serve as classifiers in the compound verb construction. The system of classification has a semantic basis, and features reminiscent of those of Australian languages are relevant: valency/transitivity, Aktionsart character and control. The inflecting verbs in Tsafiki appear to serve similar classifier functions, partitioning the set of uninflecting verbs. Ese Ejja (Takanan, Bolivia and Peru) appears to have a similar system (Vuillermet 2012).

6.2.1.2 *Lexical prefixes as classifiers*

Slavic languages have sets of aspectual prefixes that derive verbs specifying events in the perfective aspect from basic simplex verbs that are mostly imperfective in sense and specify undifferentiated activities and states (Dickey and Janda 2015: 59). For instance, in Russian only about a dozen simplex verbs are perfective in sense; the vast majority are imperfective. Corresponding to the imperfectives *pisat'* 'write' and *varit'* 'cook' are perfectives *na-pisat'* 'write' and *s-varit'* 'cook'. In some instances the prefixed form of the verb is a derived form, with a different lexical meaning, as in, for example, *pere-pisat'* 'rewrite' and *pod-pisat'* 'sign' (Janda et al. 2013: 2). These are referred to as natural perfectives and specialized perfectives respectively. Some 1,429 simplex verbs in Russian form natural perfectives with one or more of sixteen prefixes, yielding almost two thousand natural perfective verbs (Janda et al. 2013: 5).

It is generally considered that these prefixes express purely aspectual meaning. Janda et al. (2013) argue against this, and present compelling evidence that the prefixes convey additional meanings as well. Different choices of prefix for simplex verbs that take more than one prefix convey subtle meaning differences. For instance, with the prefix *za-* many verbs convey as well the inchoative sense 'change to a fixed state' or 'cover', while with the prefix *o(b)-* the additional meaning 'is acquire/impose a new feature' or 'surround'. The meaning differences are usually subtle, but are sometimes obvious, as shown by the meaning difference when *plombirovat'* 'fill, seal' takes *za-*, with the meaning 'fill teeth' vs *o(b)-* meaning 'apply a seal to secure something'.

Janda et al. (2013: 179–193) argue that criteria i.–iv. are satisfied, and thus that the prefixes serve as classifiers of the simplex verbs. Dickey and Janda (2015) extend the argument to Slavic languages generally, and argue that across this lineage the aspectual prefixes serve as classifiers. This proposal has the additional advantage that it provides a unified account of both natural perfectives and specialized perfectives.[2] Both Janda et al. (2013) and Dickey and Janda (2015) draw extensive parallels between this verb classification system and numeral classifiers in the nominal domain (see §6.1.1). In particular, they argue that in both systems classifiers serve as unitizers that contribute the meaning of discreteness to either objects (nouns) or events (verbs). By contrast, ordinary nouns and verbs in these languages specify undifferentiated and non-discrete objects or events; the classification system provides a means of giving a shape or unity to the referent object or event.

The types of meaning associated with the verbal categories in Slavic languages are remarkably similar to the meanings associated with the verbal categories in northern Australian languages. The dimension of aspect/Atkionsart is clearly involved in both natural and specialized perfectives. So also is vectorial configuration, in meanings such as 'swell, apart', 'change to a fixed state', 'apply to a surface', 'apply to bottom', 'out of a container' (Dickey and Janda 2015: 61–65, 73). Also notable is the fact that it is the telic (perfective) domain that is the locus of most (northern Australian languages) if not all distinctions (Slavic languages).

6.2.2 Numeral Classifier Systems in the Verbal Domain

Numeral classifier systems in the verbal domain are systems that are employed when verbs are quantified. The markers often occur in what appear to be reduced nominal phrases that indicate frequency (example (6.4)) or some measure of the extent or duration of the event (as in (6.5)). The reduced nominal phrase typically comprises a numeral and a member of a smallish subset of lexemes that serve as classifiers of the verb. Notably, these reduced nominal phrases contain just two units, as shown by (6.4) and (6.5). These contrast in both form and meaning with ordinary three-unit quantified NPs, as in the instrumental phrase in example (6.6). In contrast with ordinary NPs, the expressions made up of these two units do not construe a discourse referent.

(6.4) *Lìsì dǎ-le wǒ liǎng quán* Mandarin Chinese
Lisi hit-PF 1SG two fist
'Lisi hit me twice.'

(6.5) *dəən sɔ̌ɔŋ kâaw* Thai
walk two step
'walk two steps' (Matthews and Leung 2004: 453)

(6.6) *Lìsì yòng ta de liǎng ge quántóu dǎ le wǒ* Mandarin Chinese
Lisi with 3SG of two CL fist hit-PF 1SG
'Lisi hit me with his two fists.'

Zhou and McGregor (1999) and Gerner (2009) argue that these constructions in Mandarin Chinese and Kam (Kra-Dai, China) respectively satisfy criteria i.–iv. above for classification systems. In short, heads of the quantity-expressing phrases form a relatively small set compared with the set of verbs, and collocate differently with different verbs, partitioning the set of verbs into a relatively small number of sets (compared with the size of the verbal lexicon) that are partly disjoint from one another.

A number of languages of east and south-east Asia have systems of numeral classifiers of verbs, including (see Gerner 2009: 699; 2014 for fuller listings): Tibeto-Burman (e.g. Newari – Bhaskararao and Joshi 1985: 17; Hani – Li and Ersong 1986; Mandarin – Chao 1968: 312–314; Zhou and McGregor 1999; Paris 2013; Cantonese – Killingley 1983: 99–104; Matthews and Yip 1999); Kadai (e.g. Thai – Haas 1942: 205; Matthews and Leung 2004); Kra-Dai (e.g. Kam – Gerner 2009); Miao-Yao (e.g. Miao – Wang 1985); and Mon-Khmer (e.g. Vietnamese – Nguyen 1997). It seems that these systems always coexist with nominal systems of numeral classifiers. However, there are a number of languages with numeral classification systems for nouns but no corresponding systems of classification of verbs. For instance, Enfield (2019) provides an extensive discussion of systems of numeral classifiers in the nominal domain in mainland south-east Asian languages but makes no mention of verbal systems. Thus, it seems that a language has a numeral classifier system for verbs only if it has a system of numeral classification for nouns. However, it may well be that numeral classification systems of verbs are more widespread than attested in the literature, given that it is not a very well-known phenomenon.

Various other similarities exist between numeral classifier systems in the nominal and verbal domains. First, a distinction between sortal and mensural numeral classifiers is often recognized for both. In the verbal domain the distinction is accepted by Matthews and Yip (1999) for Cantonese, Gerner (2009: 713) for Kam, and Gerner (2014) more widely for east Asian languages. Sortal classifiers pick out properties that are implicit to the semantics of the verbal lexeme whereas mensural classifiers indicate a measure of the event that is not implicit to the semantics of verbal lexeme, such as some external measure of temporal extent. As in the nominal domain, I am not convinced that the distinction is always clear-cut, or that it is emic in languages with this type of verb classification system. As Gerner (2009: 713) remarks, sortal and mensural classifiers in Kam are not associated with different construction (sub)types. Nor am I convinced that only sortal classifiers count as genuine classifiers (satisfying i.–iv.), as suggested by Gerner (2014): after all, the mensural classifiers pick out atelic verbs, and the criteria are satisfied even if there is massive overlap in their partitioning of atelic verbs. The system must be taken together in its entirety.

Second, it is common to find generic classifiers in both nominal and verbal domains. In the verbal domain there may be classifiers that collocate with many different verbs, which may also collocate with other classifiers. In Mandarin Chinese, for instance, there are three generic classifiers, *cì* 'times', *huì* 'a while' and *xià* 'times, a while', comparable with the generic classifier *ge* in the nominal domain.

Third, autoclassifiers – in which a verb serves as its own event counter – are found in some verb classification systems, including Mandarin Chinese (Gerner 2014: 289–290) and Kam (Gerner 2009: 722–723). Autoclassifiers are well attested in nominal classification systems.

It seems likely that numeral classification systems of verbs are semantically motivated, perhaps invoking features comparable to at least two of the types identified for classifier systems in §6.2.1, namely Aktionsart and vectorial configuration. There is, however, rather little information on the semantics of these categorization systems. Descriptions generally outline the range of classifying elements, specifying their lexical identities without addressing in detail the meaning of the categories themselves, which is typically more schematic than the lexical meanings of the classifier units.

In Kam, for instance, classifying lexemes include nominals specifying instruments (artefactual and body part), a restricted set of verbs, and terms for units of time. The first two of these serve as the sortal classifiers. According to Gerner (2009: 730), these categorize, with a few exceptions, just those verbs that involve the semantic component of touch or contact and admit an instrumental role. Different sortal categories specify different features of the contact: by hitting contact with a physical medium, by attachment contact via a medium, or by transmission in which connection is made via an intermediate channel (Gerner 2009: 733–735; 2014: 276). Thus, sortal classifiers in Kam specify telicity and a vectorial configuration feature.[8] As in other classification systems the semantic nature of the categories emerges clearly when a given verb is multiply categorized. The verb *to*[323] 'put, apply, use' (the superscripted numerals indicate tones) admits a considerable number of alternative sortal classifications, two of which are shown in (6.7) and (6.8).

    (6.7)   *mau*[33] *to*[323] *sam*[35] *ţok*[323]   Kam
                3SG   put   three hoe
                'He used (e.g., dug with) a hoe three times.'

(6.8) *mau³³ to³²³ sam³⁵ pai⁵³*   Kam
       3SG   put   three pay.respect
       'He worshiped three times (to a god).'

6.2.3 Manner Classifier Systems

A rather poorly attested type of verb classification system is employed when events are modified by a manner expression. The Australian language Ngiyambaa has such a system (in addition to the result-oriented system mentioned on p. 146 above). There is a small set of verbs that form compounds with a modifying unit, this compound serves as an adverbial modifier in collocation with another finite verb, as shown in (6.9), where *gunung-giyi* 'pierced energetically' serves as an manner modifier of the verb *bagiyi* 'dug'.

(6.9) *winar-u*   *mingga-ø*   *gunung-giyi*   Ngiyambaa
       woman-ERG   burrow-ABS   with:energy-pierce.PST
       bagiyi
       dig.PST
       'The woman dug a burrow energetically.' (Donaldson 1980: 204)

In this construction the verb that is compounded with the manner-marker serves to categorize the main verb of the clause. Thus, in (6.9) the event of digging is categorized as one that involves a poking or piercing action. Compounding verbs all occur as main verbs in clauses, and hence are not dedicated classifiers.

There are just thirteen compounding verbs, eight transitive, and five intransitive. As the above remarks suggest, the system of classification imposed by the compounding verbs is semantically based; indeed, it is a semantically quite transparent system according to Donaldson (1980: 205). Features are involved that we have already seen for Australian verb classifier systems: valency (transitive vs intransitive), Aktionsart (for intransitive verbs an active vs inactive contrast) and vectorial configuration (for transitive verbs only, as illustrated by the 'poke' category mentioned above). But unlike the northern Australian systems, the Ngiyambaa categorization is of, not by, the main inflecting verb of the clause, and is only invoked when this verb is modified by a manner adverbial. Another difference is that the Ngiyambaa system admits little category overlap, other than between a general transitive and one of the seven other more specific transitive categories marked for vectorial configuration.

A somewhat different type of system is found in Bunun (Austronesian, Taiwan), where what Nojima (1996) refers to as lexical prefixes to adverbials classify verbs in certain constructions. There is a largish set of these lexical prefixes, many of which are formally similar to verb forms expressing similar meanings. They express general meanings like 'die', 'dream', 'burn', 'run', 'hit', 'give', and so on. These attach to adverbial roots, as in example (6.10), the collocation forming the main verb of the clause according to Nojima (1996: 16). The following verb, according to Nojima (1996: 16), is a dependent on this main verb, though it expresses the main verbal lexical content, and is more semantically specific than the lexical prefix.

(6.10) *pit-utmag-un*   *ma-pit'ia tastu-tilas*   Bunun
LP.cook-carelessly-PO AO-cook one-uncooked:rice
'(She) carelessly cooked a grain of rice in one piece, without breaking it apart.'
(Nojima 1996: 16)

The lexical prefix to the adverbial is sometimes repeated on the lexical verb itself, as in (6.11); sometimes, however, different prefixes appear on the adverbial and the lexical verb, as shown by (6.12) – perhaps reminiscent of different head and agreement classes in some gender systems (Evans 1997).

(6.11) *kis-asu-a-s*   *mabananaz-tia kis-laupa*   Bunun
LP.stab-immediately-LO-OBL   man-NPV.that LP.stab-stab
'Immediately after that, the man stabbed (the woman).' (Nojima 1996: 18)

(6.12) *tu-tmag*   *ka-huzas*   Bunun
LP.verbally-carelessly   LP.make-song
'sing songs carelessly (without due thought)' (Nojima 1996: 18)

According to Nojima (1996: 15–17) the lexical prefixes to adverbials categorize the main lexical verb. The classification is semantically based. Most verbs of cutting – including *m-astabal* 'cut (trees, branches, grass) with a sword or scythe in quick motion', *m-atistub* 'cut off', *ma-tuktuk* 'chop (e.g. wood) with axe', and *ma-valval* 'mow' – collocate with the lexical prefix *pati-* 'cut' on a modifying adverbial. However, the verb *ma-kulut* 'saw' collocates instead with *si-* 'get, pull', while *kis-laupa* 'stab' collocates with *kis-* 'stab' (Nojima 1996: 18–19). As in verb classifier systems, different choices of classifier verb are sometimes available, and express differences in construal of the lexical verb (Nojima 1996: 20–21). Although Nojima (1996) does not identify general semantic parameters of the system, it would seem that vectorial configuration and perhaps valency are relevant.

6.2.4 Instrumental Classifier Systems

A number of Amerindian and Austronesian languages show systems of instrumental markers, typically prefixes to verbs, that may serve as verb classifier systems, though information is insufficient to be entirely certain whether or not they satisfy criteria i.–iv. Indeed, they show features characteristic of both subclassification and superclassification systems (McGregor 2002b: 292–293).

The relevant markers are referred to in the Amerindianist literature as instrumental affixes, though they specify action vectors rather than instruments per se (Mithun 1999: 119). They typically specify the means or manner by which an action is performed, the kind of action vector prototypically associated with the deployment of an instrument in bringing about the event (Sapir 1930; Silver and Miller 1997: 43–44; Mithun 1999: 118–126). Northern Paiute (Uto-Aztecan) has around a score of instrumental prefixes that distinguish: body part deployed (e.g. hand, foot, nose, head, face, bum); instrument shape and manner of contact of instrument and target (e.g. long implement with edge use, long with point use); and natural forces (e.g. the sun). These semantic categories are typical of instrumental affixes cross-linguistically (Mithun 1999: 121).

These are not analysed in the literature as verb classifiers.[2] Nonetheless, they show some characteristics reminiscent of verb classification systems. As in verb classifier systems (§6.2.1) vectorial configuration seems to be the major semantic dimension marked by the prefixes, as per the remarks of the previous paragraph. Also, like verb classifier systems the number of affixes typically ranges from ten or so to a maximum of about seventy, as in Klamath (Penutian) (Mithun 1999: 122), and the system serves to create verbal lexemes, often with only partial predictability of meaning. However, it is not clear what proportion of the verbal lexicon takes instrumental affixes, and it seems that verbs collocate with a range of different prefixes. In Northern Paiute the verb -*pajui* 'split apart, break', for instance, collocates with at least seven different instrumental prefixes, including *ki-* 'bite', meaning 'break in mouth', *tsi-* 'sharp', meaning 'poke something (e.g. ice on a pond) to break it', and *ma-* 'hand', meaning 'break with hand (as in karate)' (Thornes 1997). In Central Pomo (Pomoan) *ṭáw* 'feel, sense' and *ṭʰáw* 'come open, untied' each occur with at least eleven different instrumental prefixes (Mithun 1999: 118). It could thus be that the instrumental prefixes subclassify the verbs they occur with, albeit with an apparently closed class of subclassifiers rather than an open class as in the English noun phrase.

So-called classificatory prefixes are found in various Papuan Tip Cluster Austronesian languages (Capell 1943: 237; Bradshaw 1982; Ezard 1978, 1992; cf. Margetts 1999: 115), and the Oceanic language Tinrin (New Caledonia) (Osumi 1995). These are prefixed to verbs and, like the instrumental affixes of northern American languages, specify the instrumental means by which the action is undertaken, and/or the manner in which it is performed. For instance, in the Papuan Tip Cluster language Tawala, there are five prefixes specifying the instrumental means by which the action is effected (by biting, by the feet, by a sharp knock, by hands, or just happening). Another two prefixes specify speech quality (proclaim, speak), and three specify the nature of movement (change of visibility status, cessation of motion, or movement over a significant front) (Ezard 1978: 1164–1165). The system does not seem to be conditioned by grammatical environment, but rather is lexically conditioned. Moreover, the examples Ezard provides suggest that the prefixes subdivide the events designated by a verb into types. Thus, as in the Amerindian case, the system may be a subclassifying one, again with the qualification that the set of subclassifying morphemes is closed. The situation in other Austronesian languages with these prefixes appears similar.

6.2.5 Verb Class Systems

Verb class systems are the most grammaticalized systems of verb classification, in a similar way to noun class systems, which are the most grammaticalized nominal classification systems. In both types of system the category markers are dedicated to the task of categorization. Other shared prototypical properties include: their number is typically smallish (often smaller than the number of categories in classifier systems); they are typically exhaustive, categorizing the entire lexicon of the relevant part of speech; and multiple classification of roots is typically restricted – i.e. the partitions of the verbal/nominal lexicon tend to be largely disjoint, and alternate classifications tend to be rare. There is one striking difference from noun class systems, however. The class markers in verb class systems are exclusively located on the verb itself, rather than prototypically on dependents as in noun class systems (Corbett 1991).

Two subtypes of verb class system are attested. In one type, discussed in §6.2.5.1, noun class markers are employed to mark the categories. In the other, discussed in §6.2.5.2, the class markers are restricted to the verbal domain.

6.2.5.1 *Noun class markers as verb classifiers*

The use of noun class markers with infinitival forms of verbs has been reported in various Niger-Congo languages, including many Bantu languages. Usually only one of the numerous noun class markers is employed as an infinitive marker (Forges 1983; Hadermann 1999; Maho 1999: 211–214), in which circumstances one cannot speak of classification of infinitival verbs by nominal class markers. There are, however, some Bantu languages in which infinitival forms collocate with different noun class markers (Maho 1999: 214; Schadeberg 2003: 80). In such languages it may be that verbal categories are distinguished according to the different collocating class markers, although they are not normally analysed as such in the literature.

Verb classification systems employing noun class markers is a feature of at least some Joola languages (Niger-Congo, Senegal). In Gújjolaay Eegimaa, according to Sagna (2007, 2008, 2017), infinitival forms of verbs occur in certain complement constructions, including 'want' complements (as in (6.13)), aspectual complements, continuative complements, terminative complements as well as in relational clauses (as in (6.14)). As these examples show, the infinitival forms involve a verb stem together with a noun class prefix.

(6.13)   *Appu*   *na-mammaŋ*   *e-ber*   *mámah*   Eegimaa
         Appu   RLS.3SG-want.REDUP   CL3-laugh   a-lot
         'Appu likes to laugh a lot.' (Sagna 2017: 57)

(6.14)   *gabu-rokk-ol*   *ga-kkoñ*   *si-haj*   Eegimaa
         CL5a-work-3SG.POSS   CL9-mind:cattle   CL4-domestic:animal(II.SG)
         'His/her job is to mind cattle.' (Sagna 2017: 57)

As (6.13) and (6.14) show, different noun class markers collocate with different verb stems in the infinitive. In Eegimaa fifteen different class/number prefixes collocate with infinitives, excluding the human noun class prefixes and locative class prefixes. Sagna (2007, 2008: 311; 2017) proposes that the noun class prefixes to infinitives represents a system of verb classification that is semantically motivated. The semantic criteria for the noun classes tend to carry over in a modified fashion to the verbal categories marked by the corresponding prefixes (Sagna 2008: 312). Noun class features such as shape, internal configuration, size, and individuation tend to be interpreted with verb stems in terms of internal temporal configuration (Sagna 2007). For example, the marker used with abstract nouns and liquids becomes the infinitive marker for states, and the plural class marker used for entities with a round configuration and languages becomes a marker for inherently repetitive, negative events, such as 'begging', 'slandering' or 'quarrelling'. As for numeral classifiers in the verbal domain, this type of system is dependent on the existence of a system of nominal classification.

Some lexical verbs in Eegimaa collocate with a single prefix, some with two or more. When a verb collocates with more than one prefix, one must be the prefix *e-*, the marker of CL3 singular, the default prefix that combines with the majority of nouns. Sagna (2017) presents convincing evidence that the alternations correlate with semantic differences, sometimes subtle, sometimes obvious. For instance, *su-*, CL4 plural, is used with verbs to express pluractionality – i.e. iterative or multiplicity of occurrence of an event – as shown by (6.15), whereas a single occurrence is indexed by the corresponding singular noun class marker *e-*, as in (6.16).

(6.15)　*u-m-u*　　　　*ni*　*su-roren*　*wa*　*u-baj-e*　　　　　　　Eegimaa
　　　　　PRS-CL1-MED　LOC　CL4-ask　what　CL6-happen-PFV
　　　　　'He is bothering people with questions.' (Sagna 2007)

(6.16)　*u-m-u*　　　　*ni*　*e-roren*　*wa*　*u-baj-e*　　　　　　　Eegimaa
　　　　　PRS-CL1-MED　LOC　CL3-ask　what　CL6-happen-PFV
　　　　　'He is asking what happened.' (Sagna 2007)

Sagna (2017) shows that the prefix *e-* tends to be strongly associated with transitive and telic verbs, and marks event singularity and boundedness. Alternative classifications of the same lexical verb tend to be associated with less transitive events and atelicity. For example, *-us* 'confess' collocates with CL9 *gá-* with an intransitive meaning, with CL3 *e-* with the transitive meaning (Sagna 2017: 69). In other instances of the same alternation the meaning difference relates to degree of transitivity, in accordance with the parameters of Hopper and Thompson (1980). Aktionsart, valency and perhaps also vectorial configuration are thus potential candidates for the semantic parameters underlying the system of verb classification in Eegimaa.

Other Joola languages, for example Jóola Fogny (Sapir 1965), also show lexically conditioned choices of noun class prefixes for infinitives, including some alternative choices for a single verbal lexeme. Whether these also represent verb classification systems is uncertain; the descriptions do not investigate this issue.

6.2.5.2 *Conjugation markers as verb classifiers*

Conjugation classes sometimes show characteristic conjugation markers that typically occur in the inflectional paradigms of the classes. For instance, many Pama-Nyungan languages distinguish between two and half a dozen conjugation classes, each with a characteristic marker. The bulk of verbs in these languages belong to these conjugation classes; there may be in addition a small set of irregular verbs that do not inflect according to these patterns. The prototypical shape of a verb in a Pama-Nyungan is Root(+Conjugation marker)+Inflection (Dixon 1980: 408), though morphophonemic processes and irregularities may obscure this structure. For instance, Yingkarta (Dench 1998: 40–41) has two open conjugation classes defined by the allomorph sets shown in Table 6.3.

Table 6.3 Yingkarta open conjugation classes (Dench 1998: 41)

Inflectional category	ø conjugation	l conjugation
Imperative	-ya	-ka
Future	-wu ~ -ku	-lku
Past	-purru	-lpurru
Imperfective	-npa	-npa
Present	-nyi	-lanyi
Relative (same subject)	-nhuru	-rnuru
Relative (different subject)	-tha(nu)	-rarnu
Purposive	-wura	-lkura
Apprehensional	-warangu	-lkarangu

Five of the inflections in the *l* conjugation show a characteristic *l*, which is absent in the corresponding categories in the ø conjugation. Criteria i–iv. are satisfied by the Yingkarta conjugation class system, taking – with some degree of poetic licence – *M* to be the set {ø, -*l*}: i. the bulk of the verbal domain is assigned to either the ø or the *l* conjugation; ii. in well-defined environments verbs collocate with *l* or nothing; iii. the cardinality of *M* is just two, much smaller than that of *D*, the set of regular verbs;[10] and iv. there is little if any overlap in the conjugation classes.

The conjugation classes of a number of other Pama-Nyungan languages are more or less similar to that of Yingkarta, and would also appear to satisfy criteria i.–iv. These classes are often regarded as purely morphological, with no clear-cut semantic or syntactic value (Dixon 1980: 382). Nevertheless, it seems that they are not entirely arbitrary, and there are often strong correlations between the classes and transitivity, especially for derived verb stems. In Yingkarta, for instance, in a small set of about 90 verbs, 82% of conjugation class ø were intransitive, while 88% of conjugation class *l* were transitive

(Dench 1998: 40). Some languages show stronger correlations. Thus, the Maric languages Margany and Gunya also have just two conjugation classes: an *l* class which is entirely transitive and a ø class that is entirely intransitive (Breen 1981: 275). Whether or not Aktionsart and vectorial configuration are associated with the conjugation systems of Pama-Nyungan languages remains to be tested; to date only transitivity correlations have been documented.

In some Pama-Nyungan languages the conjugation classes are largely disjoint. For example, in a lexicon of some 500 monomorphemic verbs in Dyirbal only five belong to more than one class; in Panyjima and Nyangumarta we find similar numbers of multiply classified verbs in somewhat smaller verbal lexicons. However, the conjugation classes sometimes share a more significant fraction of the verbal lexicon. Warrgamay has two conjugation classes, ø and *l*, which correlate perfectly with transitivity (Dixon 1981: 86). The vast majority of verb roots that may be assigned to the *l* class are ambi-categorial. Assigned to the *l* class they are transitive; assigned to the ø class they are intransitive. These ambi-categorial verbs comprise about two thirds of the verbal lexicon.

Conjugation classes are also found in various non-Pama-Nyungan languages of Australia. Nyulnyulan languages have largish sets of inflecting verbs that fall into two primary conjugation classes, along with irregular verbs and sometimes minor conjugation classes. These are defined in terms of the inflectional prefixes to inflecting verbs, and conjugation markers (*n- ~ na- ~ a-* and ø) show up in various places in the inflectional paradigms (McGregor 2002b: 214-219). There is again a strong correlation in Nyulnyulan languages between conjugation class and transitivity. All Nyulnyulan languages for which sufficient data exists show around a score of ambi-categorial inflecting verbs. For these inflecting verbs the correlation with transitivity is even better than in the general verbal lexicon. In the ø class the inflecting verbs are almost invariably intransitive, while assigned to the *n- ~ na- ~ a-* class they are almost invariably transitive (McGregor 2002b: 229–233). The Eastern Nyulnyulan language Yawuru shows a few exceptions where different conjugation class assignment is not associated with differences in transitivity. In these exceptions the different assignments are, however, associated with different degrees of transitivity, as per Hopper and Thompson (1980). For instance, the two verbs of speech -JIBA 'ask' and -JULKA 'tell' are assigned to both the *na-* and $ø_1$ classes. The former assignment suggests more serious impingement on the addressee than the latter assignment.

This section has shown that at least some conjugation class systems satisfy the criteria for classification systems, and that the classes may not be entirely arbitrary. Transitivity (valency) seems to be one of the major features; this feature is in a sense the correlate of gender in noun class systems. In some conjugation systems, including that of Wambaya (Mirndi), phonological properties of lexemes are relevant to the classification, as in some noun class systems.

This is not a claim that conjugation classes are always motivated. Thus, it seems that the Anindilyakwa conjugations are conditioned by neither phonology nor semantics

(Leeding 1989: 320). It may be that the conjugations of many Pama-Nyungan languages are functionless morphological elaborations, as suggested by (Dixon 1980: 382). It is likely, however, that the Pama-Nyungan inflectional classes had origins in more semantically transparent verb class systems, and ultimately verb classifier systems – see §6.4; see also Dammel and Kürschner (2018) on the diachrony of inflection classes in Germanic languages.

6.3 Grammar of Verb Classification Constructions

In this section we briefly outline an approach to the grammatical structures of the types of verb classification system identified in §6.2. To begin with, according to properties i.–iv. proposed in §6.1.2 what is common across all systems is a set of linguistic items *M* that collocate differentially in some grammatical environment with a set of verbal lexemes. These linguistic items serve – in the specified environment – as markers of the categories. That is to say, the verbal categories identified are the sets of verbs that are picked out by their collocations with the members of the set *M*. In terms of the Neo-Firthian approach outlined in §1.1.3, the members of *M* serve the textural function of category marking in the specified grammatical environment (McGregor 2002b: 266–275).

Collocation is therefore not exclusively a relation between pairs of lexical items. It can also be (or become) a grammatical relation. If the association between certain sets of linguistic items is particularly strong, it may be more than a mere statistical association: it may become a marking relation. Collocation can thus span grammar and lexicon.

In verb class systems the members of *M* are dedicated to class marking; they typically serve in no other functions in the language. This is also the case in the Gooniyandi verb classifier system, where the classifying items have no other independent usages. But the marking relation is not always the only grammatical relation present in verb classification systems. In numeral classifier systems the phrase in which the classifier occurs simultaneously serves as a type of adverbial expression of frequency or duration. (See Paris 2013: 270 for rejection of analyses of the numeral classifier in Mandarin Chinese as cognate objects, quasi objects, complements and the like.) Likewise, in manner classifier systems the phrase in which the classifier occurs simultaneously serves as a manner adverbial expression.

In verb classifier systems of the northern Australian type (§6.2.1.1) the classifier is an inflecting verb, which typically has another use as the sole lexical item of an event-specifying VP. As many commentators have remarked, in the classifying verb construction in these languages the uninflecting verb and inflecting verb together form a type of lexical compound (McGregor 2002b: 247–249). Their combination is associated with a meaning that is not entirely predictable from the meanings of the component lexical verbs, as is prototypically the case in compounding. And formally the combinations are often quite tight: the two lexemes are typically distributionally inseparable and often occur in a fixed order. (These observations remain true even in those systems in which the lexical roots are never adjacent, but always separated by inflectional material.)

It has been argued by some that the compound verb construction typical of northern Australian languages should be analysed as complex predicate constructions – for example, Wilson (1999); Amberber, Baker and Harvey (2010); Baker and Harvey (2010); Nordlinger (2010); Bowern (2014). There are problems with this analysis. Complex predicate constructions are generally understood to show two predicating lexemes that predicate jointly (Baker and Harvey 2010: 13; Butt 2010: 50). In the compound verb construction, however, just a single lexeme actually specifies the event: only the uninflecting verb serves in an event-specifying function, and thus as a predicational element as I understand the term. The other item, the uninflecting verb, categorizes the event rather than contributes to its specification. Further arguments against the complex predicate analysis are developed in McGregor (2002b: 252–266; 2006b, 2012a: 446–448); see also Dickinson (2000).

In these northern Australian systems we see further manifestation of the observation that classification lies on the border of grammar and lexicon. Compounding is of course a lexical relation. On the other hand, it emerges clearly from §6.2.1.1 that there are strong regularities in the compounds, such that at the same time one element (the inflecting verb) can be said to serve a grammatical relation of marking. By comparison, in the nominal compounds of English or Danish such regularities are not found, and no element in the compound serves as a grammatical marker.

This is not an argument for a seamless cline from lexicon to grammar as envisaged by standard SFL, Construction Grammar and Cognitive Grammar. Rather, it indicates that the same linguistic phenomenon can on the one hand show lexical features and on the other grammatical features. These features do not blur the distinction between grammar and lexicon: one aspect (compounding) is lexical, the other (marking) is grammatical. As remarked in §1.1.3 there is a sharp semiotic divide between lexicon and grammar: only the latter separates different semiotic types (aka metafunctions).

6.4 Diachrony of Verb Classification Systems

Rather little has been written on the diachrony of verb classification systems, far less than on the diachrony of nominal classification systems. In this section I provide an overview of some possible diachronic processes of development for some types of system, beginning with the most grammaticalized types, verb class systems.

Let us begin with the conjugation systems typical of Pama-Nyungan languages. According to Dixon (1980: 408–426), the consonantal conjugation markers of these languages derive from verb-root final consonants which were ultimately reanalysed as part of the inflectional material. Correspondingly, the ø conjugation class, with no marker, arose from verb roots with a final vowel. McGregor (2002b: 352–354) suggests an alternative origin in proto-Pama-Nyungan inflecting verbs. He proposes that this proto-language was like many of the languages of northern Australia in having a compound verb construction consisting of an uninflecting verbal element followed by an inflecting verb (see also Merlan 1979). The shape of the inflecting verb in this construction came to be altered over the passage of time, as it lost its categorical status as a verb. In some cases part of the erstwhile inflecting verb became reanalysed as a part of the (formerly uninflecting) verb root while the remainder was reinterpreted as the conjugation marker; in other cases the remnant of the inflecting verb became reinterpreted as the conjugation marker. The conjugation classes of some modern Pama-Nyungan languages are thus more grammaticalized than the Gooniyandi system (see p. 146 above). This scenario has it that the class system is a grammaticalization of a formerly less grammatical classifier system, a parallel development in the verbal domain to the proposed development of many noun class systems from noun classifier systems (Dixon 1980: 171; 2002: 450; Sands 1995: 285–286; Aikhenvald 2000: 272–273).

Not all conjugation systems, however, are likely to have developed from previous verb classification systems. For instance, the Nyulnyulan system probably arose via the reanalysis of the third person minimal accusative pronominal prefix in the inflecting verb as a conjugation marker (McGregor 2002b: 361). This accounts for the transitivity correlation in modern Nyulnyulan languages. (See also McGregor 2008b on the pronominal origin of some noun class markers in Worrorran languages.)

We turn now to the less grammaticalized verb classifier systems of northern Australian languages, and their possible origins and evolutionary developments. The classifiers are inflecting verbs that are deployed in another function than specifying the event. Their historical origin is clearly in lexical verbs, and most retain the ability to specify events, i.e. to occur as the lexical verbs of simple verb constructions. The classifying inflecting verbs typically number less than thirty in any language. There is also a good deal of similarity in the verbs that are used as classifiers: they are typically semantically general ones that would be expected to be highly frequent in usage, such as 'say, do', 'sit, be', 'stand', 'become', 'fall', 'go', 'carry', 'take', 'hit', 'catch, get', 'put', 'give', 'throw', and 'spear, poke'. Not infrequently a few more semantically specific and lower frequency verb will be found among the classifying verbs, as in the case of 'wander' in Nyulnyul. But these are the exceptions, and have low functional loads within their systems. (Again similarities with nominal classifier systems are apparent, where classifiers also tend to derive from semantically generic and high frequency lexical items – Aikhenvald 2000: 353–367.)

The other category of lexical item in the compound verb construction shows quite different phonotactic, morphological and syntactic properties, and clearly has a different diachronic source. Schultze-Berndt (2001) and McGregor (2001, 2002b) argue that synchronic properties of uninflecting verbs are consistent with an initial origin of many in ideophones; see also, for example, Heath (1976: 737) and Alpher (1994: 165). These ideophones occurred in collocation with inflecting verbs, providing more expressive and depictive meaning to the verbal expression. Over time these more expressive collocations came to be more frequently used and ultimately replaced many of the more mundane simple verb constructions in the expression of verbal meanings; simultaneously the set of ideophone-like lexemes expanded in number (McGregor 2002b: 341). Over time the new bi-lexical depictive expression also began to lose its expressive force, and the erstwhile ideophones came to describe rather than demonstrate (in the sense of Clark and Gerrig 1990) their referents. (See McGregor 2002b: 324–351 for fuller details.)

Central to this historical scenario is the notion that the compound verb construction, synchronically a verb classifier system, was initially driven by concerns of expressiveness. As Capell (1979: 294) put it: 'Compound conjugation is [sic] Australia developed first of all as a syntactic matter, a device probably for vividness and clarity of expression, certainly not for any grammatical reasons.' The northern Australian verb classifier system is an evolutionary exaptation; it might also be seen as in some sense an anti-spandrel: erstwhile elaboration and decoration was reinterpreted as a functional space.

The compound verb construction diffused areally across the northern part of Australia, prior to the splitting up of many of the proto-languages of the region (McGregor 2002b: 350–351). The construction itself was diffused across the proto-languages via calquing; the lexical items themselves were not borrowed. I have argued that for the Nyulnyulan (McGregor 2013a, 2018b) and Worrorran (McGregor and Rumsey 2009: 56–67) families it is possible to reconstruct not just a number of uninflecting verbs and inflecting verbs in the proto-language, but also a number of collocations of the two. Some of these collocations have remained stable over very long periods of time, and are characteristic of the families to which they are restricted. For proto-Nyulnyulan and proto-Worrorran the compound verb constructions furthermore show certain features associated with verb classifier systems in modern languages, and it is possible that even in the proto-languages these constructions were verb classifier constructions, or were well on the way to becoming classifier constructions.

To wind up this section, brief mention should be made of verbal numeral classifier systems. Matthews and Yip (1999) and Matthews and Leung (2004) suggest that numeral classifiers in the verbal domain historically derived from nominal numeral classifiers. They propose an initial construction with a verb and an NP object containing a numeral classifier. The head nominal of this NP was omitted, and the construction ultimately comprised the numeral classifier phrase alone, without a head noun. For instance, the Thai *kin sɔ̌ɔŋ kham* (eat two mouthfuls) would have derived historically from the transitive construction *kin khâw sɔ̌ɔŋ kham* (eat rice two mouthfuls). This scenario accounts for various facts about verbal numeral classifier systems, including the fact that many of the classifiers found in the verbal domain are shared with the nominal domain in languages with verbal numeral classifiers.

6.5 Concluding Remarks

Section 6.2 presents evidence that verb classification systems are not uncommon in the languages of the world. It seems likely that they are more common than attested in the literature, given that verb classification is not a grammatical phenomenon that descriptive linguists are widely aware of. To be sure, it may well be that verb classification systems are less common cross-linguistically than noun classification systems, and Bisang (2018) presents some convincing arguments as to why this should be so: effectively, that verb classifiers are less stable as classifiers than noun classifiers. Specifically, they are more likely than noun classifiers to grammaticalize into items that do not serve classificatory functions.

The approach to overt grammatical classification adopted in this chapter depends on a definition that takes distributional facts into account, including collocations of lexical and linguistic items that serve as markers of categories. This shows that Firth's notion of collocation is not just a matter of text or context, but can also be relevant to grammar. Grammaticalization processes are not restricted to lexical items becoming grammatical, but also include the reinterpretation of collocations as marking relations, ultimately blurring the division between collocation and colligation. These collocations can remain stable over long periods of time, permitting one to reconstruct them in proto-languages. The discussion of this chapter further reveals that collocations do indeed represent a part of the semantic specification of linguistic items, as suggested by Firth.

Due to space limitations we have not been able to deal with all of the important issues in verb classification systems. One of these concerns the uses of systems of verb classification. This is an issue I have investigated elsewhere for the Gooniyandi and Warrwa systems (McGregor 2002b: 363–389; 2007b), where I have suggested that one of the uses of the systems in narrative is in the foregrounding and backgrounding of events. Choice of atelic classifiers serves to background events, while telic classifiers foreground the referent event. This is reminiscent of observed correlations between aspect and grounding (e.g. Hopper 1979).

How other verb classification systems might be employed in discourse is an interesting question for future investigation. Some scholars – for example, Greenberg (1972) and Burling (1965: 259–260) – have remarked on individuation as a cognitive function of numeral classifiers in the nominal domain. Dickey and Janda (2015) take up this idea in relation to the lexical prefixes of Slavic languages, and draw a number of parallels with numeral classifiers. They propose that individuation assigns a spatio-temporal shape to the classified verb. Matthews and Leung (2004) propose a similar thing for numeral classifiers of verbs in Cantonese and Thai. It is not unreasonable to suggest that individuation plays an important role in other verb classifier systems, including the systems of northern Australian languages. In such languages the verbal lexeme itself typically conveys little in the way of semantic specification in terms of 'shape' – it is by and large unspecified for valency, Aktionsart and vectorial configuration. Only when classified does the verb take on a specific value on these dimensions.

A second issue of interest concerns how one might go about comparing systems of classification in terms of their degrees of similarity and difference from one another. I am not thinking here of categorizing systems as in §6.2, but rather the question of how to measure the similarity of two systems of the same type. Thus, McGregor (2013a) addresses the question of how similar verb classifier systems in northern Australian languages might be. Cluster analysis reveals that Nyulnyulan systems are more alike one another than they resemble the systems of nearby languages.

Third, a perennial question regarding classification systems is the Whorfian one of their relation to cognition: do overt classification systems tell us anything about the world view or cognitive style of speakers of the language? Lakoff (1986) and Allan (1977), among others, have argued that this is so for nominal classification systems. I am not aware of much relevant work in the verbal domain. One partial exception is Folli and Harley (2006). Unfortunately, however, this work is dominated by English to the virtual exclusion of all other languages, and makes no reference to systems of verb classification of the types discussed in this chapter. It mentions just the covert system of verb classification in English, according to Aktionsart, transitivity, and the opposition between unergative and unaccusative verbs. It is proposed that these event types are relevant to language acquisition and processing. It would be interesting to enquire into the possible relevance of overt verb classification systems (see also Evans and Levinson 2009).

Chapter 7

Conclusions

7.1 The Significance of Linguistic Typology

7.1.1 Linguistic Typology and Synchrony

Typology plays a central role in linguistics, and is more than a mere application of linguistic ideas or theory. Figure 7.1 displays the mutual interactions among a range of
fundamental domains of linguistics, conceived from the perspective of their orientation
and methodology rather than subject matter. It distinguishes the activities of collection
of data (fieldwork), putting this data together into a usable shape for analysis (language
documentation), analysing the data and putting it together into a coherent description
(descriptive linguistics), typology (comparing and contrasting with other languages),
and theory (the perspective from which all of these activities are undertaken). The
labels given are those appropriate to the subfields that concern the fundamental activity of language description and the production of grammars. They apply equally to other
subject domains of linguistics, whether it be the domain of language learning by the

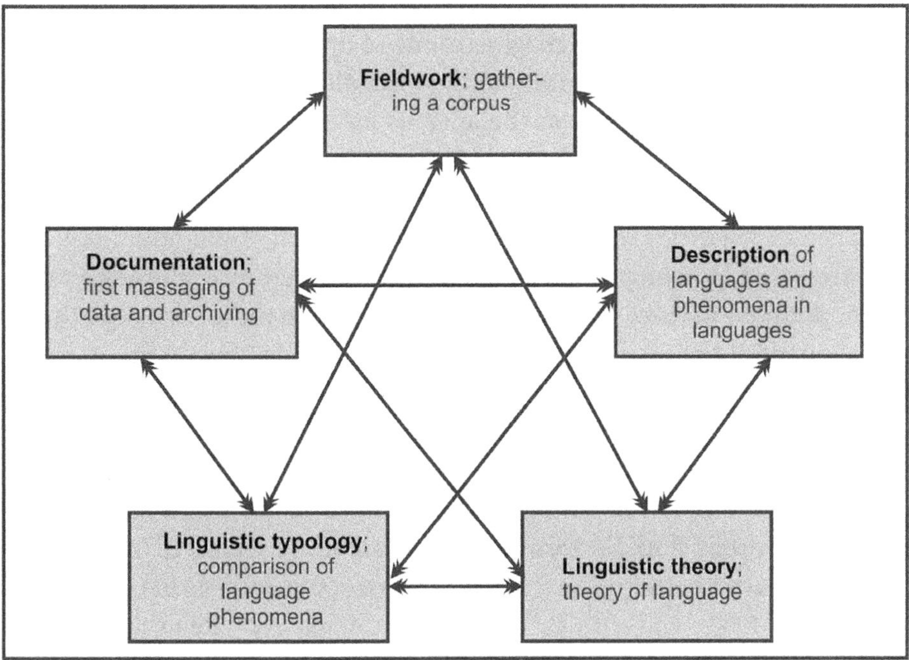

Figure 7.1 Interacting components of linguistics

child, language diachrony, sociolinguistics, psycholinguistics, or whatever – including even linguistic typology and theoretical linguistics! Whatever we do, we presumably need data, which must be organized in a usable way, analysis and description of it, comparison with other similar data sets, all of which depends on some theoretical perspective – recall Darwin's and Firth's words quoted in §1.2.4.1.

This model provides, I would argue, a more comprehensive view of the Firthian renewal of the connection than Firth's focus on just the interaction between data and theory. To illustrate the complex interaction among the components we discuss an example.

Suppose I have decided to embark on a project of describing an undocumented language of Amazonia. I will obviously need to gather a corpus of data on this language, and to do this it will be necessary to do fieldwork. The nature and focus of the fieldwork will depend on my linguistic theory, including: the sorts of information I target, whether I focus attention on gathering speaker's acceptability or grammaticality judgements, and so on. Moreover, the very nature of what is construed as data will be dependent on my theory. This should not be a one-way street. While doing fieldwork I should be thinking of the theory, and things that do not neatly fit with it. I will also be massaging the data into a usable shape, which process will be a focus of activity on my return home – typically after six to twelve months in the field. While all this is going on, I will be attempting to analyse the data, and describe the grammatical patterns in the language. The activities of documentation and description will play into one another – for instance, I will presumably want my corpus represented in a phonemic shape as soon as possible, which can only be done after serious analysis (descriptive linguistics).

As my documentation of the language expands, so my description will be refined, and this will in turn affect the documentation – for example, how I understand the meaning of a given morpheme will change as the analysis proceeds and as the documentation becomes more comprehensive. To be usable by myself – and even more so by others – a documentation will need to provide information about the meaning of the utterances that comprise it. What this means in practice is that each of the utterances will ideally be represented in phonemic form, along with an interlinear gloss line and a free translation. But none of these are givens, and all depend on the analysis and theory – as well as the minds of the interactants in the fieldwork situations. As the analysis proceeds, the understanding of both the coded meanings of the morphemes (ideally what is represented in the gloss line) and the utterance meaning of the entire utterance in its context (ideally what is represented in the free translation) will change. Changing these things has to happen as a language is better understood. There is no unassailable 'raw' data in the corpus. Both the form and the meaning are subject to improved understanding. I now have a better understanding of certain phenomena in Gooniyandi than I had in the mid-1980s, and with this my analysis of certain categories has changed; this is especially the case in the modal domain, where I would now rewrite the relevant sections of McGregor (1990a) quite differently – as well as give different glosses and free translations. This is not doctoring the data. There is no data out there, independent of human construal.

My linguistic theory will also shape my description and documentation: what sorts of phenomena I focus attention on, ignore, and how I construe the facts as components in analyses and arguments for them. For instance, if my theory is a formal one, I might focus attention on issues such as cross-clause coreference conditions in an investigation of complex sentences, and pay less attention to different construction types of complex sentences as signs and the meanings they code and implicate. The foci of interest are likely to be reversed for a Neo-Firthian.

There is, of course, always the danger that I will miss important phenomena because they are not on the radar of my linguistic theory. This is why the interaction should not be one-way: why I need to also move from the data to the theory, and why knowledge of typology is essential.

Linguistic typology is relevant at all points in these processes. It provides notions of what to expect, which is relevant to each of the above 'work packages'. Descriptivists frequently allude to Boas' advice to describe a language in its own terms. This is, of course, good advice: one should identify what is emic in a language, and organize the description around this, rather than around categories of other languages or notions in the minds of linguists. But Boas' advice does not mean that one should ignore other languages – knowledge of what to expect or not in a language, stemming from both typology and theory, guides the descriptive linguist, alerting them to phenomena that they might not otherwise have noticed or sought. Conversely, of course, descriptive work on a language will input to linguistic typology, potentially renewing it.

I have always considered that it is the exceptional and rare phenomena that are of greatest interest and significance in description, typology and theory. Indeed, my own interest in English grammar has exclusively focused on the unusual: tags to interrogatives (*are you going now, are you?* – McGregor 1995a, 1995b), so-called 'nominal tautologies' (*boys will be boys* – McGregor 1997b: 347–376), presumption invoking existentials (*there are beers and beers* – McGregor 2013d) and defenestration (§4.5; McGregor 2019b). It is only relatively recently that typologists have accorded linguistic raria the attention they deserve, with volumes such as Wohlgemuth and Cysouw (2010a, 2010b). Typological investigations of many raria are hampered by lack of information in grammars. In part this is expected and reasonable, given that a grammar must attend most to that which is usual. However, knowledge of some of the raria to be encountered in a language – and an eye for the unexpected (founded on knowledge of descriptive and typological work) – can guide fieldwork and bring to light phenomena that might be so rare in usage that they would not be likely to appear in ordinary speech within the time window of the average fieldwork project. See, for example, McGregor (2015) on four expectation-invoking constructions in Shua that are highly infrequent in use; for comparison, see McGregor (2017b) on a manner construction rather commonly employed in Shua speech, but typologically rare.

7.1.2 Linguistic Typology and Diachrony

Linguistic typology is a very different enterprise from historical-comparative linguistics, which attempts to categorize languages according to their genetic provenance. Languages can be typologically similar without being genetically related – and genetically related without being typologically similar. This does not, however, mean that typology is inherently synchronic, or that diachrony is irrelevant to it.[1] 'Everything is what it is because it got that way', as Haiman (2003: 108) has put it.

Time is relevant to all aspects of language and language use, including the system itself, which according to some extreme functionalists (e.g. Hopper 1987) is always in the process of coming into being – without ever getting there! In relation to language, we can think of time in terms of the largest periods of evolutionary history of life (even the universe) down to the smallest periods of milliseconds; for example, Durie (1998); see also LeDoux (2019). Table 7.1 provides a very gross timeline for the temporal periods most relevant to language.

Table 7.1 Gross timeline for events related to human language

Temporal period	Phenomenon
Millions of years	Evolution of biological systems and species; the emergence of the language-ready body
Tens of thousands of years	Evolution of human language in a social context
Thousands of years	Life cycle of languages
Hundreds of years	Significant language change; emergence of new varieties and languages and new grammatical phenomena (grammaticalization processes)
Decades	Human life span; noticeable changes in language systems and usage
Years	Learning ('acquisition') of the mother tongue
Months	Appearance and acceptance of new words
Days	Maximum duration of interactions (e.g. rituals)
Hours	Discourses
Minutes	Exchanges ('adjacency pairs')
Seconds	Utterances
Milliseconds	Psycholinguistic and neurolinguistic processing time

The two largest periods of time – ranging from tens of thousands of years to millions of years – relate to the evolution of human language. In keeping with functionalist and usage-based accounts, it is presumed that biology, including genetics, provided us with a language-ready body and brain, and that the evolution of language itself was primarily within its socio-cultural context (e.g. Tomasello 1999, 2008, 2014).

Normal processes of language change occur over periods of decades to thousands of years; it is normally agreed that the historical-comparative method is restricted to periods of time not exceeding about 10,000 years – after which the genetic signal becomes indistinguishable from noise.

The language system itself is learnt over a period of roughly a decade or so, within which the basic grammatical patterns of the language will have been learnt. Of course, one may gain improved skills in one's language throughout life, but this is by and large elaboration on the basics that were set in the first decade of life. New words and registerial varieties are more or less readily learnt.

The smaller temporal dimensions relate to actual usage of the system, going from what is perhaps the largest phenomena, interactive behaviours such as rituals that may extend over a number of days. But the majority of these are smaller in size, ranging from hours (for discourses) to minutes (for exchanges), related sequences of utterances (typically lasting seconds) involving interaction between speakers. At the smallest size are the milliseconds of processing time in the brain.

The various temporal dimensions have been linked in different ways by linguists of different persuasions. Many functionalists consider that the notion of function-purpose links all the temporal dimensions. Language evolved in the ways it did in order to satisfy the purposes to which it has been put in human life, beginning with the environment of the hunting-gathering lifestyle characteristic of all humans until quite recently. This function is also arguably relevant to the historical dimension of thousands of years and centuries; for instance, Halliday has proposed that certain changes occurred in English in post-scientific revolution times in response to different demands put on language (e.g. Halliday 1988b; Halliday and Martin 1993).

The semiotic components (aka metafunctions) provide a way of linking the broad functions of language with grammar itself. The hypothesis is that the systems of languages are organized emically around four of these semiotics, which structure grammar. There are (as in standard Hallidayan SFL) natural or motivated associations between the semiotic components and types of syntagmatic relations. In my view (which is not shared by other Neo-Firthians, as far as I am aware), these facilitate at the ontogenetic level the learning of the abstract system of patterns that comprises grammar. In phologenetic terms they account for features of the grammatical organization of human languages, for how and why languages developed in the ways they did. McGregor (2019a) employs this insight to develop a story of the evolutionary origins of interpersonal grammar.

Another influence on the historical development of languages comes from language learning: it is widely believed that the child leads processes of language change via their construction of a language that differs slightly from the system of their parents.

Various linguists have pointed to the influence of the millisecond domain on language change. This is fundamental to usage-based grammars, that construe changes in historical time – in particular, grammaticalization processes – as founded in use of the language system. The habitual choices made by speakers serves as a primary driving force in grammaticalization (Bybee 2010). Another perspective on this is Halliday's notion (e.g. 2002: 359) that every time a linguistic choice is made it alters the probabilities of the grammatical system slightly, and that over time this can result in change at the level of the system. Given that networks of interaction between speakers of a language clump socially and geographically, this notion can also account for synchronic variation in a language.

One of the fundamental premises that one works on when doing diachronic linguistics at the levels below the two largest is that human languages remain ultimately comparable in overall shape, that the languages spoken 10,000 or 20,000 years ago are fundamentally modern human languages. How far back this assumption can be projected is contentious, and there are vastly different answers depending on whether one assumes genetically modern humans always spoke fully modern human languages as a part of their biological heritage, or invented them in socio-cultural contexts. Linguistic typology can be expected to play some role in the temporal dimensions below the two largest. At the two largest temporal dimensions, by contrast, typology will be less useful: the proto-languages we reconstruct for our hominid ancestors need not satisfy all of the design features of human language (as per Hockett 1960), and may well be typologically distinct from modern human languages.

Thus, typology can provide the historical linguist working in temporal periods measurable in thousands of years with some means of assessing the plausibility of their reconstructions. Various linguists have evaluated the plausibility of certain historical reconstructions in the light of typological expectations (see e.g. Shields 2011: 552–556). Of course, this must be tempered by the realization that we do not know everything about possible shapes of the grammars of languages, and that the unusual does occur – we cannot necessarily rule out a reconstruction simply because it is typologically unusual or even unique.

Typology can also be employed by the historical linguist as a tool along with other tools of historical-comparative linguistics. Typology – tempered by the cautions of the previous paragraph – may be particularly relevant where the comparative method does not apply easily, for example in syntactic reconstruction. More interestingly, Nichols has proposed (1992, 2003, 2013) that by taking certain highly stable typological features into account, genetic and/or areal connections among languages can be pushed back from the 10,000 year limit of the historical-comparative method to a time depth of 30,000–60,000 years. An important challenge here is to identify these metastable features.

Typology may also be relevant at the smaller temporal dimensions as well. For example, there could be differences in the grammatical shapes of utterances in exchanges depending on the grammatical features of a language. The repetition of subject and finite element so characteristic of English exchanges (*will you go to the office tomorrow – yes I will/no, I won't*) is impossible in languages that lack free finite elements such as *will*, and/or do not distinguish a category of subject.

Evans and Levinson (2009) argue that cognitive science has tended to assume languages are cut to fundamentally the same pattern, and has given insufficient attention to variety and variation in human languages. This has impoverished cognitive science, they argue, which has underestimated the nature and variety of human cognition, as well as the place of language in it. As Levinson and Gray (2012: 171) put it:

> Language variation breeds cognitive diversity. Different languages require different processing algorithms, so that there are systematic differences in brain activation according to the language being spoken, e.g. Chinese involves more bilateral activation in word recognition … Different spatial language correlates with different spatial memory strategies … Given brain plasticity, speakers of different languages are likely to have slightly different brains … Literacy, for example, substantially rewires the brain.

This is reminiscent of Firth's emphasis on diversity and variety in language. Indeed, diversity should be instated along with reflexivity, duality of patterning, displacement, etc. as a Hockettan design feature (Hockett 1960).

If different processing strategies are invoked for different types of grammatical structure, perhaps some modes of expression for certain types of meaning are less expensive in processing terms than others. Ultimately, such cognitive differences could have implications on directions of language change.

The notion that some changes may be more natural than others plays an important role in modern thinking about historical processes in language. This provides a context for grammaticalization theory, which is concerned with 'the way grammatical forms arise and develop in space and time' (Heine 2003: 575). Much research on grammaticalization has been informed by and informs linguistic typology. For instance, the typology of noun categorization systems including classifier systems and class or gender systems has long been in a relation of mutual exchange with the grammaticalization of systems of categorization (see §6.4). It is natural in the domain of noun classification to interpret the synchronic typological variation diachronically. Recent work in grammaticalization has addressed the question of the extent to which grammaticalization pathways are universal, and the extent to which they are dependent on genetic and areal features (e.g. Narrog and Heine 2018; Bisang and Malchukov 2020). Typological characteristics of languages may thus influence the grammaticalization trajectories they follow.

7.2 Future Prospects

7.2.1 Sign Language Typology

This book has focused attention exclusively on spoken languages, languages employing the auditory-vocal medium. There are over a hundred natural human languages that employ the visual-gestural medium, namely the primary sign languages of the deaf. (*Ethnologue* currently (15-10-2019) lists 144 sign languages, the majority of which are primary languages of deaf communities – https://www.ethnologue.com/subgroups/sign-language.) These have been left out of the account because of considerations of space and because of the relative lack of reliable and depth descriptive and typological information. Fortunately, more and more descriptions of sign languages are appearing, and interest in their typology is increasing.

Deaf sign languages raise a host of issues of potential relevance to typology which might also argue for their separate treatment in linguistic typology, in preference to appending them to typologies of spoken languages. The different medium employed may have significant implications. For example, it is possible that the absence of any unit comparable to the phoneme in sign languages is a consequence of the nature of the visual-gestural medium. So also might be the preference for simultaneous expression in morphology, and thus the preponderance of fusional morphology.

Other factors that potentially play into sign language typology and structure include the sociolinguistics of transmission of the languages and the age of sign languages. Unlike most spoken languages deaf sign languages are not predominantly passed down generationally, but rather within generations, between peers. (Most deaf children have hearing parents, who are not native users of any sign language.) This sociolinguistic feature goes along with a not uncommon relatively late age of learning of sign languages as compared to spoken languages.

Most deaf sign languages are relatively young, many being traceable back just a few centuries. In traditional hunting-gathering and agricultural societies the deaf typically formed a small proportion of the population. They were by and large isolated from one another, thus restricting the emergence of full signed languages. There are a few exceptions, in isolated communities with a high incidence of genetic deafness, where so-called village sign languages arose. But by and large the majority of deaf sign languages have arisen in post-industrial times, with the bringing together of significant communities of deaf people. In a few cases these communities are so recent that it has been possible for linguists to almost observe the emergence and conventionalization of sign languages in progress – Nicaraguan Sign Language is a well-known example (Senghas, Kita and Özyürek 2004), as is also Al-Sayyid Bedouin Sign Language, which followed a somewhat different trajectory as a village sign language (Sandler et al. 2005, 2011).

Many investigators believe that the relative youth of sign languages is reflected in their higher than usual incidence of iconicity and motivation; the visual medium may also be more amenable to iconic representation than the auditory. From a Neo-Firthian perspective, sign languages offer an intriguing test case for the emic semiotic components, and more specifically the hypothesis that these are coded by distinct types of syntagmatic relation. It may also be possible to observe or infer processes of emergence of these emic phenomena from some proto-language, perhaps in a manner akin to the crystallization of the emic from an etic morass in the child's learning of the mother tongue (Halliday 1975/1977; McGregor 2019a). This has obvious implications to the evolution of human language at the largest time scales.

7.2.2 Future Prospects for a Neo-Firthian Typology

A number of significant and not uncommon grammatical phenomena have escaped the attention of Neo-Firthians (e.g. external possession constructions, as illustrated by *the farmer kissed the duckling on the lips* where there is a possessive relation between the NP *the duckling* and the NP *the lips*), while others have attracted an inordinate amount of attention (e.g. information structure and thematic relations). This seems to me to be largely a consequence of the research paradigm of the dominant Neo-Firthian theory, SFL, which pays insufficient attention to both language description and linguistic typology. Instead of focusing attention on writing descriptive grammars, and confronting the problems this raises, Neo-Firthians have attended to certain phenomena in their descriptions – naturally enough those that are accorded greatest theoretical significance. This is further exacerbated by the absence a typological angle. In this section I discuss some future prospects for mutual enrichment between Neo-Firthian linguistics and linguistic typology; this is a personal listing, and there is no implication of exhaustiveness.

As indicated in Chapter 1, non-arbitrariness in the linguistic sign has gained recognition in recent years, and along with this interest in phonological regularities in the lexicon, iconic and non-iconic (e.g. Brown, Holman and Wichmann 2013; Blasi et al. 2016). Phonaesthesia and sound symbolism have become popular topics (see references on p. 2 above; also, for the historical record, Sapir 1929; Martin 1962; Kim 1977). Aside from the typological issues these phenomena raise (e.g. how common is phonaesthesia cross-linguistically, how similar are the meanings associated with phonaesthemes, etc.), there is the question of where phonaesthesia belongs in the lexicon or grammar (e.g. Kwon and Round 2015).

Neo-Firthian theories have focused attention on the lexicon and syntax in grammar, and have said little about morphology.[2] In standard Hallidayan SFL a rank of 'morpheme' is identified, and a linear item-arrangement type of morphology assumed – the rank next above, the word, is composed of units of the morpheme rank. It is well known that there are serious difficulties with item-arrangement morphology, especially (though not exclusively) for fusional languages – or more accurately, fusional aspects of languages. Merely hiving morphology off to realization statements in system networks is not a satisfactory way of addressing the problems. There is a serious need for theory development in morphology that pays attention to the known typological diversity.

Despite the significant place of lexicon in SFL, the theory has had rather little to say about important aspects of the lexicon; the tendency has been to treat it as 'most delicate grammar', and as the output of the final choices in system networks. Even in relation to something as fundamental as parts of speech there is much that remains descriptively and theoretically unclear. Halliday (1961) proposes that the classification of parts of speech should be according to function, that is, by looking downwards from rank immediately above. However, how precisely this categorization should be effected is not explained, and I am aware of no work in SFL that establishes actual criteria for parts of speech classification in English in accordance with Halliday's strictures. I have suggested a Hallidayan way of classifying parts of speech in Gooniyandi (McGregor 1990a: 140–141; 2013b), which is very similar to the proposals of Hengeveld (1992), situated within Functional Grammar, and later elaborations of this approach.

SFL has also had rather little to say about the meanings of lexical items as such – or indeed of the meaning of grammatical items, conveniently hived off as ineffable (see §2.3.3.2). This is a domain that needs attention within Neo-Firthian linguistics both in specific languages (including English) and in the typological domain.[3] Whether Neo-Firthian approaches have anything significant to offer to the burgeoning field of semantic typology remains to be seen – though I believe they do.

In contrast with 'ordinary' verbal clauses, relational clauses (see p. 21 above) have not been extensively studied in linguistic typology, and few descriptive grammars provide more than brief treatment. These clauses have, however, been extensively studied in English within SFL (e.g. Halliday 1985: 112–128; Davidse 1992, 2000). These studies have brought to light the incredible richness of this domain, and suggest directions for further investigation in descriptive and typological work. For instance, what range of emic types of relational clause are found within a given language, and what typological generalizations are possible?

Research in this domain has the potential to contribute to theory development, by raising questions such as the range of (emic) types of relational clauses and the nature and range of grammatical relations found in them. What, for example, is the grammatical role of the verb? According to SFL, in English relational clauses the verb *be* serves in the same grammatical role as does *kiss* in *the farmer kissed the duckling* – the role of Process. However, there are reasons to doubt this, and most linguists consider *be* to be a copula: it functions to link the two expressions, and does not represent any ongoing event. The nature and theoretical status of copulas then arises, an issue that has largely been ignored in linguistics.

In quite a number of languages we find both verbal and verbless clauses expressing relational meanings. It has been observed that in some languages (e.g. Israeli) the two modes of expression are in complementary distribution according to tense (Doron 1986). In other languages, however, the two expression types are not in complementary distribution. As remarked above (p. 22), in such languages a Neo-Firthian approach (as in many other functional approaches) will presume that the alternative expressions are not entirely synonymous.

This is the case for languages of my own expertise, including Gooniyandi (McGregor 1996a). Clauses with a verb of stance (primarily 'sit', 'stand' and 'lie') construe situations within which properties are held, whereas those involving just nominal expressions in apposition do not represent situations, but merely attribute the quality of an entity in the abstract as it were. Thus, clauses in Gooniyandi can be divided into two primary types, relational (that express relations, but do not designate ongoing actions or events) and situation (that do specify ongoing events). Relational clauses are logical clauses in the sense that only logical, and not experiential grammatical relations, are found at clause level; situation clauses involve experiential relations at clause level. The same distinction can be drawn, albeit in a different way in English, depending on whether or not the verb serves as a copula or in the experiential role of Process (Halliday 1985) or State of Affairs (McGregor 1997b). This provides a prediction that can be tested on a wider sample of languages.

Aside from the relations of attribution and identification, relational clauses can express the relation of possession, as in *the computer belongs to me* and *I have a computer*.[4] For a Neo-Firthian, the range of emic possessive relational clause types in a language, and their modes of expression immediately arises. So also does the issue of the incorporation of the possessive relations into situation clauses as in *I own the computer*. One wonders whether external possession constructions can also be analysed grammatically in the same way (see McGregor 1999a for a positive answer).

Also poorly treated in description and typology are so-called existential clauses, that is, clauses like *there are three deer in my backyard*. Nor has SFL said very much about these clauses – with the notable exceptions of Davidse (1999) and Davidse and Njende (2019). Once again, the SFL assumption that these clauses designate 'processes' or ongoing events can be questioned. I would argue that these also, like relational clauses, do not express experiential meaning as clauses. Moreover, it seems misleading to refer to them as existential clauses, since they do not predicate existence – as do clauses such as *black holes exist*. Rather, they point to the presence (or absence) of something in a certain search domain, drawing attention to it. They are thus more appropriately analysed as indexical clauses, expressing textural meaning at clause level. I suggest that this Neo-Firthian approach can provide new insights into this clause type, paving the way for improved descriptions and more comprehensive typological work.

The grammatical domains of mood and modality are also areas where Neo-Firthian linguistics can learn from description and typology, as well as potentially enrich it. At the same time, I have cautioned (§1.3.2) on the danger of reifying English or SAE modal categories as universal schemes for construing modality. What Neo-Firthian approaches can offer to this domain is the assumption that it is emic categories of particular languages that matter, and that the task of the linguist is to find these – and to reject the presumption of universal modal categories. The Neo-Firthian notion of the interpersonal semiotic will also in my view provide a useful analytical tool in this domain.

Marking of grammatical relations has no significant place in SFL, though SG recognizes it as a separate type of grammatical relation, a textural one (McGregor 1997b). In linguistic typology also marking relations as such have been accorded little attention beyond Johanna Nichols' typology (1986). This typologizes markers according to their locus: whether they occur on the head or dependent within a construction. This typology has been assumed within linguistic typology ever since, albeit with some modifications. It is not, however, unproblematic. For one thing, the presumption of a dependency theory in which all constructions are analysable in head-dependent terms is questionable. For another, the identification of head and dependent in these constructions is not uncontentious, and there are often serious disagreements among grammarians (e.g. Zwicky 1985; Hudson 1987; Bauer 1990; Corbett, Fraser and McGlashan 1993). Aside from renewing the typology in terms of the locus of marking, the nature of the marking relation – what is marked, and how – should surely be accounted for.

Marking interacts with the notion of markedness, which plays a significant role in Neo-Firthian thinking (as will be clear from the discussion of various phenomena above, including optional case marking), though some typologists have argued against its usefulness (Haspelmath 2006). In view of this, there is surely a need to rethink markedness and its role in grammar.

Most grammatical theories employ somewhere or other the notion of a zero element, and Neo-Firthian (and Firthian) linguistics is no exception. The notion is nowhere to my knowledge explicitly discussed or theorized in the Firthian or SFL literature. In the majority of instances I have encountered in this literature, the term seems not to be used in reference to genuine zeroes,[5] as illustrated by zero third person singular bound pronouns in many languages (that contrast with forms with phonological substance for other persons and/or numbers) or the zero participial suffixes of the English verbs *put* and *cut* – compare the regular participial forms with an overt suffix of, for example, *walked* and *taken*. Genuine zeroes are identifiable linguistic units with meaning but lack any overt form. The only Neo-Firthian treatment I am aware of is my own, in McGregor (2003b), which attempts to specify necessary and sufficient criteria for the identification of zeroes and to propose a preliminary typology of zero elements. However, I now realize that the criteria I proposed are too restrictive, and exclude genuine instances of zero; moreover, the typology needs to be elaborated and tested on a wider sample of languages. Aside from this, there is a serious need to theorize zero.

And to this we could add other problematic semiotic entities such as the *it* of *it's raining*, *it seems that you are invoking unmotivated zeroes*, and the like. Most linguists consider – with good reason – these to be dummy elements demanded by the grammar of English. Such dummy elements are anathema to Hallidayan SFL, where they are treated as fully functional items. This is another domain where current SFL and Neo-Firthian thought needs to be refreshed by reconnection with the facts of languages.

To wind up this discussion let me return to a general issue that was raised in Chapter 1, the comparanda of typology. Assuming that we have aptly chosen our phenomena in particular languages, the question arises as to whether there is some basis on which to compare and contrast them formally; typologists are beginning to ask these questions (e.g. Borin and Saxena 2013). A more interesting question is whether some modes of expression are more 'natural' or better for certain purposes, for expressing certain meanings. And further, is it possible to predict differences of meanings on the basis of formal mode of expression? For instance, inalienable possession is expressed in some languages by morphological devices (e.g. pronominal prefixation in Nyulnyul), by apposition or juxtaposition of NPs in some (e.g. Dyirbal) and by clausal constructions (e.g. by external possession constructions in English). Are there systematic and predictable differences in the coded, inferred and contextual meanings of these constructions? A theory that assumes certain syntagmatic relations to be meaningful could make testable predictions in this domain.

Notes

Chapter 1

1 For biographical information on Firth see Robins (1961); Honeybone (2005) and Thomas (2011: 178–184); the latter two works also contain useful overviews of his thought.

2 Firth himself recognized phonaesthesia in other Germanic languages, including Norwegian, Swedish and Dutch (e.g. Firth 1957: 45; 1964: 191–193), and suggested its presence in various other languages, including Mandarin Chinese and Bantu languages (Firth 1964: 187).

3 Some Firthians have objected that Hallidayan thought diverges so much from central ideas of Firth that it cannot be seen as Neo-Firthian (e.g. Firth 1968: 9). While there is some truth to the observation, many of Halliday's ideas are firmly rooted in Firthian thought (see e.g. Kachru 2015: 87–88). An approach would hardly count as Neo-Firthian if it followed Firth to the letter. See Thomas (2011: 238–243); Webster (2015) and Davidse (2018) for biographical information on Halliday.

4 In actual practice, however, systemicists quite frequently speak of the metafunctions in their etic senses, and reify experiential, logical, interpersonal and textual meanings as a notional categorization of the functions of language. (See McGregor 2019a for some examples.)

5 It should be noted that the term *dependency* as I am using it does not refer only to head-dependent relations (hypotaxis) but also to relations between parts neither of which serves as a head (parataxis).

6 For fuller accounts of the history of typology see Ramat (2011); Graffi (2011); and Jankowsky (2013).

7 This is an oversimplification, since syllable weight is also relevant to the placement of stress, such that heavy syllables typically attract stress. Indeed, the pattern of stress depends on morae rather than syllables in this language. (See McGregor 1990a: 120–123 for details.)

8 It must also be questioned whether these four classes are sufficient for the coverage of the major grammatical functions (assuming their universality). Some languages of northern Australia cast doubt on the adequacy of the four-way distinction in that they distinguish two distinct classes of word that typically serve in event-specifying functions. The problem might be circumvented by treating them as subcategories of a single overarching category (verb). However, virtually all descriptions of these languages treat them as separate categories because their morphosyntactic and phonological properties are so different. They also raise serious difficulties for universal definitions of verbs such as proposed by Hengeveld (1992); it is beyond the scope of this brief section to discuss these problems.

9 This section deals with lexical categories. Parts of speech categories in descriptive grammars, linguistic theory and typology often include non-lexical items such as adpositions and pronouns. There seems to me to be no reason in principle why parts of speech categories should not be expanded to include all morphemes (as well as stems, as is traditionally done

– though one wonders where to stop in terms of morphologically complex items: compounds? idioms?) regardless of whether or not they are lexical items, and indeed whether or not they are free items. I have taken such an all-inclusive approach to parts of speech in my own descriptive grammars (e.g. McGregor 1990a: 135–141; 2012a: 57–64). The critera for categorization of grammatical items will, of course, be rather different to those for the categorization of lexemes. I am not aware of typologies of parts of speech that attempt to include the gamut of grammatical items.

10   To be sure, some linguists do use the term *case* in the broader sense of any morphosyntactic system that marks grammatical relations, which would also include word or phrase order, verbal agreement and cross-referencing bound pronouns attached to verbs or other units. I prefer the narrower sense of the term, though I am also happy to speak of case in systems of cross-referencing pronominals where different morphological shapes are found according to the grammatical role that the cross-referenced NP serves. This extended sense of the term *case* is also excluded from the discussion of this section.

11   Darwin Correspondence Project, 'Letter no. 3257,' accessed on 23 September 2019, https:// www.darwinproject.ac.uk/letter/DCP-LETT-3257.xml.

12   The descriptive effort within a theory cannot be judged purely by the output of descriptive grammars. But this measure does give some indication of the seriousness with which the descriptive endeavour is taken: descriptive grammars are expected to cover a wide range of grammatical phenomena and not just a select few chosen by practitioners. There are, of course, article and book length SFL treatments of particular phenomena in various languages, and accounts of the grammars of languages from an SFL perspective that do not count as descriptive grammars. For instance, Halliday (1985) can be seen as an SFL account of English grammar, but hardly as a descriptive grammar of English. (See Mwinlaaru and Xuan 2016: 31–33 for a listing of over 100 works, mostly descriptive papers.)

13   I have been generous here, as some of the works listed do not contain substantial treatments of all three core domains, phonology, morphology and syntax, and some might be better treated as applications of SFL to the description of the grammar of the language – i.e. the descriptive enterprise is subservient to the application of the theory.

14   It is easy to find examples of this tendency in Halliday's writings. For instance, in his treatment of the NP ('nominal group') he distinguishes a Qualifier role associated with material following the referent specifying item (Halliday 1985: 166–167). His motivation is purely formal: this role is realized by prepositional phrases, relative clauses, and some qualifiers that are embedded in phrases. This is taken to be a distinct role from Epithet, which indicates a property of the thing referred to (Halliday 1985: 163–164). Halliday does not present any evidence that there is a meaning difference between these. The fact that the two sets of items are effectively complementary suggests that there is just a single role. Rather than accounting for the different ordering patterns by positing distinct role signs, one could recognize a single role, and a principle of placing 'heavy' material in final position – Behaghel's law of increasing terms (1932). This does not, however, fit with the view of function as the meaning side of a sign.

15   Contra Mwinlaaru and Xuan (2016: 12), it is far from being an 'enormous contribution to the semiotic mapping of languages'. The categories of WALS are exclusively notional ones in the compilers' conceptualization.

Chapter 2

1   Among the serious problems of this theory, consider the following small selection. First, evidence is wanting that all languages actually do distinguish grammatical relations of subject and object. Second, there is ample evidence that some languages do without the part-of-speech category verb (e.g. Rijkhoff 2007). Third, various commentators have remarked that word order typology is concerned with order of phrasal units, not words. But this is not strictly true: subject and object are relations presumably served by phrases, not phrases as such; and the verb is a lexical category (of questionable universality), not a type of phrase.

2   There are no valid grounds on which to reuse roles of either intransitive or transitive clauses, as per, for example, Velupillai (2012: 244); Bickel (2011: 402) who identify one of the roles in the ditransitive with the A of transitive clauses – why not with S, and why not identify one of the other roles as O? To take their steps opens the door to replacing A by S, undermining the entire theoretical apparatus, which is founded on the assumption of different roles in clauses of different valencies that may or may not be united by grammatical patterns.

3   At least, this is how things should be. In practice, however, a number of SFL treatments of grammatical relations in languages other than English simply assume the English-specific categories of Halliday (1985). This has been a perennial criticism of SFL.

4   I gloss over a complication: some Medium NPs are occasionally marked by the ergative postposition – see further Chapter 5. This implies the need for a sharper definition that brings frequency considerations into the picture.

5   One would also expect it to be of great interest to SFL, given the centrality of meaning in the theory. However, there is a negligible amount of work on the semantics of these roles, even for English. This is perhaps a consequence of the alleged ineffability of meanings of grammatical categories (Halliday 1985: xxxiii; 1988a). While I agree in principle that the meanings of all linguistic units are ultimately ineffable, this does serve as an excuse not to make an attempt to specify their meaning in some fashion, inadequate as that may be (McGregor 1997b: 52). The failure to explicate the meanings of the roles is almost certainly one reason why typologists have remained suspicious of the claims that grammatical roles are meaningful.

6   These classifications are based on Vendler (1967), which categorises English verbs into states, achievements, accomplishments and activities. However, it seems more likely that this typology is of the experiential cores of clauses (see Figure 2.2) rather than verbs (see also Dik 1989: 90).

Chapter 3

1   This is often expressed in terms of constituenthood, that the expression must represent a single constituent. As argued in McGregor (2003a), there is a fundamental misconception here between the notion of unithood – behaving as a single item grammatically – and the grammatical relation of constituency, a completely different phenomenon.

2   The same argument applies to non-finite clauses such as English *to* and *for* clauses (*the farmer wants to kiss the duckling, the farmer was reprimanded for kissing the duckling*) and argues for a separate rank below the clause and above the phrase.

3   I leave aside here the question of the relations among the dependents: whether each separately relates to the Entity nominal as a dependent, or whether there is nesting in the structure whereby the outer dependents are dependent on the syntagms formed by the more inner ones. My suspicion is that the ordering is conventionalised in terms of lexical meaning, and does not reflect anything about nesting of dependency relations.

4   I ignore a range of more complex examples in which a negator that appears in an NP has scope over the clause, as in *no sensible person would have crossed the line then*.

5   The positioning of the first instance of the postposition between the two nominals in each example does not make these discontinuous NPs: there is nothing exceptional about the placement of the postposition after the first unit of the NP in either Gooniyandi or Nyulnyul. (See also above §3.1.1 on why PPs are a type of NP.)

Chapter 4

1   This does not mean that the connection between the clauses is never marked in any way, only that it is not marked by a morpheme. In Gooniyandi, prosodic differences exist between coordinated clauses forming a larger unit together and clauses that represent separate sentences.

2   Headless relative clauses as in *what I need is some peace and quiet* also satisfy this definition, but are not normally regarded as complements. Conversely, it is not clear that all constructions habitually treated as complement constructions really involve the complement clause in an argument role in the main clause. The paratactic type discussed by Noonan (2007: 116–118) is a case in point: it is difficult to see how a clause in a paratactic relation to another can also serve in an argument role in it. (See further §4.4 below.)

3   Other varieties of SFL also treat complex sentence constructions – for example, Hudson (1971); Fawcett (1996). I do not attempt to account for the variety of opinion in the discussion below, largely because I find the Hallidayan treatment the more insightful in most respects.

4   Textural relations may also exist between a clause and another clause or part of another clause. For instance, collocational relations can obtain between entire clauses as well as between words; and in some languages an entire clause can be employed as a sentential conjunction, linking the sentence in which it occurs to the preceding discourse. However, these are non-structural relations, and thus are not included in the discussion of this chapter.

5   Other types of extension include replacement ('instead') and subtraction ('except').

6   The fact that the relative clause is a marked clause type that does not admit free occurrence is not evidence that the syntagmatic relation it enters into is hypotaxis, as per Halliday (1985: 204–207). Examples such as (4.13) and (4.14) are relational clauses, and hence show the same dependency relations as, for example, *that is the one.*

7   In some languages adjoined relative clauses are said to exist alongside embedded ones.

8   Clark and Gerrig (1990) assume that only direct quotation involves demonstration; I have argued that this view is untenable (McGregor 1994b).

9   The notion of distancing is not a simple one, and requires further investigation (McGregor 2019b: 210). This observation is reminiscent of others. Suggestions that link the contrast between direct and indirect speech to that between representing wording and meaning, the degree of mimesis in the report, and perspective.

10 I have argued that this generic verb is monosemic in Nyulnyulan languages (McGregor 2014b), with 'say', 'do' and 'think' (among other senses) contextual interpretations of a more general meaning.

11 Note that our concern here is with the syntagmatic relation between the two clauses, not with the formal categorization of either clause. It is beyond the scope of the present chapter, however, to argue the distinctiveness of these constructions from relative clauses and the like.

12 I interpret *payi* 'OK' as a separate minor clause since as I understand it this word is an interjection that can be used as a move (albeit minor) in an interaction.

13 This statement glosses over the important issue of whether or not the putative bound clause really is bound. In some languages a marked mood is employed in both free and bound clauses – for example, in Rembarrnga (McKay 1988) and Gooniyandi (McGregor 1988), without the bound usage being in any sense fundamental. Insubordination is not an appropriate analysis in such circumstances (contra Evans 2007: 423–425). See also D'Hertefelt and Verstraete 2014 for arguments that not everything that looks like insubordination necessarily is insubordination.

14 Spronck (2015, 2017) uses the term in reference to any instance in which a framing clause is missing from an instance of reported speech or thought. As indicated above, this usage is too broad, and fails to draw a distinction between non-presence of a framing clause due to its predictability (ellipsis) and non-presence of a framing clause as a grammatical feature, not predictable from information considerations.

Chapter 5

1 This is the traditional sense of the term, and more restricted than sometimes found in the typological literature, where it may refer to circumstances in which a single case marker marks distinct grammatical relations – for example, Stolz (1996); Palancar (2002, 2009). In the scheme of these authors in a language with a single case marker that marked both the grammatical role of Agent and Instrument there would be syncretism between Agent (ergative) and Instrument cases. In my scheme this is simply a case of a single marker being used to mark different grammatical roles.

2 The term *differential case marking* is frequently used as a cover term for all four possibilities shown in the final row of Table 5.2. The problem with this terminology is that the four phenomena share little in common, and differ substantially from one another semiotically. In what follows I use the term to refer to just one of the situations.

3 Yugambeh-Bundjalung (Pama-Nyungan, Australia) is the only exception I am aware of: the ergative is obligatory on pronouns, optional on nouns referring to human and large animals, and impossible on inanimates and lower order animates (Sharpe 1996: 76).

4 For simplicity in the remainder of this section only I use the term Actor in reference to the Actor role in intransitive clauses.

5 It is not always clear from the information available on a language that it shows optional accusative marking. Descriptions sometimes disagree, some saying or implying that an accusative marker is optional while others claim that grammatical features such as animacy, definiteness, individuation or specificity govern the usage or non-usage. Nor is it always

easy to be certain that a case marker is an accusative. Languages such as Spanish and various Sino-Tibetan languages where the marker is clearly a dative or oblique are excluded.

Chapter 6

1 It is commonly believed that the noun classes of many European languages are not semantically based. However, in a seminal article Zubin and Köpcke (1986) show that gender assignment in German is not unprincipled, and follows a number of semantic, morphological and phonological regularities.

2 This distinction is not universally accepted: the contrast seems to always be etic, and there are problems in drawing a sharp boundary between the two types (e.g. Beckwith 2007: 3, 4; Lucy 2000: 332).

3 Additional problems in this approach are manifested by Passer (2016), who examines verb classifier systems in relation to features associated with other types of nominal classification and concludes that they do not represent systems of nominal classification. This type of approach can do no more than show that a particular set of phenomena is unlike others. Lacking criteria for classification systems, it cannot serve to exclude any particular system. Although I am unable to say for sure that all of the systems that go under the label of verb classifier system actually satisfy the properties identified below, the available evidence leads one to suspect that a number of systems are likely to.

4 I am not saying that this sort of system is not one of classification, or that it is not worthy of investigation. Rather, being covert it is of a somewhat different nature to the overt systems that are our concerns in this chapter.

5 These constructions show certain features typical of compounds: most notably the collocation of lexemes represents a separate lexical item. However, they are in some respects unlike the prototypical compound. Thus, in many languages the two lexical items in the compound are never adjacent, being invariably separated by inflectional material. Furthermore, it is the inflecting verb rather than the compound as a whole that takes inflections.

6 Significantly, the synonymous English borrowing *gidim-* 'get, obtain' is categorized as telic, as expected.

7 The unification further supports the notion that the prefixes are lexical ones: they clearly serve a derivational function in specialized perfectives; the meanings in natural perfectives are related, albeit rather abstract.

8 According to Gerner (2009: 733–735; 2014: 276) the features vectorial configuration and Aktionsart are not applicable in verb classification systems East Asian languages. The three contact features he identifies, however, are readily subsumed under vectorial configuration.

9 Mithun (1999: 121) specifies that the instrumental affixes are not classifiers of nominals serving in instrument roles in the clause, but says nothing about the possibility that they classify verbs.

10 We could alternatively have taken $\mathcal{M}$ to be the entire set of allomorphs in Table 6.3, resulting in a partitioning of the set of verbs effectively into two sets: the sets defined by the allomorphs in each column being identical. This approach would work for any conjugation class in which the inflections are separable from the lexical verb.

Chapter 7

1   Many – myself included – would also argue the same holds true of grammars, and that a descriptive grammar should incorporate diachrony in the story: that, at the very least, diachrony cannot be entirely ignored. See, for example, Joseph (2006) and Rankin (2006).

2   This is also true of Firthian linguistics; Robins (1959) is one of the few exceptions.

3   In the wider domain of Neo-Firthian linguistics there is, of course, the lexicographic tradition of Sinclair (e.g. 2018). Lexicography is, however, a somewhat different enterprise to semantics.

4   Again, according to SFL these clauses specify ongoing events, though the majority of linguists disagree, and would argue that *belong* and *have* serve here as copulas (e.g. Benveniste 1960/1971).

5   The first edition IFG employs zero (ø) in just one place, as a notation for present tense (contrasting with – 'past' and + 'future') (Halliday 1985: 178) – not, that is, in the linguistic sense. Something more like a linguistic zero appears in the second edition, where Halliday speaks of a 'zero alternation of the non-finite verb *being*' in non-finite dependent attributing clauses such as *with everyone too short of money* (Halliday 1994: 241). I doubt that Halliday actually means that there is a lexical zero in this alternation: I suspect this is just a (somewhat unfortunate) turn of phrase. The fourth edition of IFG adds a few more citations of zero, including zero phonemes (Halliday and Matthiessen 2014: 14), which again I suspect to be a carelessness in expression. A somewhat more puzzling 'zero' appears in an alternation in a system network in Halliday and Matthiessen (2014: 410). (More accurately, this is completely perplexing. The network shows a number of English words in scare quotes which must be interpreted as 'insert the morpheme "X"'; this can hardly be the case for 'zero'.) It transpires two pages later that the realization of 'zero' is –, presumably nothing! This is precisely the situation where I observe (McGregor 2003b: 80) that a type of linguistic zero (though certainly neither 'zero' nor *zero*) could potentially be mooted in SFG along the lines of Firth's 'zero mark' in phonology (1957: 5) (see also Jakobson 1939).

References

Agha, Asif. 1994. The semantics and pragmatics of verb classifiers in Urdu-Hindi. *Berkeley Linguistic Society* 20: 14–27.

Aikhenvald, Alexandra Y. 1994. Grammatical relations in Tariana. *Nordic Journal of Linguistics* 17(2): 201–217.

Aikhenvald, Alexandra Y. 2000. *Classifiers: A typology of noun categorisation devices.* Oxford: Oxford University Press.

Aikhenvald, Alexandra Y. 2006. Classifiers and noun classes: Semantics. In Keith Brown (ed.), *Encyclopedia of languages and linguistics*, 463–471. Oxford: Elsevier.

Akerejola, Ernest. 2005. *A text-based lexicogrammatical description of Ọ̀kọ́: A systemic functional approach.* PhD thesis, Macquarie University.

Allan, Keith. 1977. Classifiers. *Language* 53: 284–310.

Alpher, Barry. 1994. Yir-Yoront ideophones. In Leanne Hinton, Johanna Nichols and John J. Ohala (eds), *Sound symbolism*, 161–177. Cambridge: Cambridge University Press.

Alsina, Alex, Joan Bresnan and Peter Sells. 1997. Complex predicates: Structure and theory. In Alex Alsina, Joan Bresnan and Peter Sells (eds), *Complex predicates*, 1–12. Stanford, CA: CLSI Publications.

Amberber, Mengistu. 2000. Valency-changing and valency-encoding devices in Amharic. In Robert M.W. Dixon and Alexandra Y. Aikhenvald (eds), *Changing valency: Case studies in transitivity*, 312–332. Cambridge: Cambridge University Press.

Amberber, Mengistu. 2009. Differential case marking of arguments in Amharic. In Andrej L. Malchukov and Andrew Spencer (eds), *The Oxford handbook of case*, 742–755. Oxford: Oxford University Press.

Amberber, Mengistu, Brett Baker and Mark Harvey. 2010. Introduction: Complex predicates. In Mengistu Amberber, Brett Baker and Mark Harvey (eds), *Complex predicate formation: Cross-linguistic perspectives on event structure*, 1–12. Cambridge: Cambridge University Press.

Ameka, Felix K. 1992. Interjections: The universal yet neglected part of speech. *Journal of Pragmatics* 18(2–3): 101–118.

Anderson, Neil and Martha Wade. 1988. Ergativity and control in Folopa. *Language and Linguistics in Melanesia* 19: 1–16.

Andrews, Avery D. 2007. Relative clauses. In Timothy Shopen (ed.), *Language typology and syntactic description. Volume II: Complex constructions*, 206–236. Cambridge: Cambridge University Press.

Austin, Peter K. (ed.). 1988. *Complex sentence constructions in Australian languages.* (Typological Studies in Language, 15.) Amsterdam and Philadelphia: John Benjamins.

Baker, Brett and Mark Harvey. 2010. Complex predicate formation. In Mengistu Amberber, Brett Baker and Mark Harvey (eds), *Complex predicates: Cross-linguistic perspectives on event structure*, 13–47. Cambridge: Cambridge University Press.

Baker, Mark. 2000. *Lexical categories: Verbs, nouns, and adjectives.* Cambridge: Cambridge University Press.

Bakker, Dik. 2011. Language sampling. In Jae Jung Song (ed.), *The Oxford handbook of linguistic typology*, 100–127. Oxford: Oxford University Press.

Bally, Charles. 1912. Le style indirect libre en français moderne I and II. *Germanisch-Romanische Monatsschrift* IV: 549–556, 597–606.

Barnwell, Katherine G.L. 1970. *A grammatical description of Mbembe (Adun dialect): A Cross River language.* PhD thesis, University of London.

Bartens, Angela. 2000. *Ideophones and sound symbolism in Atlantic creoles.* Helsinki: Academic Scientiarum Fennica.

Bartlett, Tom. 2017. Context in systemic functional linguistics: Towards scalar supervenience? In Tom Bartlett and Gerard O'Grady (eds), *The Routledge handbook of systemic functional linguistics*, 375–390. (Routledge Handbooks in Linguistics.) London and New York: Routledge.

Bartlett, Tom and Gerard O'Grady (eds). 2017. *The Routledge handbook of systemic functional linguistics.* (Routledge Handbooks in Linguistics.) London and New York: Routledge.

Bauer, Laurie. 1990. Be-heading the word. *Journal of Linguistics* 26: 1–31.

Beckwith, Christopher I. 2007. *Phoronyms: Classifiers, class nouns, and the pseudopartitive construction.* New York: Peter Lang.

Behaghel, Otto. 1932. *Deutsche Syntax: Eine Geschichtliche Darstellung, Vol. IV, Wortstellung. Periodenbau.* Heidelberg: Carl Winters.

Benveniste, Emile. 1960/1971. The linguistic functions of 'to be' and 'to have'. In Emile Benveniste (ed.), *Problems in general linguistics*, 163–179. Coral Gables: University of Miami Press.

Bhaskararao, Peri and S. K. Joshi. 1985. A study of Newari classifiers. *Bulletin of the Deccan College Research Institute* 44: 17–31.

Bhat, D.N.S. and M.S. Ningomba. 1997. *Manipuri grammar.* München/Newcastle: Lincom Europa.

Bickel, Balthasar. 2011. Grammatical relations typology. In Jae Jung Song (ed.), *The Oxford handbook of language typology*, 399–444. Oxford: Oxford University Press.

Bisang, Walter. 2009. Serial verb constructions. *Language and Linguistics Compass* 3(3): 792–814.

Bisang, Walter. 2018. Nominal and verbal classification: A comparative perspective. In William B. McGregor and Søren Wichmann (eds), *The diachrony of classification systems*, 241–282. Amsterdam: John Benjamins.

Bisang, Walter and Andrej L. Malchukov (eds). 2020. *Grammaticalization scenarios. Areal patterns and cross-linguistic variation: A comparative handbook.* Berlin: De Gruyter Mouton.

Blake, Barry J. 1979. Pitta-Pitta. In Robert M.W Dixon and Barry Blake (eds), *Handbook of Australian languages. Volume 1*, 183–242. Canberra: Australian National University Press.

Blake, Barry J. 1983. Structure and word order in Kalkatungu: The anatomy of a flat language. *Australian Journal of Linguistics* 3: 143–175.

Blake, Barry J. 2001. *Case.* Cambridge: Cambridge University Press.

Blake, Barry J. 2017. Sound symbolism in English: Weighing the evidence. *Australian Journal of Linguistics* 37(3): 286–313.

Blankenship, Barbara. 1997. Classificatory verbs in Cherokee. *Anthropological Linguistics* 39(1): 92–110.

Blasi, Damián E., Søren Wichmann, Harald Hammarström, Peter F. Stadler and Morten H. Christiansen. 2016. Sound-meaning association biases evidenced across thousands of languages. *Proceedings of the National Academy of Sciences of the USA* 113(39): 10818–10823.

Blevins, Juliette. 2001. *Nhanda: An Aboriginal language of Western Australia.* Honolulu: University of Hawai'i Press.

Bolinger, Dwight. 1972. *That's that.* The Hague and Paris: Mouton.

Bolinger, Dwight. 1977. *Meaning and form.* London: Longmans.

Borin, Lars and Anju Saxena (eds). 2013. *Approaches to measuring linguistic differences.* (Trends in Linguistics: Studies and Monographs, 265.) Berlin: De Gruyter Mouton.

Bowern, Claire. 2014. Complex predicates in Australian languages. In Harold Koch and Rachel Nordlinger (eds), *The languages and linguistics of Australia: A comprehensive guide,* 263–327. Berlin and Boston: De Gruyter Mouton.

Bradshaw, Melvin Joel. 1982. *Word order change in Papua New Guinea Austronesian languages.* PhD thesis, University of Hawaii.

Breen, J. Gavan. 1981. Margany and Gunya. In Robert M.W. Dixon and Barry Blake (eds), *Handbook of Australian languages, Volume 2,* 275–393. Canberra: Australian National University Press.

Breeze, Mary. 1990. A sketch of the phonology and grammar of Gimira (Benchnon). In Richard Hayward (ed.), *Omotic language studies,* 1–67. London: School of Oriental and African Studies, University of London.

Bresnan, Joan and Jane Grimshaw. 1978. The syntax of free relatives in English. *Linguistic Inquiry* 9: 331–391.

Bromley, H. Myron. 1981. *A grammar of Lower Grand Valley Dani.* Canberra: Pacific Linguistics.

Brown, Cecil H., Eric W. Holman and Søren Wichmann. 2013. Sound correspondences in the world's languages. *Language* 89(1): 4–29.

Burling, Robbins. 1965. How to choose a Burmese numeral classifier? In Melford Spiro (ed.), *Context and meaning in cultural anthropology,* 243–276. New York and London: The Free Press & Collier-Macmillan.

Butler, Christopher S. 2003a. *Structure and function - a guide to three major structural-functional theories. Part 1: Approaches to the simplex clause.* Amsterdam: John Benjamins.

Butler, Christopher S. 2003b. *Structure and function - a guide to three major structural-functional theories. Part 2: From clause to discourse and beyond.* Amsterdam: John Benjamins.

Butler, Christopher S. 2019. Does functional linguistics have a 'fundamental unity'? Doing things with words in three structural-functional theories. *Functions of Language* 26(1): 64–85.

Butler, Christopher S. and Francisco Gonzálvez-García. 2014. *Exploring functional-cognitive space.* Amsterdam: John Benjamins.

Butt, Miriam. 2010. The light verb jungle: Still hacking away. In Mengistu Amberber, Brett Baker and Mark Harvey (eds), *Complex predicate formation: Cross-linguistic perspectives on event structure,* 48–78. Cambridge: Cambridge University Press.

Bybee, Joan. 2010. *Language, usage and cognition.* Cambridge: Cambridge University Press.

Caffarel, Alice M.C. 1996. *Prolegomena to a systemic functional interpretation of French grammar.* PhD thesis, University of Sydney.

Caffarel, Alice M.C. 2006. *A systemic functional grammar of French.* London: Continuum.

Caffarel, Alice M.C., James R. Martin and Christian M.I.M. Matthiessen (eds). 2004. *Language typology: A functional perspective.* (Amsterdam Studies in the Theory and History of

Linguistic Science. Series IV – Current Issues in Linguistic Theory.) Amsterdam and Philadelphia: John Benjamins.

Capell, Arthur. 1943. *The linguistic position of south-eastern Papua.* Sydney: Australasian Medical Publishing Company.

Capell, Arthur. 1979. The classification of verbs in Australian languages. In Stephen A. Wurm (ed.), *Australian linguistic studies*, 229–322. Canberra: Pacific Linguistics.

Chao, Yuan Ren. 1968. *A grammar of spoken Chinese.* Los Angeles and Berkeley: University of California Press.

Chappell, Hilary M. 2015. Introduction: Ways of tackling diversity in Sinitic languages. In Hilary M. Chappell (ed.), *Diversity in Sinitic languages*, 3–12. Oxford: Oxford University Press.

Chappell, Hilary and Jean-Christophe Verstraete. 2019. Optional and alternating case marking: Typology and diachrony. *Language and Linguistics Compass* 13(3): e12311.

Chelliah, Shobhana L. and Gwendolyn Hyslop (eds). 2011. Special issue on Optional case marking in Tibeto-Burman. *Linguistics of the Tibeto-Burman Area* 34: 2.

Chouliaraki, Lilie and Norman Fairclough. 1999. *Discourse in late modernity: Rethinking critical discourse analysis.* Edinburgh: Edinburgh University Press.

Clark, Herbert H. 2016. Depicting as a method of communication. *Psychological Review* 123(3): 324–347.

Clark, Herbert H. and Richard J. Gerrig. 1990. Quotations as demonstrations. *Language* 66: 764–805.

Clendon, Mark. 2014. *Worrorra: A language of the north-west Kimberley coast.* Adelaide: University of Adelade Press.

Comrie, Bernard. 1978. Ergativity. In Winfred P. Lehmann (ed.), *Syntactic typology: Studies in the phenomenology of language*, 329–374. Austin: University of Texas Press.

Comrie, Bernard. 1981a. Ergativity and grammatical relations in Kala Lagaw Ya (Saibai dialect). *Australian Journal of Linguistics* 1: 1–42.

Comrie, Bernard. 1981b. *Language universals and linguistic typology: Syntax and morphology.* Oxford: Basil Blackwell.

Comrie, Bernard. 1989. *Language universals and linguistic typology: Syntax and morphology.* 2nd edition. Oxford: Basil Blackwell.

Comrie, Bernard. 2000. Valency-changing derivations in Tsez. In Robert M.W. Dixon and Alexandra Y. Aikhenvald (eds), *Changing valency: Case studies in transitivity*, 360–374. Cambridge: Cambridge University Press.

Comrie, Bernard. 2013a. Alignment of case marking of full noun phrases. In Matthew S. Dryer and Martin Haspelmath (eds), *The world atlas of language structures online*, chapter 98. Munich: Max Planck Digital Library.

Comrie, Bernard. 2013b. Alignment of case marking of pronouns. In Matthew S. Dryer and Martin Haspelmath (eds), *The world atlas of language structures online*, chapter 99. Munich: Max Planck Digital Library.

Cook, Anthony. 1988. Participle sentences in Wakiman. In Peter Austin (ed.), *Complex sentence constructions in Australian languages*, 69–95. Amsterdam: John Benjamins.

Corbett, Greville G. 1991. *Gender.* Cambridge: Cambridge University Press.

Corbett, Greville G., Norman M. Fraser and Scott McGlashan. 1993. *Heads in grammatical theory.* Cambridge: Cambridge University Press.

Coupe, Alexander R. 2007. *A grammar of Mongsen Ao.* Berlin: Mouton de Gruyter.

Coupe, Alexander R. 2011. On core case marking patterns in two Tibeto-Burman languages of Nagaland. *Linguistics in the Tibeto-Burman Area* 34(2): 21–47.

Craig, Colette. 1986a. Introduction. In Colette Craig (ed.), *Noun classes and categorization: Proceedings of a symposium on categorization and noun classification, Eugene, Oregon, October 1983*, 1–10. Amsterdam: John Benjamins.

Craig, Colette (ed.). 1986b. *Noun classes and categorization: Proceedings of a symposium on categorization and noun classification, Eugene, Oregon, October 1983*. (Typological Studies in Language.) Amsterdam: John Benjamins.

Craig, Colette. 1994. Classifier languages. In R.E. Asher and J.M.Y. Simpson (eds), *The encyclopedia of language and linguistics, volume 2*, 565–569. Oxford: Pergamon Press.

Croft, William. 1994. Semantic universals and classifier systems. *Word* 45: 145–171.

Croft, William. 2000. Parts of speech as language universals and language-particular categories. In Petra M. Vogel and Bernard Comrie (eds), *Approaches to the typology of word classes*, 65–102. Berlin: Mouton de Gruyter.

Crowley, Terry. 1981. The Mpakwithi dialect of Anguthimri. In Robert M.W. Dixon and Barry Blake (eds), *Handbook of Australian languages, Volume 2*, 147–194. Canberra: Australian National University Press.

Crowley, Terry. 1983. Uradhi. In Robert M.W. Dixon and Barry Blake (eds), *Handbook of Australian languages, Volume 3*, 307–428. Canberra: Australian National University Press.

Crowley, Terry. 1995. Inalienable possession in Paamese grammar. In Hilary M. Chappell and William B. McGregor (eds), *The grammar of inalienability: A typological perspective on body part terms and the part-whole relation*, 383–432. Berlin and New York: Mouton de Gruyter.

D'Hertefelt, Sarah. 2015. *Insubordination in Germanic: A typology of complement and conditional constructions*. PhD thesis, KU Leuven.

D'Hertefelt, Sarah and Jean-Christophe Verstraete. 2014. Independent complement constructions in Swedish and Danish: Insubordination or dependency shift. *Journal of Pragmatics* 60: 89–102.

Dammel, Antje and Sebastian Kürschner. 2018. The diachrony of inflectional classes in four Germanic languages: What happens after transparency is lost? In William B. McGregor and Søren Wichmann (eds), *The diachrony of classification systems*, 283–314. Amsterdam: John Benjamins.

Davidse, Kristin. 1992. A semiotic approach to relational clauses. *Occasional Papers in Systemic Linguistics* 6: 99–131.

Davidse, Kristin. 1999. The semantics of cardinal versus enumerative existential constructions. *Cognitive Linguistics* 10(3): 203–250.

Davidse, Kristin. 2000. Semiotic and possessive models in relational clauses: Thinking with grammar about grammar. *Revista Canaria Estudios Ingleses* 40: 13–35.

Davidse, Kristin. 2017. Systemic functional linguistics and the clause: The experiential metafunction. In Tom Bartlett and Gerard O'Grady (eds), *The Routledge handbook of systemic functional linguistics*, 79–95. London and New York: Routledge.

Davidse, Kristin. 2018. A tribute to M. A. K. Halliday (1925–2018). *Functions of Language* 25(2): 205–228.

Davidse, Kristin and Ngum Meyuhnsi Njende. 2019. Enumerative *there*-clauses and *there*-clefts: Specification and information structure. *Acta Linguistica Hafniensia* 52(2): 160–191.

de Roeck, Marijke. 1994. A functional typology of speech reports. In Elisabeth Engberg-Pedersen, L. Falster Jakobsen and L. Schack Rasmussen (eds), *Function and expression in Functional Grammar*, 331–351. Berlin: Mouton de Gruyter.

DeLancey, Scott. 1985. On active typology and the nature of agentivity. In Frans Plank (ed.), *Relational typology*, 47–60. Berlin: Mouton de Gruyter.

DeLancey, Scott. 2006. The blue bird of ergativity. Unpublished manuscript. Available at: http://celia.cnrs.fr/FichExt/Documents%20de%20travail/Ergativite/3dDelancey.pdf (accessed 5 December 2019).

Dench, Alan C. 1998. *Yingkarta*. München and Newcastle: Lincom Europa.

Dickey, Stephen M. and Laura A. Janda. 2015. Slavic aspectual prefixes and numeral classifiers: Two kinds of lexico-grammatical unitizers. *Lingua* 168: 57–84.

Dickinson, Connie. 2000. Complex predicates in Tsafiki. *Proceedings of the Annual Meeting of the Berkeley Linguistics Society* 26: 27–37.

Dickinson, Connie. 2003. *Complex predicates in Tsafiki*. PhD thesis, University of Oregon.

Dik, Simon C. 1986. On the notion 'functional explanation'. *Belgian Journal of Linguistics* 1: 11–52.

Dik, Simon C. 1989. *The theory of functional grammar. Part 1: The structure of the clause*. Dordrecht: Foris Publications.

Dik, Simon C. 1997a. *The theory of functional grammar. Part 1: The structure of the clause*. Berlin: Mouton de Gruyter.

Dik, Simon C. 1997b. *The theory of functional grammar. Part 2: Complex and derived constructions*. Berlin: Mouton de Gruyter.

Dingemanse, Mark. 2012. Advances in the cross-linguistic study of ideophones. *Language and Linguistics Compass* 6(10): 654–672.

Dixon, Robert M.W. 1972. *The Dyirbal language of North Queensland*. Cambridge: Cambridge University Press.

Dixon, Robert M.W. 1977. *A grammar of Yidiny*. Cambridge: Cambridge University Press.

Dixon, Robert M.W. 1979. Ergativity. *Language* 55: 59–138.

Dixon, Robert M.W. 1980. *The languages of Australia*. Cambridge: Cambridge University Press.

Dixon, Robert M.W. 1981. Wargamay. In Robert M.W. Dixon and Barry Blake (eds), *Handbook of Australian languages, Volume 2*, 1–144. Canberra: Australian National University Press.

Dixon, Robert M.W. 1982. *Where have all the adjectives gone? And other essays in semantics and syntax*. Berlin: Mouton.

Dixon, Robert M.W. 1983. Nyawaygi. In Robert M.W. Dixon and Barry Blake (eds), *Handbook of Australian languages, Volume 3*, 431–525. Canberra: Australian National University Press.

Dixon, Robert M.W. 1986. Noun classes and noun classification in typological perspective. In Colette Craig (ed.), *Noun classes and categorization: Proceedings of a symposium on categorization and noun classification, Eugene, Oregon, October 1983*, 105–112. Amsterdam: John Benjamins.

Dixon, Robert M.W. 1987. Studies in ergativity: Introduction. *Lingua* 71: 1–16.

Dixon, Robert M.W. 1994. *Ergativity*. Cambridge: Cambridge University Press.

Dixon, Robert M.W. 2002. *Australian languages: Their nature and development*. Cambridge: Cambridge University Press.

Dixon, Robert M.W. 2006. Complementation strategies in Dyirbal. In Robert M.W. Dixon and Alexandra Y. Aikhenvald (eds), *Complementation: a cross-linguistic typology*, 263–279. Oxford: Oxford University Press.

Dixon, Robert M.W. 2010a. *Basic linguistic theory. Volume 1: Methodology.* Oxford: Oxford University Press.

Dixon, Robert M.W. 2010b. *Basic linguistic theory. Volume 2: Grammatical topics.* Oxford: Oxford University Press.

Dixon, Robert M.W. and Alexandra Y. Aikhenvald (eds). 2006. *Complementation: A cross-linguistic typology.* Oxford: Oxford University Press.

Donaldson, Tamsin. 1980. *Ngiyambaa: The language of the Wangaaybuwan.* Cambridge: Cambridge University Press.

Donohue, Mark. 1997. Tone systems in New Guinea. *Linguistic Typology* 1(3): 347–386.

Doron, Edit. 1986. The pronominal 'copula' as an agreement clitic. In H. Borer (ed.), *The syntax of pronominal clitics*, 313–332. New York: Academic Press.

Dowty, David. 1979. *Word meaning and Montague grammar.* Dordrecht: Reidel.

Drach, Erich. 1963 [1937]. *Grundgedanken der deutshen Satzlehre.* Darmstadt: Wissenschaftliche Buchgesellschaft.

Dryer, Matthew S. 1992. The Greenbergian word order correlations. *Language* 68: 81–138.

Dryer, Matthew S. 1997. Are grammatical relations universal? In Joan Bybee, John Haiman and Sandra A. Thompson (eds), *Essays on language function and language type: Dedicated to T. Givón*, 115–143. Amsterdam and Philadelphia: John Benjamins.

Dryer, Matthew S. 2007. Noun phrase structure. In Timothy Shopen (ed.), *Language typology and syntactic description. Volume II: Complex constructions*, 151–205. Cambridge: Cambridge University Press.

Du Bois, John W. 1987. The discourse basis of ergativity. *Language* 63: 805–855.

Du Bois, John W. 2003. Discourse and grammar. In Michael Tomasello (ed.), *The new psychology of language: Cognitive and functional approaches to language structure. Volume 2*, 47–87. Mahwah, NJ and London: Lawrence Erlbaum.

Durie, Mark. 1985. *A grammar of Acehnese.* Dordrecht: Foris.

Durie, Mark. 1987. Grammatical relations in Acehnese. *Studies in Language* 11: 365–399.

Durie, Mark. 1997. Grammatical structures in verb serialization. In Alex Alsina, Joan Bresnan and Peter Sells (eds), *Complex predicates*, 289–354. Stanford, CA: CLSI Publications.

Durie, Mark. 1998. The temporal mediation of structure and function. In Michael Darnell, Edith Moravcsik, Frederick Newmeyer, Michael Noonan and Kathleen Wheatley (eds), *Functionalism and formalism in linguistics. Volume 1: General papers*, 417–443. Amsterdam and Philadelphia: John Benjamins.

Eckert, Penelope. 2018. *Meaning and linguistic variation: The third wave in sociolinguistics.* Cambridge: Cambridge University Press.

Eddaikra, Djafar and Paul Tench. 1992. The pharyngealization system in Algerian spoken Arabic. In Paul Tench (ed.), *Studies in systemic phonology*, 77–86. London: Pinter.

Enfield, Nicholas J. 2019. *Mainland Southeast Asian languages: A concise typological introduction.* Cambridge: Cambridge University Press.

Enfield, Nicholas J., A. Kelly and S. Sprenger. 2004. *Max-Planck-Institut für Psycholinguistik Annual Report, 2004.* Nijmegen: Max-Planck-Institut für Psycholinguistik.

Epps, Patience. 2008. *A grammar of Hup.* Berlin and New York: Mouton de Gruyter.

Epps, Patience. 2011. Linguistic typology and language documentation. In Jae Jung Song (ed.), *The Oxford handbook of language typology*, 634–649. Oxford: Oxford University Press.

Essegbey, James. 2019. *Tutrugbu (Nyangbo) language and culture*. Leiden and Boston: Brill.

Evans, Nicholas. 1995. *A grammar of Kayardild: With historical-comparative notes on Tangkic*. Berlin: Mouton de Gruyter.

Evans, Nicholas. 1997. Head classes and agreement classes in the Mayali dialect chain. In Mark Harvey and Nicholas Reid (eds), *Nominal classification in Aboriginal Australia*, 105–146. Amsterdam/Philadelphia: John Benjamins.

Evans, Nicholas. 2003. *Bininj Gun-wok: A pan-dialectal grammar of Mayali, Kunwinjku and Kune*. Canberra: Pacific Linguistics.

Evans, Nicholas. 2007. Insubordination and its uses. In Irina Nikolaeva (ed.), *Finiteness: Theoretical and empirical foundations*, 366–431. Oxford: Oxford University Press.

Evans, Nicholas. 2009. Insubordination and the grammaticalisation of interactive presuppositions. Paper presented at conference *Methodologies in determining morphosyntactic change*, Osaka. Available at: http://www.r.minpaku.ac.jp/ritsuko/english/symposium/pdf/symposium_0903/Evans_handout.pdf (accessed 5 December 2019).

Evans, Nicholas. 2011. Semantic typology. In Jae Jung Song (ed.), *The Oxford handbook of linguistic typology*, 504–533. Oxford: Oxford University Press.

Evans, Nicholas. 2013. Some problems in the typology of quotation: A canonical approach. In Dunstan Brown, Marina Chumakina and Greville G. Corbett (eds), *Canonical morphology and syntax*, 66–98. Oxford: Oxford University Press.

Evans, Nicholas and Stephen C. Levinson. 2009. The myth of language universals: Language diversity and its importance for cognitive science. *Behavioral and Brain Sciences* 32: 429–492.

Evans, Nicholas and Honoré Watanabe 2016a. The dynamics of insubordination: An overview. In Nicholas Evans and Honoré Watanabe (eds), *Insubordination*, 1–37. Amsterdam and Philadelphia: John Benjamins.

Evans, Nicholas and Honoré Watanabe (eds). 2016b. *Insubordination*. (Typological Studies in Language 115.) Amsterdam and Philadelphia: John Benjamins.

Everett, Daniel L. 2005. Cultural constraints on grammar and cognition in Pirahã: Another look at the design features of human language. *Current Anthropology* 42(4): 621–646.

Ezard, Bryan. 1978. Classificatory prefixes of the Massim Cluster. In Stephen A. Wurm and Lois Carrington (eds), *Second International Conference on Austronesian linguistics: Proceedings 2, Eastern Austronesian*, 1159–1180. Canberra: Pacific Linguistics.

Ezard, Bryan. 1992. Tawala derivational prefixes: A semantic perspective. In Malcolm Ross (ed.), *Papers in Austronesian linguistics 2*, 147–250. Canberra: Pacific Linguistics.

Fairclough, Norman. 1995. *Critical discourse analysis: The critical study of language*. London: Longman.

Fawcett, Robin P. 1980. *Cognitive linguistics and social interaction: Towards an integrated model of a systemic functional grammar and the other components of a communicating mind*. Heidelberg: Julius Groos.

Fawcett, Robin P. 1996. A systemic functional approach to complementation in English. In Margaret Berry, Christopher Butler, Robin Fawcett and Guowen Huang (eds), *Meaning and form: Systemic functional interpretations. Meaning and choice in language: Studies for Michael Halliday*, 297–366. Norwood, NJ: Ablex.

Fehn, Anne-Maria. 2014. *A grammar of Ts'ixa (Kalahari Khoe)*. PhD thesis, Universität zu Köln.

Fillmore, Charles. 1968. The case for case. In Emmon Bach and Robert T. Harms (eds), *Universals in linguistic theory*, 1–90. New York: Holt, Rinehart & Winston.

Firth, John R. 1957. *Papers in linguistics 1934-1951.* London: Oxford University Press.

Firth, John R. 1964. *The tongues of men and Speech.* London: Oxford University Press.

Firth, John R. 1968. *Selected papers of J. R. Firth 1952-59.* Ed. by Frank R. Palmer. London and Harlow: Longmans.

Foley, William A. 2000. The languages of New Guinea. *Annual Review of Anthropology* 29: 357–404.

Foley, William A. and Robert D. Van Valin. 1984. *Functional syntax and universal grammar.* Cambridge: Cambridge University Press.

Folli, Raffaella and Heidi Harley. 2006. What language says about the psychology of events. *Trends in Cognitive Sciences* 10(3): 91–92.

Fontaine, Lise, Tom Bartlett and Gerard O'Grady (eds). 2013. *Systemic functional linguistics: Exploring choice.* Cambridge and New York: Cambridge University Press.

Forges, G. 1983. La classe de l'infinitif en Bantu. *Africana Linguistica* IX: 259–263.

Fry, John. 2003. *Ellipsis and wa-marking in Japanese conversation.* New York and London: Routledge.

Fujii, N. and T. Ono. 2000. The occurrence and non-occurrence of the Japanese direct object marker o in conversation. *Studies in Language* 24: 1–39.

Gabelentz, Georg von der. 1901 [1891]. *Die Sprachwissenschaft: Ihre Aufgaben, Methoden und bisherigen Ergebnisse.* Leipzig: Tauchnitz.

Gaby, Alice. 2017. *A grammar of Kuuk Thaayorre.* Berlin: De Gruyter.

Gerner, Matthias. 2009. Instruments as verb classifiers in Kam (Dong). *Linguistics* 47(3): 697–742.

Gerner, Matthias. 2014. Verb classifiers in East Asia. *Functions of Language* 21(3): 267–296.

Geytenbeek, Brian and Helen Geytenbeek. 1971. *Gidabal grammar and dictionary.* Canberra: Australian Institute of Aboriginal Studies.

Gildea, Spike and Francesc Queixalós (eds). 2010. *Ergativity in Amazonia.* (Typological Studies in Language, 89.) Amsterdam and Philadelphia: John Benjamins.

Givón, Talmy. 1985. Ergative morphology and transitivity gradients in Newari. In Frans Plank (ed.), *Relational typology,* 89–107. Berlin: Mouton de Gruyter.

Givón, Talmy. 1995. *Functionalism and grammar.* Amsterdam: John Benjamins.

Glass, Amee and Dorothy Hackett. 1970. *Pitjantjatjara grammar: A tagmemic view of the Ngaanyatjara (Warburton Ranges) dialect.* Canberra: Australian Institute of Aboriginal Studies.

Goddard, Cliff. 1982. Case systems and case marking in Australian languages: A new interpretation. *Australian Journal of Linguistics* 2: 167–196.

Goldberg, Adele E. 1995. *Constructions: A construction grammar approach to argument structure.* Chicago and London: University of Chicago Press.

Graffi, Giorgio. 2011. The pioneers of linguistic typology: From Gabelentz to Greenberg. In Jae Jung Song (ed.), *The Oxford handbook of linguistic typology,* 25–42. Oxford: Oxford University Press.

Gras, Pedro. 2016. Revisiting the functional typology of insubordination: Insubordinate que-constructions in Spanish. In Nicholas Evans and Honoré Watanabe (eds), *Insubordination,* 113–143. Amsterdam and Philadelphia: John Benjamins.

Green, Ian P. 1989. *Marrithiyel: A language of the Daly River region of Australia's Northern Territory.* PhD thesis, Australian National University.

Greenberg, Joseph H. 1963. Some universals of grammar with particular reference to the order of meaningful elements. In Joseph H. Greenberg (ed.), *Universals of language,* 73–113. Cambridge, MA: MIT Press.

Greenberg, Joseph H. 1972. Numeral classifiers and substantival number: Problems in the genesis of a linguistic type. *Working Papers in Language Universals* 9: 1–40.

Grinevald, Colette. 2000. A morphological typology of classifiers. In Gunter Senft (ed.), *Systems of nominal classification*, 50–92. Cambridge: Cambridge University Press.

Guirardello, Raquel. 1999. *A reference grammar of Trumai*. PhD thesis, Rice University.

Güldemann, Tom. 2008. *Quotative indexes in African languages: A synchronic and diachronic survey*. Berlin and New York: Mouton de Gruyter.

Güldemann, Tom. 2012. Thetic speaker-instantiating quotative indexes as a cross-linguistic type. In Isabelle Buchstaller and Ingrid van Alphen (eds), *Quotatives: Cross-linguistic and cross-disciplinary perspectives*, 117–142. Amsterdam/Philadelphia: John Benjamins.

Haacke, Wilfrid H.G. 2013. Syntax: !Gora. In Rainer Vossen (ed.), *The Khoesan languages*, 340–347. London and New York: Routledge.

Haas, Mary R. 1942. The use of numeral classifiers in Thai. *Language* 18: 201–205.

Haas, William. 1957. Zero in linguistic description. *Studies in linguistic analysis. Special volume of the Philological Society*, 33–53. Oxford: Blackwell.

Hadermann, Pascale. 1999. Les formes nomino-verbales de classes 5 et 15 dans les langues bantoues du Nord-Ouest. In Larry M. Hyman and Jean-Marie Hombert (eds), *Bantu historical linguistics*, 431–471. Stanford: CSLI Publications.

Haig, Geoffrey. 2010. Alignment. In Silvia Luraghi and Vit Bubenik (eds), *Continuum companion to historical linguistics*, 250–268. London and New York: Continuum.

Haiman, John. 1979. Hua, a Papuan language of New Guinea. In Timothy Shopen (ed.), *Languages and their speakers*, 35–89. Cambridge: Winthrop.

Haiman, John. 1983. Iconic and economic motivation. *Language* 59: 782–819.

Haiman, John. 2003. Explaining infixation. In John Moore and Maria Polinsky (eds), *The nature of explanation in linguistic theory*, 105–120. Stanford, CA: The Center for the Study of Language and Information.

Haiman, John and Sandra Thompson. 1988. *Clause combining in grammar and discourse*. Amsterdam: John Benjamins.

Hale, Ken. 1976. The adjoined relative clause in Australia. In Robert M.W. Dixon (ed.), *Grammatical categories in Australian languages*, 78–105. Canberra: Australian Institute of Aboriginal Studies.

Hale, Ken. 1983. Warlpiri and the grammar of non-configurational languages. *Natural Language and Linguistic Theory* 1: 5–47.

Halliday, Michael A.K. 1961. Categories of the theory of grammar. *Word* 17: 241–292.

Halliday, Michael A.K. 1966. Typology and the exotic. In Angus McIntosh and Michael A.K. Halliday (eds), *Patterns of language: Papers in general, descriptive and applied linguistics*, 165–182. London: Longmans.

Halliday, Michael A.K. 1967. Notes on transitivity and theme in English, Parts 1 and 2. *Journal of Linguistics* 3: 37–81, 199–244.

Halliday, Michael A.K. 1968. Notes on transitivity and theme in English, Part 3. *Journal of Linguistics* 4: 179–215.

Halliday, Michael A.K. 1973. *Explorations in the functions of language*. London: Edward Arnold.

Halliday, Michael A.K. 1975/1977. *Learning how to mean: Explorations in the development of language and meaning*. London: Edward Arnold.

Halliday, Michael A.K. 1978. *Language as social semiotic: The social interpretation of language and meaning*. London: Arnold.

Halliday, Michael A.K. 1985. *An introduction to functional grammar*. London: Edward Arnold.

Halliday, Michael A.K. 1988a. On the ineffability of grammatical categories. In James D. Benson, Michael J. Cummings and William S. Greaves (eds), *Linguistics in a systemic perspective*, 27–52. Amsterdam: John Benjamins.

Halliday, Michael A.K. 1988b. On the language of physical science. In M. Ghadessy (ed.), *Registers of written English: Situational factors and linguistic features*, 162–178. London: Pinter.

Halliday, Michael A.K. 1992. A systemic interpretation of Peking syllable finals. In Paul Tench (ed.), *Studies in Systemic Phonology*, 98–121. London and New York: Pinter.

Halliday, Michael A.K. 1994. *An introduction to functional grammar*. 2nd edition. London: Edward Arnold.

Halliday, Michael A.K. 1996. Systemic functional grammar. In Keith Brown and Jim Miller (eds), *Concise encyclopedia of syntactic theories*, 321–325. Oxford: Pergamon.

Halliday, Michael A.K. 2002. *On grammar*. London and New York: Continuum.

Halliday, Michael A.K. 2003 [1985]. Systemic background. In Jonathan J. Webster (ed.), *The collected works of M.A.K. Halliday*. Volume 3. *On language and linguistics*. 185–198. London and New York: Bloomsbury Academic.

Halliday, Michael A.K. 2008. *Complementarities in language*. Beijing: The Commercial Press.

Halliday, Michael A.K. 2013. Meaning as choice. In Lise Fontaine, Tom Bartlett and Gerard O'Grady (eds), *Systemic functional linguistics: Exploring choice*, 15–36. Cambridge: Cambridge University Press.

Halliday, Michael A.K. and Ruqaiya Hasan. 1976. *Cohesion in English*. London: Longman.

Halliday, Michael A.K. and James R. Martin. 1993. *Writing science: Literacy and discursive power*. London: The Falmer Press.

Halliday, Michael A.K. and Christian M.I.M. Matthiessen. 2014. *Halliday's introduction to functional grammar*. 4th edition. London and New York: Routledge.

Harvey, Mark. 2002. *A grammar of Gaagudju*. Berlin and New York: Mouton de Gruyter.

Harvey, Mark and Robert Mailhammer. 2018. Reconstructing remote relationships: Proto-Australian noun class prefixation. *Diachronica* 34(4): 470–515.

Hasan, Ruqaiya. 1996. Semantic networks: A tool for the analysis of meaning. In Carmel Cloran, David Butt and Geoff Williams (eds), *Ways of saying, ways of meaning: Selected papers of Ruqaiya Hasan*, 104–131. London: Cassell.

Haspelmath, Martin. 1993. *A grammar of Lezgian*. Berlin and New York: Mouton de Gruyter.

Haspelmath, Martin (ed.). 2004. *Coordinating constructions*. (Typological Studies in Language, 58.) Amsterdam/Philadelphia: John Benjamins.

Haspelmath, Martin. 2006. Against markedness (and what to replace it with). *Journal of Linguistics* 42: 25–70.

Haspelmath, Martin. 2007. Coordination. In Timothy Shopen (ed.), *Language typology and syntactic description. Volume II: Complex constructions*, 1–51. Cambridge: Cambridge University Press.

Haspelmath, Martin. 2010a. Comparative concepts and descriptive categories in crosslinguistic studies. *Language* 86(3): 663–687.

Haspelmath, Martin. 2010b. Framework-free grammatical theory. In Bernd Heine and Heiko Narrog (eds), *The Oxford handbook of linguistic analysis*, 341–365. Oxford: Oxford University Press.

Haspelmath, Martin. 2016. The challenge of making language description and comparison mutually beneficial. *Linguistic Typology* 20(2): 299–303.

Haynie, Hannah J., Claire Bowern and Hannah LaPalombara. 2014. Sound symbolism in the languages of Australia. *PLoS ONE* 9: 1–16.

Heath, Jeffrey. 1976. North-East Arnhem land. In Robert M.W. Dixon (ed.), *Grammatical categories in Australian languages*, 735–740. Canberra: Australian Institute of Aboriginal Studies.

Heath, Jeffrey. 1984. *Functional grammar of Nunggubuyu*. Canberra: Australian Institute of Aboriginal Studies.

Heine, Bernd. 2003. Grammaticalization. In Brian D. Joseph and Richard D. Janda (eds), *The handbook of historical linguistics*, 575–601. Oxford: Blackwell.

Hellwig, Birgit. 2006. Complement clause type and complementation strategies in Goemai. In Robert M.W. Dixon and Alexandra Aikhenvald (eds), *Complementation: A cross-linguistic typology*, 204–223. Oxford: Oxford University Press.

Hengeveld, Kees. 1992. Parts of speech. In Michael Fortescue, Peter Harder and Lars Kristoffersen (eds), *Layered structure and reference in a functional perspective: Papers from the functional grammar conference in Copenhagen 1990*, 29–55. Amsterdam: John Benjamins.

Hengeveld, Kees. 1996. Adverbial clauses in the languages of Europe. In Betty Devrietend, Louis Goossens and Johan van der Auwera (eds), *Complex structures: A functionalist perspective*, 119–147. Berlin: Mouton de Gruyter.

Hengeveld, Kees and J. Lachlan Mackenzie. 2008. *Functional Discourse Grammar: A typologically-based theory of language structure*. Oxford and New York: Oxford University Press.

Hercus, Luise A. 1982. *The Bagandji language*. Canberra: Pacific Linguistics.

Hill, Clair. 2015. The noun phrase in Umpila. Unpublished manuscript.

Hill, Jane H. 2005. *A grammar of Cupeño*. Berkeley, Los Angeles, and London: University of California Press.

Hinton, Leanne, Johanna Nichols and John J. Ohala (eds). 1994. *Sound symbolism*. Cambridge: Cambridge University Press.

Hockett, Charles F. 1960. The origin of speech. *Scientific American* 203(3): 88–96.

Holmes, Janet. 1986. Functions of *you know* in women's and men's speech. *Language in Society* 15: 1–22.

Honeybone, Patrick. 2005. Firth, J. R. (John Rupert). In Siobhan Chapman and Christopher Routledge (eds), *Key thinkers in linguistics and the philosophy of language*, 80–86. Edinburgh: Edinburgh University Press.

Hook, Peter E. 1974. *The compound verb in Hindi*. Ann Arbor: The University of Michigan Centre for South and Southeast Asian Studies.

Hopper, Paul. 1979. Aspect and foregrounding in discourse. In Talmy Givón (ed.), *Discourse and syntax*, 213–241. New York: Academic Press.

Hopper, Paul. 1987. Emergent grammar. *Berkeley Linguistics Society* 13: 139–157.

Hopper, Paul and Sandra Thompson. 1980. Transitivity in grammar and discourse. *Language* 56: 251–299.

Hopper, Paul and Sandra Thompson. 1984. The discourse basis for lexical categories in universal grammar. *Language* 60: 703–772.

Hopper, Paul and Elizabeth Traugott. 2003. *Grammaticalization*. Cambridge: Cambridge University Press.

Hsieh, Fuhui and Shuanfan Huang. 2006. The pragmatics of case marking in Saisiyat. *Oceanic Linguistics* 45(1): 91–109.

Huddleston, Rodney. 1988. Constituency, multi-functionality and grammaticalisation in Halliday's Functional Grammar. *Journal of Linguistics* 24(1): 137–174.

Hudson, Joyce, Eirlys Richards, Pompy Siddon and Peter Skipper. 1978. *The Walmajarri: An introduction to the language and culture.* Darwin: Summer Institute of Linguistics, Australian Aborigines Branch.

Hudson, Richard. 1971. *English complex sentences: An introduction to systemic grammar.* Amsterdam: North Holland.

Hudson, Richard. 1987. Zwicky on heads. *Journal of Linguistics* 23: 109–132.

Iggesen, Oliver A. 2004. *Case-asymmetry: A world-wide typological study on lexeme-class-dependent deviations in morphological case inventories.* PhD thesis, Universität Bremen.

Jaeger, T. Florian. 2006. *Redundancy and syntactic reduction in spontaneous speech.* PhD thesis, Stanford University.

Jaeger, T. Florian. 2010. Redundancy and reduction: Speakers manage syntactic information density. *Cognitive Psychology* 61: 23–62.

Jakobson, Roman. 1939. Signe zéro. *Mélanges de linguistique offerts à Charles Bally*, 143–152. Genève: Georg and Cie.

Janda, Laura A., Anna Endresen, Julia Kuznetsova, Olga Lyashevskaya, Anastasia Makarova, Tore Nesset and Svetlana Sokolova. 2013. *Why Russian aspectual prefixes aren't semantically empty: Prefixes as verb classifiers.* Bloomington, IN: Slavica.

Jankowsky, Kurt R. 2013. Comparative, historical, and typological linguistics since the eighteenth century. In Keith Allan (ed.), *The Oxford handbook of the history of linguistics*, 635–654. Oxford: Oxford University Press.

Jian, Wang. 2015. Bare classifier phrases in Sinitic languages: A typological perspective. In Hilary M. Chappell (ed.), *Diversity in Sinitic languages*, 110–133. Oxford: Oxford University Press.

Jones, Barbara. 2011. *A grammar of Wangkajunga: A language of the Great Sandy Desert of North Western Australia.* Canberra: Pacific Linguistics.

Joseph, Brian D. 2006. The historical and cultural dimensions in grammar formation: The case of Modern Greek. In Felix K. Ameka, Alan Dench and Nicholas Evans (eds), *Catching language: The standing challenge of grammar writing*, 549–564. Berlin and New York: Mouton de Gruyter.

Kachru, Braj B. 2015. 'Socially realistic linguistics': The Firthian tradition. In Jonathan J. Webster (ed.), *The Bloomsbury companion to M. A. K. Halliday*, 72–93. London and New York: Bloomsbury.

Kashyap, Abhishek K. 2019. Language typology. In Geoff Thompson, Wendy L. Bowcher, Lise Fontaine and David Schönthal (eds), *The Cambridge handbook of Systemic Functional Linguistics*, 767–792. Cambridge: Cambridge University Press.

Keenan, Edward L. 1985. Relative clauses. In Timothy Shopen (ed.), *Language typology and syntactic description. Volume II: Complex constructions*, 141–170. Cambridge: Cambridge University Press.

Keenan, Edward L. and Bernard Comrie. 1977. Noun phrase asscessibility and universal grammar. *Linguistic Inquiry* 8: 63–99.

Kelly, John. 1992. Systems for open syllabics in North Welsh. In Paul Tench (ed.), *Studies in systemic phonology*, 87–97. London: Pinter.

Kießling, Roland. 2018. Niger-Congo numeral classifiers in a diachronic perspective. In William B. McGregor and Søren Wichmann (eds), *The diachrony of classification systems*, 33–75. Amsterdam: John Benjamins.

Kilian-Hatz, Christa. 2008. *A grammar of Modern Khwe (Central Khoisan)*. Köln: Rüdiger Köppe.

Kilian-Hatz, Christa. 2013. Syntax: Kxoe subgroup: Khwe. In Rainer Vossen (ed.), *The Khoesan languages*, 356–378. London and New York: Routledge.

Killingley, Siew-Yue. 1983. *Cantonese classifiers: Syntax and semantics*. Newcastle upon Tyne: Grevatt & Grevatt.

Kim, Kong-On. 1977. Sound symbolism in Korean. *Journal of Linguisics* 13(1): 67–75.

Kimball, Geoffrey D. 1991. *Koasati grammar*. Lincoln and London: University of Nebraska Press and American Indian Studies Research Institute, Indiana University.

Kimps, Ditte and Kristin Davidse. 2008. Illocutionary force and conduciveness in imperative constant polarity tag questions: A typology. *Text & Talk* 28(6): 699–722.

Kimps, Ditte, Kristin Davidse and Bert Cornillie. 2014. A speech function analysis of tag questions in British English spontaneous dialogue. *Journal of Pragmatics* 66: 64–85.

Kimps, Ditte, Kristin Davidse and Gerard O'Grady. 2019. English tag questions eliciting knowledge or action: A comparison of the speech function and exchange structure models. *Functions of Language* 26(1): 86–111.

Kite, Suzanne and Stephen Wurm. 2004. *The Duuŋidjawu language of southeast Queensland: Grammar, texts and vocabulary*. Canberra: Pacific Linguistics.

Kittilä, Seppo and Andrej L. Malchukov. 2009. Varieties of accusative. In Andrej L. Malchukov and Andrew Spencer (eds), *The Oxford handbook of case*, 549–561. Oxford: Oxford University Press.

Kofod, Frances M. 1978. *The Miriwung language (East Kimberley): A phonological and morphological study*. MA thesis, University of New England.

König, Christa. 2006. Marked nominative in Africa. *Studies in Language* 30(4): 655–732.

König, Christa. 2008a. *Case in Africa*. Oxford: Oxford University Press.

König, Christa. 2008b. The marked-nominative languages of eastern Africa. In Bernd Heine and Derek Nurse (eds), *A linguistic geography of Africa*, 251–271. Cambridge: Cambridge University Press.

König, Christa. 2009. Marked nominatives. In Andrej L. Malchukov and Andrew Spencer (eds), *The Oxford handbook of case*, 535–548. Oxford: Oxford University Press.

Kuhn, Thomas S. 1970. *The structure of scientific revolutions*. Chicago: The University of Chicago Press.

Kumakhov, Mukhadin, Karina Vamling and Zara Kumakhova. 1996. Ergative case in the Circassian languages. *Working Papers, Lund University, Dept. of Linguistics* 45, 93–111.

Kuno, Susumu. 1973. *The structure of the Japanese language*. Cambridge, MA: MIT Press.

Kurumada, Chigusa and T. Florian Jaeger. 2012. Communicatively efficient language production and case-marker ellipsis in Japanese. Unpublished manuscript.

Kwon, Nahyun. 2015. *The natural motivation of sound symbolism*. PhD thesis, University of Queensland.

Kwon, Nahyun and Erich R. Round. 2015. Phonaesthemes in morphological theory. *Morphology* 25(1): 1–27.

Lacroix, René. 2009. Laz relative clauses in a typological and areal perspective. In Peter K. Austin, Oliver Bond, Monik Charette, David Nathan and Peter Sells (eds), *Proceedings of Conference on language documentation and linguistic theory 2*, 205–210. London: SOAS.

Lakoff, George. 1986. Classifiers as a reflection of mind. In Colette Craig (ed.), *Noun classes and categorization: Proceedings of a symposium on categorization and noun classification, Eugene, Oregon, October 1983*, 13–51. Amsterdam: John Benjamins.

Lambrecht, Knud. 1994. *Information structure and sentence form: Topic, focus, and the mental represention of discourse referents*. Cambridge: Cambridge University Press.

Lang, Adrienne. 1975. *Semantics of classificatory verbs in Enga*. Canberra: Pacific Linguistics.

Langacker, Ronald W. 1987. *Foundations of cognitive grammar. Volume 1*. Stanford, CA: Stanford University Press.

Langacker, Ronald W. 1991. *Foundations of cognitive grammar. Volume II: Descriptive applications*. Stanford, CA: Stanford University Press.

Langacker, Ronald W. 2008. Subordination in cognitive grammar. In Barbara Lewandowska-Tomaszczyk (ed.), *Asymmetric events*, 137–149. Amsterdam/Philadelphia: John Benjamins.

LaPolla, Randy J. 1992. 'Anti-ergative' marking in Tibeto-Burman. *Linguistics of the Tibeto-Burman Area* 15(1): 1–9.

LaPolla, Randy J. 1995. 'Ergative' marking in Tibeto-Burman. In Yoshio Nishi, James A. Matisoff and Yasuhiko Nagano (eds), *New horizons in Tibeto-Burman morphosyntax*, 189–228. Osaka: National Museum of Ethnology.

LaPolla, Randy J. 2008. Relative clause structures in the Rawang language. *Language and Linguistics* 9(4): 797–812.

LaPolla, Randy J. 2016. On categorization: Stick to the facts of the languages. *Linguistic Typology* 20(2): 365–375.

LeDoux, Joseph. 2019. *The deep history of ourselves: The four-billion-year story of how we got conscious brains*. New York: Viking.

Lee, Hanjung. 2007. Case ellipsis at the grammar/pragmatics interface: A formal analysis from a typological perspective. *Journal of Pragmatics* 39: 1465–1481.

Lee, Jennifer R. 1987. *Tiwi today: A study of language change in a contact situation*. Canberra: Pacific Linguistics.

Leeding, Velma J. 1989. *Anindilyakwa phonology and morphology*. PhD thesis, University of Sydney.

Lehmann, Christian. 1988. Towards a typology of clause linkage. In John Haiman and Sandra A. Thompson (eds), *Clause combining in grammar and discourse*, 181–225. Amsterdam: John Benjamins.

Levin, Beth. 1993. *English verb classes and alternations: A preliminary investigation*. Chicago and London: The University of Chicago Press.

Levinson, Stephen C. 2000. *Presumptive meanings: The theory of generalized conversational implicature*. Cambridge, MA and London: The MIT Press.

Levinson, Stephen C. and Russell D. Gray 2012. Tools from evolutionary biology shed new light on the diversification of language. *Trends in Cognitive Sciences* 16(3): 167–173.

Li, Chao. 2007. Split ergativity and split intransitivity in Nepali. *Lingua* 117: 1462–1482.

Li, Charles N. 1986. Direct and indirect speech: A functional study. In Florian Coulmas (ed.), *Direct and indirect speech*, 29–45. Berlin: Mouton de Gruyter.

Li, Charles N. and Ranier Lang. 1979. The syntactic irrelevance of an ergative case in Enga and other Papuan languages. In Frans Plank (ed.), *Ergativity: Towards a theory of grammatical relations*, 307–324. London: Academic Press.

Li, Charles N. and Sandra Thompson. 1981. *Mandarin Chinese: A functional reference grammar.* Berkeley: University of California Press.

Li, Eden Sum-hung. 2007. *A systemic functional grammar of Chinese.* London: Continuum.

Li, Eden Sum-hung. 2017. The nominal group in Chinese. In Tom Bartlett and Gerard O'Grady (eds), *The Routledge handbook of systemic functional linguistics*, 338–353. London and New York: Routledge.

Li, Yongsui and Wang Ersong. 1986. *Haniyu Jianzhi [An outline grammar of Hani].* Beijing: Nationalities' Press.

Lidz, Liberty. 2011. Agentive marking in Yongning Na (Mosuo). *Linguistics in the Tibeto-Burman Area* 34(2): 49–72.

Liljegren, Henrik. 2008. *Towards a grammatical description of Palula: An Indo-Aryan language of the Hindu Kush.* PhD thesis, Stockholm University.

Lock, Graham. 1992. Non-segmental phonology and variable rules: Investigating variation in Singapore Mandarin nasal finals. In Paul Tench (ed.), *Studies in systemic phonology*, 122–134. London: Pinter.

Louagie, Dana. 2017. *A typological study of noun phrase structures in Australian languages.* PhD thesis, KU Leuven.

Louagie, Dana. 2020. *Noun phrases in Australian languages: A typological study.* (Pacific Linguistics, 662.) Berlin and Boston: De Gruyter Mouton.

Louagie, Dana and Jean-Christophe Verstraete. 2015. Personal pronouns with determining functions in Australian languages. *Studies in Language* 39(1): 158–197.

Louagie, Dana and Jean-Christophe Verstraete. 2016. Noun phrase constituency in Australian languages: A typological study. *Linguistic Typology* 20(1): 25–80.

Lu, Man, Jeroen van de Weijer, Chris Sinha and Zhengguang Liu. 2019. Optional ergative marking in Tujia. *Lingua* 223: 46–66.

Lucy, John A. 2000. Systems of nominal classification: A concluding discussion. In Gunter Senft (ed.), *Systems of nominal classification*, 326–341. Cambridge: Cambridge University Press.

Luk, Ellison and Maïa Ponsonnet. 2019. Discourse and pragmatic functions of the Dalabon 'ergative' case-marker. *Australian Journal of Linguistics* 39(3): 287–328.

Lyons, John. 1968. *Introduction to theoretical linguistics.* Cambridge: Cambridge University Press.

Maho, Jouni. 1999. *A comparative study of Bantu noun classes.* Göteborg: Acta Universitatis Gothoburgensis.

Malchukov, Andrej L. and Peter de Swart. 2009. Differential case marking and actancy variations. In Andrej L. Malchukov and Andrew Spencer (eds), *The Oxford handbook of case*, 339–355. Oxford: Oxford University Press.

Malchukov, Andrej L. and Andrew Spencer (eds). 2009. *The Oxford handbook of case.* (Oxford Handbooks in Linguistics.) Oxford: Oxford University Press.

Mardale, A. 2010. Eléments d'analyse du marquage différentiel de l'objet dans les langues romanes. *Faits de langue - Les cahiers* 2: 161–197.

Margetts, Anna. 1999. *Valence and transitivity in Saliba an Oceanic language of Papua New Guinea.* PhD thesis, Catholic University of Nijmegen.

Martin, James R. 1996. Transitivity in Tagalog: A functional interpretation of case. In Margaret Berry, Christopher Butler, Robin Fawcett and Guowen Huang (eds), *Meaning and form: Systemic functional interpretations - meaning and choice in language: Studies for Michael Halliday*, 229–296. Norwood, NJ: Ablex.

Martin, Samuel E. 1962. Phonetic symbolism in Korean. *American Studies in Altaic Linguistics (Uralic and Altaic Series)* 13: 177–189.

Martins, Silvana and Valter Martins. 1999. Makú. In Robert M.W. Dixon and Alexandra Y. Aikhenvald (eds), *The Amazonian languages*, 251–267. Cambridge: Cambridge University Press.

Matthews, Peter H. 1966. The concept of rank in Neo-Firthian linguistics. *Journal of Linguistics* 2: 101–109.

Matthews, Stephen and Tommi Tsz-Cheung Leung. 2004. Verbal vs. nominal classifier constructions in Cantonese and Thai. In Somsonge Burusphat (ed.), *Papers from the Eleventh Annual Meeting of the Southeast Asian Linguistics Society, 2001*, 445–459. Tempe, Arizona: Arizona State University.

Matthews, Stephen and Virginia Yip. 1999. Verbal and nominal classification: Syntactic and semantic parallels in Cantonese and beyond. Paper presented at *Symposium on verb classification*, ALT-III, Amsterdam.

Matthiessen, Christian M.I.M. 2004. Descriptive motifs and generalizations. In Alice M.C. Caffarel, James R. Martin and Christian M.I.M. Matthiessen (eds), *Language typology: A functional perspective*, 537–673. Amsterdam/Philadelphia: John Benjamins.

Maw, Joan. 1992. Tone groups and reported speech in Swahili. In Paul Tench (ed.), *Studies in systemic phonology*, 161–174. London: Pinter.

Mayer, Mercer. 1967. *A boy, a dog and a frog*. New York: Dial Books for Young Readers.

McGregor, William B. 1984. *A grammar of Kuniyanti: An Australian Aboriginal language of the Southern Kimberley, Western Australia*. PhD thesis, University of Sydney.

McGregor, William B. 1988. Mood and subordination in Kuniyanti. In Peter Austin (ed.), *Complex sentence constructions in Australian languages*, 37–67. Amsterdam: John Benjamins.

McGregor, William B. 1989a. Discourse basis of ergative marking in Gooniyandi. *La Trobe University Working Papers in Linguistics* 2: 127–158.

McGregor, William B. 1989b. Phrase fracturing in Gooniyandi. In L. Marácz and Peter Muysken (eds), *Configurationality: The typology of asymmetries*, 207–222. Dordrecht: Foris Publications.

McGregor, William B. 1990a. *A functional grammar of Gooniyandi*. Amsterdam: John Benjamins.

McGregor, William B. 1990b. The metafunctional hypothesis and syntagmatic relations. *Occasional Papers in Systemic Linguistics* 4: 5–50.

McGregor, William B. 1991. The concept of rank in systemic linguistics. In Eija Ventola (ed.), *Functional and systemic linguistics: Approaches and uses*, 121–138. Berlin and New York: Mouton de Gruyter.

McGregor, William B. 1992a. The semantics of ergative marking in Gooniyandi. *Linguistics* 30(2): 275–318.

McGregor, William B. 1992b. Systemic phonology of Gooniyandi. In Paul Tench (ed.), *Studies in systemic phonology*, 19–43. London: Pinter.

McGregor, William B. 1994a. Complex sentence constructions in Nyulnyul, Western Australia. *Functions of Language* 1(1): 25–66.

McGregor, William B. 1994b. The grammar of reported speech and thought in Gooniyandi. *Australian Journal of Linguistics* 14(1): 63–92.

McGregor, William B. 1995a. *The English 'tag question': A new analysis, is(n't) it?* In Peter Fries and Ruqaiya Hasan (eds), *On subject and theme: A discourse functional perspective*, 91–121. Amsterdam: John Benjamins.

McGregor, William B. 1995b. Ja hear that didja? Interrogative tags in Australian English. *Te Reo* 38: 3–35.

McGregor, William B. 1996a. Attribution and identification in Gooniyandi. In Margaret Berry, Christopher Butler, Robin Fawcett and Guowen Huang (eds), *Meaning and form: Systemic functional interpretations. Meaning and choice in language: Studies for Michael Halliday*, 395–430. Norwood, NJ: Ablex.

McGregor, William B. 1996b. Sound symbolism in Gooniyandi. *Word* 47(3): 339–364.

McGregor, William B. 1997a. Functions of noun phrase discontinuity in Gooniyandi. *Functions of Language* 4(1): 83–114.

McGregor, William B. 1997b. *Semiotic grammar*. Oxford: Clarendon Press.

McGregor, William B. 1998. 'Optional' ergative marking in Gooniyandi revisited: Implications to the theory of marking. *Leuvense Bijdragen* 87: 491–534.

McGregor, William B. 1999a. External possession constructions in Nyulnyulan languages. In Doris L. Payne and Immanuel Barshi (eds), *External possession*, 429–448. Amsterdam: John Benjamins.

McGregor, William B. 1999b. The medio-active construction in Nyulnyulan languages. *Studies in Language* 23(3): 531–567.

McGregor, William B. 2001. Ideophones as the source of verbs in Northern Australian languages. In F.K. Erhard Voeltz and Christa Kilian-Hatz (eds), *Ideophones*, 205–221. Amsterdam/Philadelphia: John Benjamins.

McGregor, William B. 2002a. Ergative and accusative patterning in Warrwa. In Kristin Davidse and Béatrice Lamiroy (eds), *The nominative & accusative and their counterparts*, 285–317. Amsterdam: John Benjamins.

McGregor, William B. 2002b. *Verb classification in Australian languages*. Berlin and New York: Mouton de Gruyter.

McGregor, William B. 2003a. A fundamental misconception of modern linguistics. *Acta Linguistica Hafniensia* 35: 39–64.

McGregor, William B. 2003b. The nothing that is, the zero that isn't. *Studia Linguistica* 57(2): 75–119.

McGregor, William B. 2004. *The languages of the Kimberley, Western Australia*. London: RoutledgeCurzon.

McGregor, William B. 2005. Semantics and pragmatics of ergative marking in Kimberley languages. Unpublished manuscript.

McGregor, William B. 2006a. Focal and optional ergative marking in Warrwa (Kimberley, Western Australia). *Lingua* 116(4): 393–423.

McGregor, William B. 2006b. The grammar of complex predicate constructions in Warrwa and other Nyulnyulan languages. Paper presented at *Workshop on Complex Predicates*, ALS 2006 Conference, University of Queensland.

McGregor, William B. 2007a. A desiderative complement construction in Warrwa. In Jeff Siegel, John Lynch and Diana K. Eades (eds), *Language description, history and development: Linguistic indulgence in memory of Terry Crowley*, 27–40. Amsterdam: John Benjamins.

McGregor, William B. 2007b. Discourse uses of verbal classification systems in Warrwa (Nyulnyulan). Paper presented at workshop *The Representation of Actions, States and Events in Classification Systems: Universals and Typological Diversity*, in ICLC-10, Kraków.

McGregor, William B. 2007c. Ergative marking of intransitive subjects in Warrwa. *Australian Journal of Linguistics* 27(2): 201–229.

McGregor, William B. 2008a. Complementation as interpersonal grammar. *Word* 59(1): 25–53.

McGregor, William B. 2008b. The origin of noun classes in Worrorran languages. In Claire Bowern, Bethwyn Evans and Luisa Miceli (eds), *Morphology and language history: In honour of Harold Koch*, 185–200. Amsterdam/Philadelphia: John Benjamins.

McGregor, William B. 2009. Introduction. In William B. McGregor (ed.), *The expression of possession*, 1–12. Berlin and New York: Mouton de Gruyter.

McGregor, William B. 2010. Optional ergative case marking systems in a typological-semiotic perspective. *Lingua* 120(7): 1610–1636.

McGregor, William B. 2012a. *The Nyulnyul language of Dampier Land, Western Australia.* Canberra: Pacific Linguistics.

McGregor, William B. 2012b. Why there is an ergative but no absolutive case in Gooniyandi (and nearby languages). Unpublished manuscript.

McGregor, William B. 2013a. Comparing linguistic systems of categorisation. In Lars Borin and Anju Saxena (eds), *Approaches to measuring linguistic differences*, 387–427. Berlin: De Gruyter Mouton.

McGregor, William B. 2013b. Lexical categories in Gooniyandi, Kimberley, Western Australia. In Jan Rijkhoff and Eva van Lier (eds), *Flexible word classes: Typological studies of underspecified parts of speech*, 221–246. Oxford and New York: Oxford University Press.

McGregor, William B. 2013c. Optionality in grammar and language use. *Linguistics* 51(6): 1147–1204.

McGregor, William B. 2013d. There are existential constructions and existential constructions: Presumption invoking existentials in English. *Folia Linguistica* 47(1): 139–181.

McGregor, William B. 2014a. Connate roles in Nyulnyul: Non-nuclear grammatical relations within the core. In Nicole Delbecque, Karen Lahousse and Willy Van Langendonck (eds), *Non-nuclear cases*, 67–93. Amsterdam: John Benjamins.

McGregor, William B. 2014b. The 'say, do' verb in Nyulnyul, Warrwa, and other Nyulnyulan languages is monosemic. In Klaus Robering (ed.), *Events, arguments, and aspects: Topics in the semantics of verbs*, 301–327. Amsterdam/Philadelphia: John Benjamins.

McGregor, William B. 2015. Four counter-presumption constructions in Shua (Khoe-Kwadi, Botswana). *Lingua* 158: 54–75.

McGregor, William B. 2017a. There's grammar and there's grammar just as there's usage and there's usage. *English Text Construction* 10(2): 199–232.

McGregor, William B. 2017b. Unusual manner constructions in Shua (Khoe-Kwadi, Botswana). *Linguistics* 55(4): 857–897.

McGregor, William B. 2018a. Emergence of optional accusative case marking in Khoe languages. In Ilja A. Seržant and Alena Witzlack-Makarevich (eds), *Diachrony of differential argument marking*, 243–279. Berlin: Language Sciences Press.

McGregor, William B. 2018b. The history of verb classification in Nyulnyulan languages. In William B. McGregor and Søren Wichmann (eds), *The diachrony of classification systems*, 315–351. Amsterdam: John Benjamins.

McGregor, William B. 2019a. The evolutionary origins of interpersonal grammar. *Functions of Language* 26(1): 112–135.

McGregor, William B. 2019b. Reported speech as a dedicated grammatical domain – and why defenestration should not be thrown out the window. *Linguistic Typology* 23(1): 207–219.

McGregor, William B. in preparation. *A grammar of Warrwa, Kimberley, Western Australia.*

McGregor, William B. and Alan L. Rumsey. 2009. *Worrorran revisited: The case for genetic relations among languages of the Northern Kimberley region of Western Australia.* Canberra: Pacific Linguistics.

McGregor, William B., Eva Schultze-Berndt and Thekla Wiebusch. 2007. Verb classification systems in the languages of the world. Unpublished manuscript.

McGregor, William B. and Jean-Christophe Verstraete (eds). 2010. Special issue section of *Lingua*, Optional ergative marking. *Lingua* 120(7).

McKay, Graham. 1988. Figure and ground in Rembarrnga complex sentences. In Peter Austin (ed.), *Complex sentence constructions in Australian languages*, 7–36. Amsterdam: John Benjamins.

McLellan, Marilyn J. 1992. *A study of the Wangurri language.* PhD thesis, Macquarie University.

Merlan, Francesca. 1979. On the prehistory of some Australian verbs. *Oceanic Linguistics* 18(1): 33–112.

Merlan, Francesca. 1981. Some functional relations among subordination, mood, aspect and focus in Australian languages. *Australian Journal of Linguistics* 1: 175–210.

Merlan, Francesca. 1983. *Ngalakan grammar, texts, and vocabulary.* Canberra: Pacific Linguistics.

Merlan, Francesca, Steven Powell Roberts and Alan Rumsey. 1997. New Guinea 'classificatory verbs' and Australian noun classification: A typological comparison. In Mark Harvey and Nicholas Reid (eds), *Nominal classification in Aboriginal Australia*, 63–103. Amsterdam/Philadelphia: John Benjamins.

Minashima, Hiroshi. 2001. On the deletion of accusative case markers in Japanese. *Studia Linguistica* 55(2): 175–190.

Mithun, Marianne. 1988. The grammaticalization of coordination. In John Haiman and Sandra A. Thompson (eds), *Clause combining in grammar and discourse*, 331–359. Amsterdam and Philadelphia: John Benjamins.

Mithun, Marianne. 1999. *The languages of native North America.* Cambridge: Cambridge University Press.

Mithun, Marianne. 2008. The extension of dependency beyond the sentence. *Language* 84: 69–119.

Mithun, Marianne and Wallace Chafe. 1999. What are S, A, and O? *Studies in Language* 23(3): 569–596.

Mithun Williams, Marianne. 1976. *A grammar of Tuscarora.* New York: Garland.

Mock, Carol C. 1992. A systemic phonology of Isthmus Zapotec prosodies. In James Benson and William Greaves (eds), *Systemic perspectives on discourse: Selected theoretical papers from the 9th International Systemic Workshop*, 141–159. Norwood, NJ: Ablex.

Mohanan, Tara. 1994. *Argument structure in Hindi.* Stanford, CA: CSLI.

Monaghan, James. 1979. *The Neo-Firthian tradition and its contribution to general linguistics.* Tuebingen: Niemeyer.

Moravcsik, Edith A. 1978. On the distribution of ergative and accusative patterns. *Lingua* 45: 233–279.

Moravcsik, Edith A. 2013. *Introducing language typology.* New York: Cambridge University Press.

Mwinlaaru, Isaac N. and Winfred Wenhui Xuan. 2016. A survey of studies in systemic functional language description and typology. *Functional Linguistics* 3(8): 1–41.

Myhill, J. 1992. *Typological discourse analysis: Quantitative approaches to the study of linguistic function.* Oxford and Cambridge, MA: Blackwell.

Naish, Constance. 1979. *A syntactic study of Tlingit.* Dallas, TX: Summer Institute of Linguistics.

Narrog, Heiko and Bernd Heine (eds). 2018. *Grammaticalization from a typological perspective.* Oxford: Oxford University Press.

Neidle, Carol and Joan Cottle Poole Nash. 2015. American Sign Language. In Julie Bakken Jepsen, Goedele De Clerck, Sam Lutalo-Kiingi and William B. McGregor (eds), *Sign languages of the world: A comparative handbook,* 31–70. Berlin/Boston and Preston: De Gruyter Mouton and Ishara Press.

Nekes, Hermann and Ernest A. Worms. 2006. *Australian languages.* Berlin and New York: Mouton de Gruyter.

Nguyen, Dinh H. 1997. *Vietnamese.* Amsterdam: John Benjamins.

Nichols, Johanna. 1986. Head-marking and dependent-marking grammar. *Language* 62: 56–119.

Nichols, Johanna. 1992. *Linguistic diversity in space and time.* Chicago: University of Chicago Press.

Nichols, Johanna. 2003. Diversity and stability in language. In Brian D. Joseph and Richard D. Janda (eds), *The handbook of historical linguistics,* 283–310. Oxford: Blackwell.

Nichols, Johanna. 2013. Macrofamilies, macroareas, and contact. In Raymond Hickey (ed.), *The handbook of language contact,* 361–379. Malden and Oxford: Wiley-Blackwell.

Nojima, Motoyasu. 1996. Lexical prefixes of Bunun verbs. *Gengo Kenkyu* 110: 1–27.

Noonan, Michael. 2007. Complementation. In Timothy Shopen (ed.), *Language typology and syntactic description. Volume II: Complex constructions,* 52–150. Cambridge: Cambridge University Press.

Nordlinger, Rachel. 2010. Complex predicates in Wambaya: Detaching predicate composition from syntactic structure. In Mengistu Amberber, Brett Baker and Mark Harvey (eds), *Complex predicate formation: Cross-linguistic perspectives on event structure,* 237–258. Cambridge: Cambridge University Press.

Nuckolls, Janice B. 1999. The case for sound symbolism. *Annual Review of Anthropology* 28: 225–252.

Ochs, Elinor. 1982. Ergativity and word order in Samoan child language. *Language* 58(3): 646–671.

Ochs, Elinor. 1988. *Culture and language development: Language acquisition and language socialization in a Samoan village.* Cambridge: Cambridge University Press.

Ogden, R. 2006. Firthian phonology. In Keith Brown (ed.), *Encyclopedia of language and linguistics, volume 4,* 485–487. Oxford: Elsevier.

Okell, John. 1969. *A reference grammar of colloquial Burmese.* London: Oxford University Press.

Osumi, Midori. 1995. *Tinrin grammar.* Honolulu: University of Hawai'i Press.

Palancar, Enrique L. 2002. *The origin of agent markers.* Berlin: Akademie.

Palancar, Enrique L. 2009. Varieties of ergative. In Andrej L. Malchukov and Andrew Spencer (eds), *The Oxford handbook of case,* 562–571. Oxford: Oxford University Press.

Paris, Marie-Claude. 2013. Verbal reduplication and verbal classifiers in Chinese. In Guangshun Cao, Hilary Chappell, Redouane Djamouri and Thekla Wiebusch (eds), *Breaking down the barriers: Interdisciplinary studies in Chinese linguistics and beyond, volume 1,* 257–278. Taipei: Institute of Linguistics, Academica Sinitica.

Pascual, Esther. 2014. *Fictive interaction: The conversation frame in thought, language, and discourse.* Amsterdam and Philadelphia: John Benjamins.

Passer, Matthias B. 2016. (What) Do verb classifiers classify? *Lingua* 174: 16–44.

Patz, Elisabeth. 2002. *A grammar of the Kuku Yalanji language of North Queensland*. Canberra: Pacific Linguistics.

Payne, John R. 1985. Complex phrases and complex sentences. In Timothy Shopen (ed.), *Language typology and syntactic description. Volume II: Complex constructions*, 3–41. Cambridge: Cambridge University Press.

Pike, Kenneth L. 1948. *Tone languages: A technique for determining the number and type of pitch contrasts in a language, with studies in tonemic substitution and fusion*. Ann Arbor: University of Michigan Press.

Pike, Kenneth L. 1959. Language as particle, wave, and field. *The Texas Quarterly* 2(2): 37–54.

Prakasam, V. 1972. *A systemic treatment of certain aspects of Telugu phonology*. D.Phil. thesis, University of York.

Prakasam, V. 1992. Length in Telugu. In Paul Tench (ed.), *Studies in systemic phonology*, 70–76. London: Pinter.

Primus, Bestrice. 2011. Case-marking typology. In Jae Jung Song (ed.), *The Oxford handbook of language typology*, 303–321. Oxford: Oxford University Press.

Queixalós, Francesc and Spike Gildea. 2010. Manifestations of ergativity in Amazonia. In Spike Gildea and Francesc Queixalós (eds), *Ergativity in Amazonia*, 1–25. Amsterdam and Philadelphia: John Benjamins.

Quesada, J. Diego. 1999. Ergativity in Chibchan. *Sprachtypol. Univ. Forsch. (STUF)* 52(1): 22–51.

Ramat, Paolo. 2011. The (early) history of linguistic typology. In Jae Jung Song (ed.), *The Oxford handbook of linguistic typology*, 9–24. Oxford: Oxford University Press.

Rankin, Robert L. 2006. The interplay of synchronic and diachronic discovery in Siouan grammar-writing. In Felix K. Ameka, Alan Dench and Nicholas Evans (eds), *Catching language: The standing challenge of grammar writing*, 527–547. Berlin and New York: Mouton de Gruyter.

Reid, Nicholas J. 1997. Class and classifier in Ngan'gityemerri. In Mark Harvey and Nicholas Reid (eds), *Nominal classification in Aboriginal Australia*, 165–228. Amsterdam/Philadelphia: John Benjamins.

Reid, Nicholas J. 2000. Complex verb collocations in Ngan'gityemerri: A non-derivational strategy for encoding valence alternations. In Robert M.W. Dixon and Alexandra Y. Aikhenvald (eds), *Changing valency: Case studies in transitivity*, 333–359. Cambridge: Cambridge University Press.

Reid, Wallis. 1980. Meaning and narrative structure. *Columbia University Working Papers in Linguistics* 5: 12–19.

Reinhart, Tanya 1975. Whose main clause? (Point of view in sentences with parentheticals). In Susumu Kuno (ed.), *Harvard studies of syntax and semantics: Volume 1*, 127–171. Cambridge, MA: Department of Linguistics, Harvard University.

Rijkhoff, Jan. 2002. *The noun phrase*. Oxford: Oxford University Press.

Rijkhoff, Jan. 2007. Word classes. *Language and Linguistics Compass* 1(6): 709–726.

Rijkhoff, Jan. 2008a. Descriptive and discourse-referential modifiers in a layered model of the noun phrase. *Linguistics* 46(4): 789–829.

Rijkhoff, Jan. 2008b. Layers, levels and contexts in Functional Discourse Grammar. In Daniel García Velasco and Jan Rijkhoff (eds), *The noun phrase in Functional Discourse Grammar*, 63–115. Berlin and New York: Mouton de Gruyter.

Rijkhoff, Jan. 2014. Modification as a propositional act. In María de los Ángeles Gómez Gonzáles, Francisco José Ruiz de Ibáñez and Francisco Gonzálvez-García (eds), *Theory and practice in functional-cognitive space*, 129–150. Amsterdam: John Benjamins.

Rijkhoff, Jan. 2016. Crosslinguistic categories in morphosyntactic typology: Problems and prospects. *Linguistic Typology* 20(2): 333–363.

Rijkhoff, Jan and Dik Bakker. 1998. Language sampling. *Linguistic Typology* 2(3): 263–314.

Rijkhoff, Jan, Dik Bakker, Kees Hengeveld and Peter Kahrel. 1993. A method of language sampling. *Studies in Language* 17(1): 169–203.

Robins, Robert H. 1959. In defence of WP. *Transactions of the Philological Society* 58(1): 116–144.

Robins, Robert H. 1961. John Rupert Firth: Obituary. *Language* 37: 191–200.

Robins, Robert H. 1967. *A short history of linguistics*. London: Longman.

Rose, David. 2001. *The Western Desert code: An Australian cryptogrammar*. Canberra: Pacific Linguistics.

Round, Erich and Lesley Stirling. 2015. Universals of split argument coding and morphological neutralization: Why Kala Lagaw Ya is not as bizarre as we thought. *Australian Journal of Linguistics* 35(3): 251–281.

Rumsey, Alan L. 1982. *An intra-sentence grammar of Ungarinjin, North-western Australia*. Canberra: Pacific Linguistics.

Rumsey, Alan L. 1990. Wording, meaning, and linguistic ideology. *American Anthropologist* 92: 346–361.

Rumsey, Alan L. 2000. Bunuba. In Robert M.W. Dixon and Barry Blake (eds), *The handbook of Australian languages, Volume 5*, 34–152. Melbourne: Oxford University Press Australia.

Sagna, Serge. 2007. Do noun class markers classify verbs in Gújjolaay Eegimaa? Paper presented at workshop *The Representation of Actions, States and Events in Classification Systems: Universals and Typological Diversity*, in ICLC-10, Kraków.

Sagna, Serge. 2008. *Formal and semantic properties of the Gújjolaay Eegimaa: (A.k.a Banjal) nominal classification system*. PhD thesis, University of London.

Sagna, Serge. 2017. Morphological alternation and event delimitation in Eegimaa. *Italian Journal of Linguistics* 29(1): 53–74.

Sakel, Jeanette. 2006. Verb classification in Mosetén. Paper presented at COST Workshop on Verb Classification, Humboldt University.

Sakel, Jeanette. 2007. The verbness markers of Mosetén from a typological perspective. In Bernhard Wälchli and Matti Miestamo (eds), *New challenges in typology: Broadening the horizons and redefining the foundations*, 315–335. Berlin: Mouton de Gruyter.

Sandler, Wendy, Mark Aronoff, Irit Meir and Carol Padden. 2011. The gradual emergence of phonological form in a new language. *Natural Language and Linguistic Theory* 29(2): 503–543.

Sandler, Wendy, Irit Meir, Carol Padden and Mark Aronoff. 2005. The emergence of grammar: Systematic structure in a new language. *Proceedings of the National Academy of the Sciences of the United States of America* 102(7): 2661–2665.

Sands, Kristina. 1995. Nominal classification in Australia. *Anthropological Linguistics* 37: 247–346.

Sapir, Edward 1929. A study in phonetic symbolism. *Journal of Experimental Psychology* 12: 225–239.

Sapir, Edward. 1930. Southern Paiute, a Shoshonean language. *Proceedings, American Academy of Arts and Sciences* 65(1): 1–296.

Sapir, J. David 1965. *A grammar of Diola-Fogny: A language spoken in the Basse-Casamance region of Senegal*. Cambridge: Cambridge University Press.

Saunders, Thomas. 1997. *The verbal semantics of Ungarinyin: A preliminary study*. BA (Hons) thesis, Australian National University.

Saxena, Anju. n.d. Ergative/absolutive alternation in Lhasa Tibetan. Unpublished manuscript.

Schachter, Paul. 1985. Parts-of-speech systems. In Timothy Shopen (ed.), *Language typology and syntactic description. Volume 1*, 3–61. Cambridge: Cambridge University Press.

Schachter, Paul and Fé T. Otanes. 1972. *Tagalog reference grammar*. Berkeley: University of California Press.

Schachter, Paul and Timothy Shopen. 2007. Parts-of-speech systems. In Timothy Shopen (ed.), *Language typology and syntactic description. Volume I: Clause structure*, 1–60. Cambridge: Cambridge University Press.

Schadeberg, Thilo C. 2003. Derivation. In Derek Nurse and Gérard Philippson (eds), *The Bantu languages*, 71–89. London and New York: Routledge.

Schmid, Hans-Jörg. 2013. Is usage more than usage after all? The case of English *not that*. *Linguistics* 51(1): 75–116.

Schultze-Berndt, Eva. 2000. *Simple and complex verbs in Jaminjung: A study of event categorisation in an Australian language*. PhD thesis, Catholic University of Nijmegen.

Schultze-Berndt, Eva. 2001. Ideophone-like characteristics of uninflected predicates in Jaminjung (Australia). In F.K. Erhard Voeltz and Christa Kilian-Hatz (eds), *Ideophones*, 355–374. Amsterdam/Philadelphia: John Benjamins.

Schultze-Berndt, Eva and Serge Sagna. 2010. Towards a typology of overt verb classification. Paper presented at *COST Action 31 Final Conference. Categorizing human experience: Classification in languages and knowledge systems*. Ecole Normale Superieure, Paris.

Schultze-Berndt, Eva and Candide Simard. 2012. Constraints on noun phrase discontinuity in an Australian language: The role of prosody and information structure. *Linguistics* 50(5): 1015–1058.

Scott, Graham. 1986. On ergativity in Fore and other Papuan languages. In *Papers in New Guinea Linguistics, 18*, 167–175. Canberra: Pacific Linguistics.

Seifart, Frank. 2018. The semantic reduction of the noun universe and the diachrony of nominal classification. In William B. McGregor and Søren Wichmann (eds), *The diachrony of classification systems*, 9–32. Amsterdam: John Benjamins.

Senft, Gunter (ed.). 2000. *Systems of nominal classification*. (Language, Culture and Cognition.) Cambridge: Cambridge University Press.

Senghas, Ann, Sotaro Kita and Asli Özyürek. 2004. Children creating core properties of language: Evidence from an emerging sign language in Nicaragua. *Science* 305: 1779–1782.

Sharpe, Margaret. 1996. *An introduction to the Yugambeh-Bundjalung language and its dialects*. Armidale: The author.

Shields, Kenneth. 2011. Linguistic typology and historical linguistics. In Jae Jung Song (ed.), *The Oxford handbook of linguistic typology*, 551–567. Oxford: Oxford University Press.

Shopen, Timothy (ed.). 1985. *Language typology and syntactic description. Volume II: Complex constructions*. Cambridge: Cambridge University Press.

Shopen, Timothy (ed.). 2007. *Language typology and syntactic description. Volume II: Complex constructions*. Cambridge: Cambridge University Press.

Shore, Susanna. 1992. *Aspects of a systemic-functional grammar of Finnish*. PhD thesis, Macquarie University.

Siewierska, Anna. 1984. Phrasal discontinuity in Polish. *Australian Journal of Linguistics* 4(1): 57–71.

Siewierska, Anna. 2013. Alignment of verbal person marking. In Matthew S. Dryer and Martin Haspelmath (eds), *The world atlas of language structures online*, chapter 100. Munich: Max Planck Digital Library.

Silver, Shirley and Wik R. Miller. 1997. *American Indian languages: Cultural and social contexts.* Tucson: The University of Arizona Press.

Silverstein, Michael. 1976. Hierarchy of features and ergativity. In Robert M.W. Dixon (ed.), *Grammatical categories in Australian languages*, 112–171. Canberra: Australian Institute of Aboriginal Studies.

Silverstein, Michael. 1986. Classifiers, verb classifiers and verbal categories. *Berkeley Linguistics Society* 12: 497–514.

Sinclair, John (ed.). 2018. *Collins COBUILD Advanced learner's dictionary.* (Collins COBUILD Dictionaries for Learners.) Glasgow: HarperCollins.

Slonimska, Anita and Seán G. Roberts. 2017. A case of systematic sound symbolism in pragmatics: Universals in *wh*-words. *Journal of Pragmatics* 116: 1–20.

Song, Jae Jung (ed.). 2011. *The Oxford handbook of linguistic typology.* (Oxford Handbooks in Linguistics.) Oxford: Oxford University Press.

Spronck, Stef. 2015. *Reported speech in Ungarinyin [["…"] -ma-]: Grammar and social cognition in a language of the Kimberley region, Western Australia.* PhD thesis, Australian National University.

Spronck, Stef. 2017. Defenestration: Deconstructing the frame-in relation in Ungarinyin. *Journal of Pragmatics* 114: 104–133.

Spronck, Stef and Tatiana Nikitina. 2019. Reported speech forms a dedicated syntactic domain: Typological arguments and observations. *Linguistic Typology* 23(1): 119–159.

Stolz, Thomas. 1996. Some instruments are really good companions – some are not: On syncretism and the typology of instrumentals and comitatives. *Theoretical Linguistics* 23(1/2): 113–200.

Suter, Edgar. 2010. The optional ergative in Kâte. In John Bowden, Nikolaus P. Himmelmann and Malcolm Ross (eds), *A journey through Austronesian and Papuan linguistic and cultural space: Papers in honour of Andrew K. Pawley*, 423–437. Canberra: Pacific Linguistics.

Swartz, Stephen. 1988. Pragmatic structure and word order in Warlpiri. In Peter Austin, Leone Dunn, Stephen M. Swartz et al. (eds), *Papers in Australian Linguistics, 17*, 151–166. Canberra: Pacific Linguistics.

Talmy, Leonard. 1978. Figure and ground in complex sentences. In Joseph Greenberg (ed.), *Universals of human language, Volume 4, Syntax*, 625–649. Stanford, CA: Stanford University Press.

Taylor, A.J. 1970. *Syntax and phonology of Motu (Papua): A transformational approach.* PhD thesis, Australian National University.

Taylor, Charles. 1985. *Nkore-Kiga.* London, Sydney, Dover and New Hampshire: Croom Helm.

Tchekhoff, Claude. 1981. *Simple sentences in Tongan.* Canberra: Pacific Linguistics.

Terrill, Angela. 2002. *Dharumbal: The language of Rockhampton, Australia.* Canberra: Pacific Linguistics.

Teruya, Kazuhiro. 2007. *A systemic functional grammar of Japanese.* London: Continuum.

Thomas, Margaret. 2011. *Fifty key thinkers on language and linguistics.* London and New York: Routledge.

Thompson, Geoff, Wendy L. Bowcher, Lise Fontaine and David Schönthal (eds). 2019. *The Cambridge handbook of Systemic Functional Linguistics.* Cambridge: Cambridge University Press.

Thompson, Sandra A., Robert E. Longacre and Shin Ja J. Hwang. 2007. Adverbial clauses. In Timothy Shopen (ed.), *Language typology and syntactic description. Volume II: Complex constructions*, 237–300. Cambridge: Cambridge University Press.

Thornes, Tim. 1997. Instrumental prefixes in Northern Paiute. Paper presented at *Second Meeting of the Association for Linguistic Typology*, Eugene.

Tomasello, Michael. 1999. *The cultural origins of human cognition*. Cambridge MA: Harvard University Press.

Tomasello, Michael. 2003. *Constructing a language: A usage-based theory of language acquisition*. Cambridge, MA and London: Harvard University Press.

Tomasello, Michael. 2008. *Origins of human communication*. Cambridge, MA and London: The MIT Press.

Tomasello, Michael. 2014. *A natural history of human thinking*. Cambridge, MA and London: Harvard University Press.

Tomasello, Michael and Michael Jeffrey Farrar. 1986. Joint attention and early language. *Child Development* 57(6): 1454–1463.

Tomlin, Russell (ed.). 1987. *Coherence and grounding in discourse*. Amsterdam: John Benjamins.

Tournadre, Nicolas. 1991. The rhetorical use of the Tibetan ergative. *Linguistics of the Tibeto-Burman Area* 14(1): 93–107.

Tournadre, Nicolas. 1995. Tibetan ergativity and the trajectory model. In Yoshio Nishi, James A. Matisoff and Yasuhiko Nagano (eds), *New horizons in Tibeto-Burman morphosyntax*, 261–275. Osaka: National Museum of Ethnology.

Tournadre, Nicolas. 1996. *Ergativité en tibétain: approche morphosyntaxique de la langue parlée*. Paris and Leuven: Peeters.

Townsend, David J. and Thomas G. Bever. 1977. *Main and subordinate clauses: A study in figure and ground*. Bloomington: Indiana University Linguistics Club.

Traugott, Elizabeth Closs. 2003. Constructions in grammaticalization. In Brian D. Joseph and Richard D. Janda (eds), *The handbook of historical linguistics*, 624–647. Oxford: Blackwell.

Trubetzkoy, Nikolai S. 1969. *Principles of phonology*. Berkeley and Los Angeles: University of California Press.

Trudgill, Peter. 2011. *Sociolinguistic typology: Social determinants of linguistic complexity*. Oxford: Oxford University Press.

Tsunoda, Tasaku. 1981. Split case-marking patterns in verb-types and tense/aspect/mood. *Linguistics* 19: 389–438.

Urban, Matthias. 2011. Conventional sound symbolism in terms for organs of speech: A cross-linguistic study. *Folia Linguistica* 45(1): 199–214.

Van de Velde, Freek. 2007. Interpersonal modification in the English noun phrase. *Functions of Language* 14(2): 203–230.

van Lier, Eva and Jan Rijkhoff. 2013. Flexible word classes in linguistic typology and grammatical theory. In Jan Rijkhoff and Eva van Lier (eds), *Flexible word classes: Typological studies of underspecified parts of speech*, 1–30. Oxford and New York: Oxford University Press.

Van Valin, Robert D. 1993. A synopsis of role and reference grammar. In Robert D. Van Valin (ed.), *Advances in role and reference grammar*, 1–164. Amsterdam: John Benjamins.

Vandelanotte, Lieven. 2004. Deixis and grounding in speech and thought representation. *Journal of Pragmatics* 36: 489–520.

Vandelanotte, Lieven. 2009. *Speech and thought representation in English: A cognitive-functional approach*. Berlin and New York: Mouton de Gruyter.

Velupillai, Viveka. 2012. *An introduction to linguistic typology*. Amsterdam/Philadelphia: John Benjamins.

Vendler, Z. 1967. *Linguistics in philosophy*. Ithica, NY: Cornell University Press.

Verstraete, Jean-Christophe. 2002. Mood and clause combining in Australian languages. Unpublished manuscript.

Verstraete, Jean-Christophe. 2005a. The semantics and pragmatics of composite mood marking: The non-Pama-Nyungan languages of northern Australia. *Linguistic Typology* 9(2): 223–268.

Verstraete, Jean-Christophe. 2005b. Two types of coordination in clause combining. *Lingua* 115: 611–626.

Verstraete, Jean-Christophe. 2007. *Rethinking the coordinate-subordinate dichotomy: Interpersonal grammar and the analysis of adverbial clauses in English*. Berlin and New York: Mouton de Gruyter.

Verstraete, Jean-Christophe. 2010. Animacy and information structure in the system of ergative marking in Umpithamu. *Lingua* 120: 1637–1651.

Verstraete, Jean-Christophe, Sarah D'Hertefelt and An Van linden. 2012. A typology of complement insubordination in Dutch. *Studies in Language* 36(1): 123–153.

Voeltz, F.K. Erhard and Christa Kilian-Hatz (eds). 2001. *Ideophones*. (Typological Studies in Language, 44.) Amsterdam/Philadelphia: John Benjamins.

Vološinov, V. 1973. *Marxism and the philosophy of language*. New York and London: Seminar Press.

Vuillermet, Marine. 2012. *A grammar of Ese Ejja, a Takanan language of the Bolivian Amazon; Grammaire de l'ese ejja, langue takana d'Amazonie bolivienne*. PhD thesis, Université Lumière Lyon 2.

Wales, Katie. 2013. Alice in ego-land: The rhetoric of inanimate objects that talk. *Babel: The Language Magazine* 4: 35–37.

Walsh, Michael. 1976. Ergative, locative and instrumental case inflections: Murinjpata. In Robert M.W. Dixon (ed.), *Grammatical categories in Australian languages*, 405–408. Canberra: Australian Institute of Aboriginal Studies.

Walsh, Michael. 1997. Noun classes, nominal classification and generics in Murrinhpatha. In Mark Harvey and Nicholas Reid (eds), *Nominal classification in Aboriginal Australia*, 255–292. Amsterdam/Philadelphia: John Benjamins.

Wang, Fushi. 1985. *Miaoyu Jianzhi [An outline grammar of Miao]*. Beijing: Nationalities' Press.

Webster, Jonathan J. 2015. Michael Alexander Kirkwood (M. A. K.) Halliday – a brief biography. In Jonathan J. Webster (ed.), *The Bloomsbury companion to M. A. K. Halliday*, 3–14. London and New York: Bloomsbury.

Whorf, Benjamin L. 1956. *Language, thought and reality: Selected writings of Benjamin Lee Whorf*. Cambridge, MA: MIT Press.

Wilkins, David P. 1989. *Mparntwe Arrernte (Aranda): Studies in the structure and semantics of grammar*. PhD thesis, Australian National University.

Willemsen, Jeroen. in preparation. *A grammar of Reta*. PhD thesis, Aarhus University.

Willemsen, Jeroen and Ehm Hjort Miltersen. 2020. The expression of vulgarity, force, severity and size: Phonaesthemic alternations in Reta and in other languages. *Studies in Language* 44(3): 659–699.

Willett, Michael. 2014. *A study of the productivity of twelve English onset phonesthemes*. PhD thesis, University of Cardiff.

Williams, Corinne J. 1980. *A grammar of Yuwaalaraay.* Canberra: Pacific Linguistics.

Wilson, Stephen. 1999. *Coverbs and complex predicates in Wagiman.* Stanford, CA: CSLI Publications.

Wohlgemuth, Jan and Michael Cysouw (eds). 2010a. *Rethinking universals: How rarities affect linguistic theory.* (Empirical Approaches to Language Typology, 45.) Berlin and New York: Mouton de Gruyter.

Wohlgemuth, Jan and Michael Cysouw (eds). 2010b. *Rara & rarissima: Documenting the fringes of linguistic diversity.* (Empirical Approaches to Language Typology, 46.) Berlin and New York: De Gruyter Mouton.

Wurm, Stephen A. 1976. Accusative marking in Duungidjawu (Waga-Waga). In Robert M.W. Dixon (ed.), *Grammatical categories in Australian languages,* 106–111. Canberra: Australian Institute of Aboriginal Studies.

Xiaoqing, Ouyang. 1986. *The clause complex in Chinese.* MA thesis, University of Sydney.

Yaguchi, Michiko. 2001. The function of the non-deictic *that* in English. *Journal of Pragmatics* 33: 1125–1155.

Yali, Ou and Liu Chengyu. 2014. A systemic functional matrix of Chinese phonology. *Linguistics & the Human Sciences* 10(3): 220–246.

Zhou, Xiaokang and William B. McGregor. 1999. Verbal classification in Mandarin Chinese. Paper presented at *Symposium on verb classification,* ALT-III, Amsterdam.

Zubin, David A. and Klaus-Michael Köpcke. 1986. Gender and folk taxonomy: The indexical relation between grammatical and lexical categorization. In Colette Craig (ed.), *Noun classes and categorization: Proceedings of a symposium on categorization and noun classification, Eugene, Oregon, October 1983,* 139–180. Amsterdam: John Benjamins.

Zuckermann, Ghil'ad. 2006. Complement clauses types in Isralei. In Robert M.W. Dixon and Alexandra Y. Aikhenvald (eds), *Complementation: A cross-linguistic typology,* 77–92. Oxford: Oxford University Press.

Zwicky, Arnold. 1985. Heads. *Journal of Linguistics* 21: 1–30.

Author Index

Language Index

Subject Index

CPSIA information can be obtained
at www.ICGtesting.com
Printed in the USA
BVHW061151190921
617040BV00004B/30